Changing Lives

Changing Lives:
Life Stories of Asian Pioneers in Women's Studies

Edited by the Committee on
Women's Studies in Asia
Foreword by Florence Howe

The Feminist Press
at The City University of New York
New York

Published by The Feminist Press at The City University of New York, 311 East 94 Street, New York, New York 10128. All rights reserved.

First published by Kali for Women, India.
99 98 97 96 95 5 4 3 2 1

Library of Congress Cataloging-in-Publication Data
Changing lives : Life stories of Asian pioneers in women's
  studies / edited by the Committee on Women's Studies in
  Asia ; foreword by Florence Howe.
      p.   cm.
  Rev. ed. of: Women's studies, women's lives, ©1994.
  ISBN 1-55861-108-8. — ISBN 1-55861-109-6 (pbk.)
  1. Women's studies—Asia. 2. Women's studies—Study and
teaching—Asia. 3. Women scholars—Asia. I. Committee on
Women's Studies in Aisa.   II. Women's studies, women's lives.
HQ1181.A78W66 1995
305.42'095—dc20   94-48660
                                                        CIP

Cover art: *Peru: Machu Picchi Revisited* by Betty La Duke, 1981,
acrylic, 68 x 54 inches.
Cover design: Tina Malaney
Text design: Tina Malaney

Printed in the United States of America on acid-free paper by
McNaughton & Gunn, Inc.

This publication is made possible, in part, by public funds from
the New York State Council on the Arts. The Feminist Press is also
grateful to Mariam Chamberlain, Joanne Markell, and Genevieve
Vaughan for their generosity.

Contents

Contents

Committee on Women's Studies in Asia

Barbara Lazarus is Associate Provost for Academic Projects at Carnegie Mellon University, Pittsburgh, USA. An educational anthropologist, Dr. Lazarus has served as Dean at Carnegie Mellon University and Wellesley College. She has worked in the area of changing roles of women in Asia since 1979 and has written widely on the subject.

Cho Hyoung teaches sociology at Ewha Women's University, Seoul, Korea. She represented her country at the UNESCO-sponsored Meeting of Experts in Women's Studies and Social Sciences in Asia, held in New Delhi in 1983.

Fanny M. Cheung is Reader in Psychology at The Chinese University of Hong Kong and Programme Coordinator of graduate studies in Clinical Psychology. Concurrently, she is the Programme Director of the Gender Research Programme, at The Chinese University, an interdisciplinary research programme initiated by her in 1985.

Hiroko Hara is associated with the Women's Studies programme at Ochanomizu University, Tokyo. In 1990 she was the first woman to be elected President of the Japanese Anthropological Association.

Konta Intan Damanik teaches Economics at Universitas Kristen Satya Wacana, Salatiga, Indonesia. She is actively involved in promoting women's studies in Indonesia and organized a six-university consultation on the subject in 1990.

Lucia Pavia Ticzon is co-founder and first director of the Women's Resource and Research Center (WRRC) at Miriam College Foundation, Inc., Quezon City, Philippines. She is a leturer at the College, is the WRRC's Programme Officer for Women's Studies Development and a practitioner of Organization Development and Planning. She is also one of the three coordinators of Isis International in Manila.

Malavika Karlekar is a Senior Fellow at the Centre for Women's Development Studies, New Delhi. She is the author of *Poverty and Women's Work,* (1982) and of *Voices from Within—Early Personal Narratives of Bengali Women* (1991).

Manorama Barnabas was the Executive Associate for Women's Concerns of the United Board for Christian Higher Education in Asia, New York, 1987-91. She has taught Philosophy and Women's Studies in India and the US. She was named Elisabeth Luce Moore Distinguished Professor to Taiwan in 1979-80. She has written extensively on the challenges facing higher education in traditional societies.

Maria Ascuncion Azcuna is a member of the Institute of Women's Studies at St. Scholastica's College in Manila.

Nora Lan-hung Chiang (Huang) teaches Geography at the National Taiwan University, Taipei and was Coordinator of the Women's Research Center located at the Population Studies Center of the University, 1985-89. She has published extensively and was the Elisabeth Luce Moore Distinguished Professor in Hong Kong, 1990-91.

Pilwha Chang is Chair of the Department of Women's Studies at Ewha Women's University, Seoul, Korea.

Yasuko Muramatsu is a development economist teaching at Tokyo Woman's Christian University. Dr. Muramatsu was the 1982-83 Elisabeth Luce Moore Distinguished Professor to Indonesia. In 1985-86 she was a Bunting Fellow at Radcliffe College and was the Director of the International Group for the Study of Women's '88 Tokyo Symposium on *Women and Communication in an Age of Science and Technology.*

Acknowledgements

M any people and resources have contributed to the making of this book. The United Board for Christian Higher Education in Asia, based in New York City, provided moral and financial support for the project from the beginning. We are grateful for their sustained interest in our work. Our thanks to the Ford Foundation, Jakarta, Indonesia for a publication grant and to the federation of Asian Women's Assoiciation, Taipei, Taiwan, for an early grant which encouraged us to press on.

Our book has proved to be a labor of love of many people—women and men—who contributed in important ways with ideas and critiques as well as introduced us to many sources of information. To the essayists in *Women's Studies, Women's Lives* our deep appreciation for their willingness to share personal joys and trials so generously, and our sincere gratitude for their insights and ideas as well as for the time and energy they devoted to this work.

In any endeavor of this sort, it is impossible to give adequate thanks to each individual. However, we particularly acknowledge: Paul T. Lauby, President Emeritus of the United Board of Christian Higher Education in Asia who helped initiate and nurture this project; David W. Vikner, President, Patricia L. Magdamo, Vice President, Donald P. McComb, Director of Finance and Administration, and Carmen Dagnino, at the United Board who were helpful in many and special ways; Barbara Gimbel, Chair of the United Board's Women's Concerns Committee for her support; and Dorothy O. Helly, of Hunter College, whose early advice helped to define the work.

The Committee on Women's Studies in Asia which was

formed to coordinate work on this volume brought to fruition the dream of colleagues in Asia and the United States. Each member has given unstintingly of her time and the outcome is the result of voluntary efforts of all the scholars involved. The institutions: Tokyo Woman's Christian University; The Chinese University of Hong Kong; Centre for Women's Development Studies, New Delhi; Women's Resource and Research Center, Quezon City, the Philipines; St Scholastica's College, Manila; Ewha Women's University, Seoul, Korea; National Taiwan University, Taipei; Satya Wacana University, Salatiga, Indonesia; Ochanomizu University, Tokyo; Carnegie Mellon University, Pittsburgh, USA and the United Board for Christian Higher Education in Asia—cooperated with their faculty to make this work possible. We thank them.

Early on in the project a distribution of responsibilities was made: Malavika Karlekar and Barbara Lazarus worked on and edited *Women's Studies, Women's Lives*. Manorama Barnabas, Fanny Cheung, Lucia Pavia Ticzon and Yasuko Murmatsu are writing and editing a second volume, *A Resource Guide for Women's Studies*. As Chairperson of the editorial team, Yasuko Muramatsu has been deeply involved in the whole project. We appreciate each other's contributions and are thankful for the opportunity and the challenge of working well together over these last years.

Manorama Barnabas
January 1994

Publisher's note: *The editors and publishers regret not being able to individually acknowledge the photographers whose pictures we carry here. While every attempt has been made to trace them, sometimes this has not been possible, particularly with family photographs. For this, our apologies.*

Foreword

As a publisher over the past twenty-four years, I have rarely written a foreword to one of our own books. But I felt compelled to write this one for two reasons, one professional, one personal—as though we could separate those two aspects of our lives. But I will try to be clear about what I mean, and begin with the professional.

In the spring of 1990, a small group of Philippine women visited me at The Feminist Press. We held a seminar, with several Press staff joining us in the library. Together the two groups talked about their work. We described our activist origins, the research we did in the 1970s, the inservice teaching to stimulate school systems, and the international publishing that began in the 1980s. They described their activist work and their involvement in women's studies, both research and teaching. They also described a five-year women's studies project in the region that might soon be ready for publication.

In addition, one of the two books they described is the volume by the Committee on Women's Studies in Asia you have opened: the story of women's studies in Asia, as told through various generations of pioneers from eleven different countries. I said I was eager to read the books they might publish.

Several days later, we met again at Hunter College where the Fourth Interdisciplinary Congress on Research on Women had begun. They asked me to meet with them that afternoon, and in a small space in one of the lounges, they proposed that The Feminist Press become the publisher of their women's studies regional project. "Oh, no," I said, trying to keep the conversation light, "I'm very flattered, but you can't have an American imperialist publisher." "No, no," Lucia Pavia Ticzon replied, speaking for the group, "We've thought about it, and we've decided that you're *international*, not American." We went round this conversation several times, until I could no longer manage the joking tone in the midst of tears. They were in earnest about The Feminist Press as an international institution. "Why don't you publish it yourselves?" I took a deep breath. "Why not establish a publishing arm?—you do everything else." They explained that they had no time for publishing now, and no expertise. Perhaps in the future. But the offer held. I said I'd be delighted to *co-publish*, but I thought that they ought to have an Asian publisher, and I suggested Kali for Women in India.

And that is, of course, what eventually the Committee chose to do.

The personal story begins when I read the manuscript of this book in 1994, for more than twenty-five years ago, I was one of a group of U.S. "pioneers" *changing lives*. Again and again, in the thirteen memoirs in this volume, I recognized my own experience, for I too, like so many in the West, had come to women's studies through personal encounters with the men in my life, and through intellectual discoveries affecting my professional life. I am by nature and nurture a crusty, tough, street-reared person, not easily brought to tears. But again, I found my eyes filling despite myself as I read essay after essay. I remembered what it was like to be shocked by colleagues who, allegedly for your own good, told you not to "waste your time" on the narrow subject of women, certainly not on poor women, or women in some kind of trouble.

As I read about the husbands and children who needed to be told by fearful women that family work had to be shared among all of them, not pressed as a second and third job on mother, I remembered my own timid rebellion about the laundry. And I remembered all the days of my youth when I had to pick up my father's and brother's clothes where they had dropped them on the floor and carry them to the bathroom hamper. My mother believed that men were totally exempt from household labor, and my young cries of "unfair" fell on deaf ears.

Why are these life stories important to an American and Canadian audience now both generations older and younger than the Asian "pioneer" writers? For "pioneer" women of my generation, the stories will help us remember our own changing lives, and perhaps suggest that we tell our own stories for daughters and sons and granddaughters and grandsons and those who will follow them. For "pioneer" women of the two following generations, these stories will make palpable the experiences privileged academic women share, despite profound cultural differences. It may also—and here I am being idealistically hopeful—remind the several "pioneer" generations in the West that in Asia, women's studies "pioneers" have not broken the connection between themselves and the least privileged women of their countries. Perhaps it is too optimistic to expect one book to make a difference, but for women's studies pioneers the world over, books have been lifelines. *Changing Lives* will remind all of us outside Asia that experiences shared and relayed through women's studies worldwide can indeed cross cultural borders to produce unforeseen, positive, and permanent changes in critical consciousness.

Florence Howe

Introduction

Why was I born a member of the female sex?... had I been a
boy, and had news of my mother's condition, then no matter
where I had been, like a bird I would have flown to her side.
What am I to do now! I am a caged bird.
Rassundari Debi, India, 1868[1]

I don't want to be identified as a bonsai or a wild tree. I don't
want to be sentenced to my present form of existence. As a
human subject, I am expressing continuously the life that
flows through me. I have limited control over what flows
through me. But I have ample space to grasp its meaning, to
learn, unlearn and relearn. Beyond my present form of existence, the world is wide open and free. Nobody, no boundaries
can imprison my consciousness.
Thanh-Dam Truong, Vietnam, 1990[2]

Women's studies, women's lives

A decade and a half after the International Women's Year is
not too early for some enquiry and introspection into what,
for lack of a better phrase, have been the gains and losses. This
volume attempts to do so through the stories of women who
have responded variously to a challenging phase in contemporary history. These stories speak of individual experiences,
anxieties and solutions. A common thread running through all
is an awareness that, for each essayist, life changed after she
began teaching and researching about women. While a few,
more than others, may have some questions regarding the future and direction of women's studies, or its status in academia,

1

each knows that her perceptions, expectations and priorities are very different today from what they were when she started out.

By questioning existing structures, whether within the home or outside, women's studies has provided its practitioners with a distinctive way of looking at the world. It is not important whether they continue to work in the field or not. What is relevant is that wherever they are and will be, their view will be one borne of a range of experiences during a vital period of their lives. For when the personal and that which does not directly affect one find affinity, the outcome is bound to be an almost irreversible change in perceptions and expectations. This, perhaps more than any other transient success, is what remains, a much valued gain for those who have cared to search. Many of the essayists speak not only of their own personal lives, but also comment at length on women's studies and where it has brought them intellectually. For women's studies entered the world of academia at a crucial moment and has helped in the process of expanding methodologies and bases of enquiry; above all, it has provided the individual researcher with a new confidence.

The move towards a re-evaluation of established methodologies and theoretical premises[3] helps to contextualize women's studies in a wider intellectual framework. The development of a discourse on women in the academy appears inextricably connected to the development of the women's movement. Indeed, some believe that women's studies is a response to the need to provide the women's movement with a theoretical foundation.[4] All of this, however, sounds a bit like putting the proverbial cart before the horse: in the first instance, we need to establish what we mean by women's studies.

Definitions of new disciplines are often many and at times contradictory, if not confusing. Put simply, women's studies which was talked of as an area of research, teaching and action only after 1975, the International Women's Year, concentrates on gender as a category of analysis in the same manner that caste, religion, class, and status groups have so far been used by social scientists.[5] It is now generally accepted that while "sex" refers to physiological distinctions, gender is "a cultural construct, a set of learned behaviour patterns."[6] Women's studies emphasizes that a focus on gender as a category of analysis means that it now becomes an important indicator within studies where the focus may be on other variables. Thus, in order to provide a complete picture of peasant uprisings or of a tribal or "native" community there is a need to look not only at class and ethnic factors, but also at gender as a significant variable. In emphasizing the need for social scientists to be gender-sensitive, women's studies is staking a claim to restructure entire knowledge systems and social science methodologies.[7]

Again, there is an important body of opinion which believes that incorporation into existing disciplines as courses or papers may be preferable to marginalization (some call it ghettoization) as a relatively new, independent area of study. These debates, which were initiated some years ago,[8] raise important questions not only about the status of women's studies but also about the identity of those interested in this growing area. To put it simply, women's studies scholars—and certainly those represented in this volume—are those who have established themselves in various disciplines prior to their interest in women's studies. The very nature of the area lends itself to interdisciplinary methodology, analysis, and networking. Ideally, to work across disciplines, a researcher needs to be familiar with more than one subject. This is not always possible particularly as academic requirements stress specialization in a single area.[9] Nonetheless, in sociology and social anthropology— for instance, economic anthropology, political sociology, sociologies of religion, education, medicine, and so on—stretch across disciplines; similar exercises increasingly characterize women's studies as scholars look to new data sources and methodologies to enrich their area of work. It is possible of course that in the process researchers may be open to criticism from purists in various parent disciplines. However, this is a risk worth taking as research across disciplines often results in investigations into hitherto neglected areas and the emergence of new perspectives. Essential for interdisciplinary research is the use of a range of methodologies, many of which are relatively new. These are some of the challenges which the women's studies scholar has to recognize and take on.

Is women's studies different from a range of earlier studies that have focused on women? Can studies in the social sciences prior to 1975, which deal with the status of women, their employment, education, multiple roles, patterns of marriage, and so on, also be regarded as work in women's studies? One answer to these questions would be that if such studies do not envisage women as an oppressed category, they do not fall within the ambit of this new area of work. This answer can be countered by a further question: Is it necessary to have a prior belief in the existence of subjugation, oppression, and discrimination for work on gender to qualify as women's studies? Or is it important to read, study, and analyze a problem in accordance with the norms of certain rigorous theoretical and research methods and then come to conclusions based on relevant findings? But are these two approaches mutually exclusive? Is it not time to acknowledge that no activity can be free from the intellectual, social, and ethical baggage of the teacher, the learner, the reader? That commitment to a cause and intellectual rigor can go together? A related question asks whether women's studies belongs to academia alone the way, for instance, quantum physics does? Or can it also justifiably imply action, intervention, and consciousness-raising in the interests of justice and equity? If these are broadly defined to include a conscientious teacher's or researcher's committed handling of the subject matter and students, then most would agree that women's studies, like some facets of other social science disciplines, involves action. Here action and intervention imply the teacher's ability to influence the thinking of her or his students as well as of the impact of research findings on policy formulation and administrative strategies. In other words, women's studies further restates a belief that knowledge creation has to reflect perceptions of the real world with all its warts and blemishes.

An approach on which there is less agreement is one which defines action as working for structural change. Here the external agent acts as a catalyst. That this agent may be a researcher is evident from the increasing popularity of the participatory research method. Maintaining that "actors in the situation are not merely objects of someone else's study but are actively influencing the process of knowledge generation and elaboration," participatory research challenges notions of objectivity, neutrality, and value-free judgements.[10] The situation thus represented is the product of the collaborative processes of researcher and respondent.[11] Participatory research has been used effectively, for instance, in women's studies,[12] the sociology of education,[13] and the study of movements and grassroots organization.[14] We already know that critiques of existing methods, frameworks, and viewpoints are being questioned, and not only by those in women's studies. The limitations of an approach that speaks of objective distance, of facts alone, and of absolute truths have already been mentioned. Scholars such as Sandra Harding[15] point out that so-called objectivity is in fact the objectivity of male discourse. It is now time to make space for the feminist standpoint, to redefine objectivity. One of the practical fallouts of this disillusionment which established post-Enlightenment modes of thought is the projection of the subject as an active agent in the construction of knowledge. Methodologically, the voices of the observer, of the students, and of the teacher, become as important as that of the object of study. To hear those voices, the methodological tools of literary and autobiographical analysis,[16] oral histories,[17] life histories,[18] and case studies,[19] become vital. More specifically, women's studies has much to share with the fieldwork-based traditions in sociology and social anthropology; in fact, notions of objectivity versus subjectivity, of taking sides and yet trying to remain "intact," and ultimately questions about the role of the fieldworker are those which have concerned sociologists and social anthropologists for some decades now.[20]

Women's studies does not claim exclusive rights to any of these approaches; at the same time, its emphasis on reflexivity and on knowledge as shared experience has led to its use in unique and distinctive ways. Today it shares much with postmodern discourse, but draws the line at a total loss of context and the demise of the subject. It finds attractive the belief that the observer and the observed, the teacher and the taught, the reader and the text collaborate in the act of interpretation and creation. A dialogue and a mutuality characterize these relationships; but, caution anthropologists for instance, these must be within the parameters of location and context.[21] Feminist anthropologists Marilyn Strathern, Micaela di Leonardo, and Susan Gal point to the lack of "parity between the authorship of the anthropologist and the informant."[22] In other words, authorship of a piece of writing is the product of an individual's specific context, background, and experience.

The quest for common creations sometimes overlooks that the one initiating the process is often a woman from an advantaged social, educational, and even racial background. She brings a specific baggage with her despite her best attempts at incorporating the Other into discourse. Her worldview, categories of analysis, dialogic tools, and modes of translation are determined by her culture and training.[23] Thus the new reality—or the one the researcher/teacher hopes to have

created through the involved participation of her respon-
dents/students—may in fact reflect a privileged view, her understanding of another's world. While this dilemma charac-
terizes any situation where one attempts to represent the
Other, it is particularly significant when a vast divide sepa-
rates those in an essentially hierarchical relationship. Nor
need it be limited to contexts of First World researcher and
Third World researched alone.[24] The differences and inequalities within any one culture can equally pose a moral dilemma
for the one involved in the act of creating a new reality.

In an interesting interface with Clifford Geertz, Ngugi Wa
Thiong'o, and others, Jack Goody is concerned with the loss of
context and a "wider frame."[25] In short, enough thought is not
only not given to the situated observer and where she has
come from, but also giving space to essentialism and the narrowly local can ultimately be limiting and inward-looking. To
elaborate on these points a bit more, in their commitment to
look for other voices, postmodernists can logically justify religious fundamentalism and a range of cultural beliefs about
femininity and masculinity. In some senses these are inevitable
developments of an intellectual freedom of a very special
kind. At the same time it is necessary to be aware of the dangers of extreme relativism.

All of this is not to suggest that the time has come to bring
down the curtain on any activity that involves interfacing
with those in different life situations. It is only to acknowledge that there can never be any perfect piece of research nor
any one reality. Women's studies is uniquely situated to join
this exciting debate as an active partner. The fact that most researchers and teachers in the area are women provides an um-
bilical link between theory and praxis. Each essayist in this
volume, then, approaches the feminist credo "the personal is
political" in her own way. In doing so, she allows us entry into
her private world as well as that of the public persona. As involved readers we must surely relate to what is being offered,
each in our individual ways.

Looking for patterns

This volume was originally conceived of as part of a resource
book on women's studies in Asia. Potential contributors were
requested "to write about your life and your interest in
women's studies." Soon enough, the Editorial Committee was

overwhelmed by the response: essays poured in thick and fast and clearly an entire book was in the making. Each piece went well beyond a mere mechanical recounting of professional careers and varied experiences. As editors, we have tried to interfere as little as possible with differing idiomatic uses of English and turns of phrase. Given their particular situation, a few essayists, more than others, dwell on the personal. Yet, interestingly, none deal with conflicts over sexual preferences and identity in the area. This is perhaps because discussions on personal sexuality are as yet something many Asian feminists are not prepared to bring into the open. Most authors prefer a more formal account of "why women's studies?" or "what has it done for us professionally?" These disparate vignettes have provided enough insights and information to enable us to draw out some recurrent themes and areas of concern.

Writing about oneself can be a demanding task; there is much to conceal, many fears, anxieties, doubts. Yet, once one is able to overcome the initial hesitation and face oneself, there is plenty to be discovered, learned, accepted. Nor is the process of self-discovery the same for all, as is clear from our authors' accounts. In the present context, the move to women's studies provided many the opportunity for self-analysis. A few initially backed off, only to come back to it later. Others reacted to the rigid structures of academia and to male indifference, if not contempt, to a growing area of concern. Political oppression, the trauma of fieldwork among the poor, the penetrating questions of a research student—these and more led to our authors' search for a new psychological and intellectual space. These autobiographical writings of thirteen women who have shaped women's studies in their countries have gone far beyond the expectations not only of the editors but also of the authors themselves. They provide valuable insights into the social structure of various societies, differing academic systems, the status of women, and, of course, the anxieties and joys of women discovering a new form of self-expression. Some, more than others, deal with the personal aspects of their odyssey; others are deeply concerned with the academic status and legitimacy of women's studies.

Our essayists are all Asians but, as their stories tell us, very different forces shaped their lives. Most are in their forties, at a crucial stage of their academic careers and personal lives; while the Editorial Committee tried to contact scholars from as many

7

Asian countries as they could, earlier commitments as well as an inability to complete work within our timeframe meant that many who were interested had to decline. Thus our Asia consists of Pakistan, India, Vietnam, Hong Kong, China, Taiwan, Korea, the Philippines, Japan, and Indonesia. The volume is not all-inclusive subject- or country-wise, nor do its contributors claim to be the main voices in women's studies in their countries. Nonetheless, juxtaposing personal responses, hopes, and aspirations against a backdrop of at times suffocating family norms and rigid academic structures, helps us develop a picture of women's studies in a vibrant part of the world.

Despite intra- and inter-country variations, it is possible to trace some common patterns. To begin, the family is of vital importance in the lives of most of our authors. In conventional socio-economic and historical analysis, the family has been viewed as a homogenous unit: internal inequalities in power, authority and resource allocation have been ignored or not taken into account either at the level of research and policy, or in the minds of its members. In the Asian context, the public face of family unity and cooperation is a much-vaunted ideal. Of course, research from the West indicates that the entire notion of the family, its composition, roles, and obligations, is in a state of flux. Declining fertility, delayed childbirth, rising divorce rates, an increasing number of man-woman relationships which may or may not end in marriage, and, in fact, relationships among those of the same sex all seriously question the traditional notion of the family as a domestic unit with a distinct age and hierarchy structure.[26] Despite their exposure to the West and western ways of life, the essayists were almost uniform in their overall commitment to the family; some, however, had started questioning dominant values; the resultant tensions and anxieties which this process brought are very much evident in several essays.

Each of the authors in *Changing Lives* writes of some significant events that influenced her decision to enter the field of women's studies. For some, it was a poignant awareness of what it meant to be a woman which led to questioning later on. Li Xiaojiang (China) felt that the advent of menstruation had an important impact on her own understanding of herself and of her relationships. Her powerful description evokes a series of at times conflicting images:

During the course of my secondary education, most of my girl classmates began to menstruate. Girl students had a nickname for menstruation: "ill luck." When a girl was in her "ill luck" she was exempt from attending hours of PE and from doing manual labour. Boys jealously complained of girls' privileges.... I regard the day of my first menstruation as monstrously ominous. It was during the early stage of the Cultural Revolution. On that day my father was hauled out to parade in the streets and lanes by Red Guards; he was in disgrace. He was dragged along tied with a rope; a placard with humiliating and abusive words hung from his neck and dangled on his chest, and an ugly fool's cap was crushed on his head.... One of them [the guards] poured a big bottle of ink on his head. My heart shrank at such a grim sight and, driven by impulse, I was on the point of rushing to his rescue when I felt a drastic twinge in the lower part of my abdomen. A flow of hot liquid trickled down the inner sides of my thigh ... suddenly it dawned on me what the flow meant. And tears began to run down my cheeks. It was an instant of bewilderment; the ink that was poured on my father's head, my menstrual discharge, and my tears churning like a whirlpool. I seemed to be engulfed. I felt a deep sense of humiliation in my status as a woman and as a daughter.

Noemi Alindogan-Medina (the Philippines) observed that as a child she worked long hours at child-minding, cooking, and washing while "the boys were nowhere to be found." Mothers were important figures; Thanh-Dam Truong's (Vietnam) description of her matri-focal family ("father was away most of the time for work and other related activities") is striking. While her mother encouraged her daughters to study, she was nonetheless tense about their sexual vulnerability; her daughters attributed their mother's at times harsh behavior to this fear. Aurora Javate (the Philippines) noted that

Our family of six girls and one boy provided me with my first exposure to women's power as the daily affairs of the household were efficiently run by the women without much help from the men in the family.... My grandmother, a strong-willed woman who excelled in the kitchen as she did in daily discourse with my grandfather, was as assertive as any modern-day feminist. While tending to her *botica* (drug store) ... my mother reared all seven of us. In these two women, I saw qualities of resourcefulness, tenacity, self-reliance, and forbearance in the face of adversity— qualities that would later shape my own worldview of women.

Tension between the family and the traditional role of women on the one hand, and the desire for higher education—

and indeed the need to break out of an incarcerating mold—pervades most essays. Nearly all were educated in Great Britain and the United States; Konta Damanik (Indonesia) came to India for her pre-Ph.D. work. Experiences varied from Thanh-Dam's contrasting of the civil rights movement with events in Vietnam to Fanny Cheung's (Hong Kong) frank comment that she was a disinterested observer of the U.S. women's movement. However, all admit that, intellectually and emotionally, the experience of study abroad was useful. In many ways distance from home provided a much needed perspective on their lives; yet once back, decisions had to be taken and responsibilities faced. Most were expected to marry, rear children, and, if necessary, combine domesticity with a career. Cho Hyoung's (Korea) description of her changed perceptions after a few years of marriage and exposure to a different world is, in many ways, extremely telling:

> I married a man of my choice while I was in graduate school. He was a thoughtful person who knew how to help out his student wife. We had a child after I had passed my qualifying exams. Our marriage seemed to go all right until after three years of involuntary separation—he was completing his doctoral dissertation in the U.S. and I went through the resocialization process in Korea. . . . When he came back to Korea, I suddenly found that he was a typical Korean man; a demanding and domineering husband and father of his child. He was happy to have a working wife, particularly in such a prominent job as that of a university professor, but he hated to see her preoccupied with outside activities and especially with the women's movement, women's studies, or anything in that line. He was even hostile to that sort of "unwomanly" activity.
>
> While I was becoming more and more critical of the dictatorial, patriarchal, and vulgar capitalistic arrangement of Korean society, he was entering into it as a conformist. At home it meant not only two marriages, but two different worlds, espousing contradictory perspectives.

They were separated in 1979. Prior to her going to the U.S. for her Ph.D., Nora Lan-hung Chiang (Taiwan) was constantly told by her mother-in-law that she "should sacrifice my own interest for my family." Things were even more difficult when she returned home.

> When I came back to Taiwan with my husband, I was stunned to discover my subservient status within the extended family,

where daughters-in-law did not eat with the menfolk and spent all their time caring for the family. The attitude of the older generation to those younger was patriarchal and condescending. It was very oppressive for someone used to living in a freer society. I began to realize that I would need to struggle if I wanted to keep my identity intact and be different from other women. This was particularly so in respect to my work. I did not adjust well and was constantly angry and frustrated. I also felt humiliated. However, I was luckier than many Chinese women at that time as I was living in the city and not with the extended family. Nowadays, it is common for a young couple to live by themselves when they first get married.

She ultimately adjusted and did not walk out of her marriage; nor did Li Xiaojiang who had planned "to remain single all my life." However, things changed when "unaccountably I fell in love." After her marriage, she realized that compromises with notions of independence were inevitable. She writes:

> After I married I soon discovered that I was hindered in every direction when I sought to think and act in keeping with the willpower, independence, values, and conduct of my unmarried days. My husband and my son, family chores, and my family's social connections all could turn out to be one sort of obstruction or another if I persisted in following my earlier path.... On the other hand, it would have been like a death sentence had I been forced to part with my husband and his family.... As long as I was unwilling to part with my husband and family, I had to assume all the consequences which stemmed from this unwillingness. And no sooner had I volunteered to assume all the consequences than I realized I had been lured into another trap.

The familial pattern of contrary pulls, opposing loyalties, and inevitable compromises followed. We can now pause and ask whether the Asian woman, no matter how "liberated," "emancipated," or professional she may be, can ever overcome her guilt, her ambivalence? Is she not then very different from her western sisters? Does she have the same options as they do? We feel that there is a difference. Once again, it is the family and its ideology which directs personalities, decides on courses of action, and weaves invisible webs of compliance, if not complicity. Women like Thanh-Dam who have chosen not to return home, or Konta and Yasuko Muramatsu (Japan) who have remained single, or Cho Hyoung who walked out of a bad marriage have, to a certain extent, escaped the dilemmas and guilt of the married professional woman. Nevertheless, on the whole, the Asian emphasis (and here we know that we may be accused of generalizing) on a collective identity, on an individuality which is shaped by the requirements of the whole, exerts a pervasive influence on women's lives. These stories speak of women's attempts at redefining their identities, but the context invariably remains the family. The struggle to be free is, in the ultimate analysis, the struggle to be free from the family's right to establish parameters and frames of reference. At the same time, it is the family that provides an anchor, a much-needed ballast in a fast-changing world. In the ensuing confusion and bewilderment, the women's movement and women's studies become invaluable supports, forms of emotional and intellectual sustenance in a difficult situation. Yasuko and Konta may remain single, yet the demands of the extended family encroach on their psychic and physical space. To be a woman is to learn to cope with, above all, a range of pressures and obligations. Not all of these are justified, nor even legitimate, but in order to refuse, our authors know that the costs can be enormous and, of course, unfair. At the same time, these are strong women for whom there is a symbiosis between personal evolution and growth and women's studies.

Apart from the local level politics of the family—if it can be so put—a number have been involved in the women's movement and the wider political arena. Fareeha Zafar (Pakistan), Noemi, and Aurora's feminist activism was deeply influenced by political events within their countries: persistent instability and corruption increased their desire to participate in alternate structures. On the other hand, the Communist movement directed the motivations and activities of Li Xiaojiang and Liang Jun (China). Aline Wong (Singapore) is a minister in the government. Irrespective of whether they were involved or committed politically to a particular ideology or party, all the authors were influenced by the fact that women's studies has a symbiotic relationship with the women's movement. For some, being an academic as well as an activist did not pose any dilemma; for others, such as Yasuko and Malavika Karlekar (India), the issue was a real one. As Yasuko writes:

> Even after women's studies was introduced in Japan in the early 1970s, I did not immediately relate my research to it. I took the

position: "I will retain an interest in it, but women's studies is not for me."

As she explains later, part of her hesitation arose out of doubts over the theoretical underpinnings of women's studies. For Malavika the issues were not dissimilar; when she decided to give up university teaching and go in for full-time research on women, she had some doubts. Was she making a mistake? Would she regret her voyage into an uncharted world? Yet, the die was cast, as teaching no longer satisfied her fully. At the same time, field research brought with it uncomfortable questions of how to construct another reality.

If we go back to the discussion at the beginning of this chapter, women's studies, more than many other disciplines, is better equipped to enable a collaborative construction of knowledge; a sharing of experiences is its *raison d'etre* and the underlying principle of the sisterhood notion. Further, a belief in the injustice of existing social and political systems has led sensitive academics like Thanh-Dam to enquire first hand what exploitation means:

> ... I became involved with organizations set up by prostitutes themselves in Western Europe and, to a lesser extent, in the United States and Canada. Although the involvement was of short duration—during the First and Second World Whores Congresses in Amsterdam and Brussels—I soon discovered that differentiation ran much deeper. I felt compelled to understand its deeper roots.... Emotions such as anger, guilt, embarassment, and despair have been part of the process of looking, finding, talking, reading, thinking, and writing. Experiencing these emotions has helped me grasp the meaning of power at its center as well as its extremities.

Not dissimilar emotions led Malavika to study the lives of sweeper women, perhaps the most oppressed and stigmatized community in Indian society.

The costs of change

Entering a new field and forging a new way have had very real personal and professional costs for these women. Disappointment, unhappiness, withdrawal of approval, and public disclaimers are typical; Cho Hyoung's resolve was strengthened after a senior sociologist asked her, "Why should a promising young sociologist like you spend so much time and energy on trivial matters such as women and poverty?" Her reaction was not uncharacteristic of many women who have chosen to journey on. In reviewing the lives of women who are among the pioneers in women's studies in Asia, one is struck by the nature of oppression, personal and otherwise, and of individual triumphs.

Out of the personal and professional experiences of the authors, from their tentative and not-so-tentative entry in the field, we see the development of new ways of working together and the formation of new kinds of groups and organizations. We also go through some of their tribulations with them as they take on obdurate colleagues and academic structures. Centers for research on women have been initiated at institutions for higher education. Some tentatively and/or for external reasons, such as the one at Tokyo Woman's Christian University, others by the deliberate policy of the women involved. Many of these have developed a new kind of working style, one which is less hierarchical and more nurturant than traditional academic institutions. Lessons learned from developing these groups that the authors share should prove useful to scholars in the future. In addition to the development of centers at institutions of higher education, a number of women have developed women's groups that are independent of academia.

A review of the experiences of the thirteen pioneers provides, in microcosm, a picture of some of the key questions facing women's studies scholars in Asia today. While many of the authors were, at some time in their careers, trained abroad, a search for a non-western reference point pervades the essays. The role of the family in the context of women's studies in Asia emerges as a major force. A strong commitment to others plays itself out in a few dramatic themes. For some, action on behalf of other women is a necessary agenda for women's studies; for others, there is a strong need expressed for theory-building in economics, sociology, philosophy, and, indeed, even in more technical fields. There is also an overall interest in women in development and its expansion.

While, on the face of it, the insights and self-analysis, as well as information, in these essays should be a source of hope, we must also share some reservations. Most of those in women's studies are women. Is this because women automatically have greater and better access to women's lives and women's problems than men? Or is women's studies a "typical

14

soft option for girls?" A number of authors raise a second disturbing issue: the tendency for a certain unselective amateurishness among people doing research on women. Some students, indeed professionals as well, seem to think that any woman can tackle the subject, guided merely by a combination of good intentions, empathy, and common sense.

Again, theory-building and action sometimes appear as complementary activities, and sometimes as dramatic divisions among our scholars. Some, for example, express concern about women's studies without an adequate theoretical base, while others feel that academic neglect is to blame. Thus, Li Xiaojiang notes:

> What will women's studies be like in the future? Our projects connected with women's studies will develop on the basis of successes of previous projects. It is probable that our future journey to further promote women's studies in China will be easier than our past. Perhaps unjustifiable pressure will be less often applied and opprobrium will no longer be so profusely cast in our direction. Still, I do not think I can be too optimistic.

We cannot comment on the contemporary concerns of the women in women's studies without reflecting on another important, emerging theme: a focus on gender rather than only women. Sometimes this emerges as a commitment to changing men and women, sometimes as an interest in understanding differences in public and private roles, not merely an increase in opportunities for women to move into those occupational roles traditionally held by men. There is now a subtle difference in perceptions and expectations: earlier, the dominant male view was that defenseless women need to be taken care of. Even if they worked for a wage, they should not, for instance, be put on night shifts, sent down mine pits and quarries, or posted to sensitive violence-prone areas. Now a distinct edge of aggression, of competitiveness, is vying with the more comfortable, superior attitude of paternalistic protection. But feminists across the board—and our authors are good examples of this position—know what they want. Tolerance of condescension and accommodative gestures—essential components of a patriarchal ideology—find little space in their scheme of things. This often means going it alone and doing things the way they feel they should be done. As we read, surely we must share and empathize. For no matter where we have come from, women's studies celebrates the right to reach out, to reflect, and to question.

Malavika Karlekar
Barbara Lazarus

Notes

1. Quoted on p. 116 of M. Karlekar's *Voices from Within: Early Personal Narratives of Bengali Women,* New Delhi: Oxford University Press, 1992.

2. From Thanh-Dam Truong, "Passage to Womanhood and Feminism," in this volume.

3. For more detailed discussion on this see the following texts: R. Blackburn, *Ideology in Social Science—Readings in Critical Social Theory,* Glasgow: Fontana, 1972; B.N. Ganguli, *Ideology and Social Sciences,* New Delhi: Arnold Heinemann, 1974; C. Geertz, *The Interpretation of Culture,* New York: Basic Books, 1973, "Local Knowledge and its Limits: Some *Obiter Dicta,*" *Yale Journal of Criticism* 5, no. 2, (Spring 1992), and *Local Knowledge—Further Essays in Interpretive Anthropology,* New York: Basic Books, 1992; Institute of Economic Growth, *Relevance in Social Science Research,* Delhi: Vikas, 1982; D.P. Mukherjee, "Lament for Economics," *The Economic Weekly* 2, 46, no. 14 (1959); L. Stone and G. Campbell, "The Use and Misuse of Surveys in International Development: An Experiment from Nepal," *Human Organization* 43, no. 1 (1984); and V. Turner and E. Bruner, *The Anthropology of Experience,* Urbana and Chicago: University of Illinois Press, 1986.

4. There are several different perspectives on this debate, some of which can be found in: G. Bonder, "Women's Studies and the Epistemological Criticisms of the Paradigms in the Human Sciences," mimeo, 1982; E.N. Chow, "Theoretical Frameworks and Methodology of Women's/Gender Studies in Relation to Sinicization," in *Proceedings of the Conference on Gender Roles and Changing Society,* Taipei: National Taiwan University, 1989; Dai-hyun Chung, "Nature of Women's Problems and Feminology," in *Journal of Korean Women's Studies* 1 (1985); N. Desai et al., "Women's Studies and Social Sciences in India," mimeo, 1982; M. Evasco, "In Quest of a Philippines Context for Women's Studies," unpublished paper, Philippines Social Science Center, 1988; M. Karlekar, "Women's Studies in the Eighties: State of the Discipline in USA and India," in *Samya Shakti, A Journal of Women's Studies* 1, no. 1 (1982); Wan Sharping, "The Emergence of Women's Studies in China," in *Women's Studies International Forum* 11, 5 (1988), and Amaryllis Torres, *The Filipino Woman in Focus: A Book of Readings,* Bangkok: Unesco, 1989.

5. See P. Abbott and C. Wallace, *An Introduction to Sociology: Feminist Perspectives,* London: Routledge and Kegan Paul, 1991;

B. Agarwal, "Conceptualising Women's Studies: Some Notes," mimeo, 1986; U. Kalpagam, "Gender in Economics—The Indian Experience," in *Economic and Political Weekly* 21, no. 41, *Review of Women's Studies*, October 1986; D. Lockwood, "Class, Status and Gender" in Rosemary Crompton and Michael Mann (eds.), *Gender and Stratification*, Cambridge, Polity Press; H. Moore, *Feminism and Anthropology*, Minneapolis, University of Minnesota Press; and R. Wallace (ed.), *Feminism and Sociological Theory*, Newbury Park: Sage, 1989.

6. P. Caplan, *The Cultural Construction of Sexuality*, London: Tavistock, 1987, p. 1.

7. See, for instance, V. Mazumdar, "Social Science Research and the Problems of Inequality: The Women's Dimension," mimeo, 1987; M. Millman and R. M. Kanter (eds.), *Another Voice: Feminist Perspectives on Social Life and Social Science*, New York: Garden City; 1975; D. Smith, "Sociological Theory: Methods of Writing Patriarchy," in R. Wallace (ed.), *Feminism and Sociological Theory*, Newbury Park: Sage, 1989.

8. G. Bowles and R. Duelli Klein discuss this in their *Theories of Women's Studies*, Berkeley: University of California Press, 1983, as do N. Desai et al., op. cit. See also *SIGNS Special Issue: Feminist Theory* 7, no. 3 (Spring 1982), and C. Stimpson, "Women's Studies: Its Presence and Promise in the Present," mimeo, 1982.

9. B. Agarwal, "Conceptualising Women's Studies: Some Notes," mimeo, 1986.

10. R. Tandon, "Participatory Evaluation and Research: Main Concepts and Issues," in W. Fernandes and R. Tandon, *Participatory Research as a Process of Liberation*, New Delhi: Indian Social Institute, 1981, p. 21.

11. See O. Fals Borda (ed.), *The Challenge of Social Change*, London: Sage, 1985, and "Investigating Reality in Order to Transform It," in *Dialectical Anthropology* 4, no. 1 (1979); Paolo Freire, *Pedagogy of the Oppressed*, Harmondsworth: Penguin Books, 1970 and *Cultural Action for Freedom*, Harmondsworth: Penguin, 1974; and M.D.A. Rehman, "The Theory and Practice of Participatory Action Research," in Fals Borda (ed.), *The Challenge of Social Change*, op. cit.

12. Several studies have documented this. Among these are: Narayan Banerjee, "Alternative Development Perspective for Tribal Women," mimeo, New Delhi: Centre for Women's Development Studies, 1984; S. Harding (ed.); *Feminism and Methodology*, Bristol, P.A.: Open University Press, 1987; P. Lather, "Feminist Perspectives on Empowering Research Methodologies," in *Women's Studies International Forum* 2, no. 4, 1988; V. Mazumdar, "Peasant Women Organise for Empowerment," New Delhi, Centre for Women's Development Studies, Occasional Paper No 13, 1989, and *Women of the Forest* (forthcoming), H. Roberts (ed.), *Doing Feminist Research*, London: Routledge and Kegan Paul, 1981; and K. Sharma, "Women and Participatory Development," in M.

Krishna Raj (ed.), *Women's Studies in India—Some Perspectives,* Bombay: Popular Prakashan, 1986.

13. B. Jackson and S. Jackson, *Childminder—A Study in Action Research,* London: Routledge and Kegan Paul, 1979; and T. La Belle, "From Consciousness-Raising to Popular Education in Latin America and the Caribbean," in *Comparative Education* (May 1987).

14. S. Muntemba (ed.), *Rural Development and Women—Lessons from the Field,* Geneva: International Labour Organisation, 1985; G. Omvedt, *We Will Smash This Prison!* New Delhi: Orient Longman, 1979; A. Touraine, *The Voice and the Eye,* Cambridge: Cambridge University Press, 1983.

15. S. Harding, *Feminism and Methodology,* op. cit.

16. Recent examples of these are: A. Basu, "The Reformed Family, Women Reformers: A Case Study of Vidyagauri Nilkanth," in *Samya Shakti: A Journal of Women's Studies,* 4 and 5, New Delhi, (1983); S. Benstock, *The Private Self: Theory and Practice of Women's Autobiographical Writings,* Chapel Hill: University of North Carolina Press, 1988; J. Braxton, *Black Women Writing Autobiography,* Philadelphia: Temple University Press, 1990; M. Karlekar, *Voices from Within,* op. cit.; C. Heilbrun, *Writing a Woman's Life,* New York: Ballantine Books, 1988; C.S. Lakshmi, *The Face Behind the Mask—Women in Tamil Literature,* New Delhi: Vikas, 1984; M. Mukherjee, "The Unperceived Self: A Study of Nineteenth Century Biographies," in K. Chanana (ed.), *Socialisation, Education and Women,* New Delhi: Orient Longman, 1988; V. Rao, "Thumri as Feminine Voice," in *Economic and Political Weekly* 25, no. 17 (April 1990); and K. Sangari and S. Vaid (eds.), *Recasting Women: Essays in Colonial History,* New Delhi: Kali for Women, 1989.

17. J. Bodnar, "Power and Memory in Oral History," in *Journal of American History* (1989); Stree Shakti Sangathana, *We Were Making History: Life Histories of Women in the Telangana People's Struggle,* New Delhi: Kali for Women, 1989; J. Vansina, *Oral Tradition: A Study in Historical Methodology,* London, 1965.

18. M. Agar, "Stories, Background Knowledge and Themes: Problems in Analysis of Life History Narrative," in *American Ethnologist* 7 (1980); and *Speaking of Ethnography,* Sage: Los Angeles, 1980; S. Bhave, *Pan on Fire,* New Delhi: Indian Social Institute, 1989; V. Crapanzano et al., "Personal Testimony: Narratives of the Self in the Social Sciences and the Humanities," *ITEMS,* Social Science Research Council, 40, no. 2 (June); A. Das Gupta et al., "Revati: A Survey That Was Not," in *Samya Shakti* 4 and 5; S. Geiger, "Women's Life Histories: Method and Content," in *SIGNS* 2, no. 2; J. Modell, "Stories and Strategies," in *International Journal of Oral History* (Winter 1983), and "The Performance of Talk," ibid (Winter 1987); and C. Robertson, "In Pursuit of Life Histories: The Problem of Bias," in *FRONTIERS* 7, no. 2.

19. F. Cheung and R. Yuen, "Psychological and Social Characteristics

Related to Social Participation among Working-Class Housewives in Hong Kong," Occasional paper no. 22, Centre for Hong Kong Studies, 1987; Hiroko Hara, Yasuko Muramatsu, and Chie Minami (eds), *Cushokigyo no Onnatachi* (Women in Small and Medium-scale Idustry), Tokyo: Miraisha, 1987; Nora Lan-hung Chiang (Huang), "The Migration of Rural Women to Taipei," in James Fawcett et al., *Women in the Cities of Asia—Migration and Urban Adaptation*, Colorado: Westview Replica edition, 1974; N. Desai, "Reinforcing and Relaxing Factors in Gender-Based Inequitous Relations in the Family," unpublished paper, 1991, and M. Karlekar, *Poverty and Women's Work—A Study of Sweeper Women in Delhi*, New Delhi: Vikas, 1982; S. Jetley, "Women's Work and Family Strategies: Meerut District, Western Uttar Pradesh, India," unpublished report, 1988; L. Gulati, *Profiles in Female Poverty*, New Delhi: Hindustan Publishing Corporation, 1981; M. Mitra, "Women's Work and Household Survival Strategies: A Case Study of Santhal Women's Lives and Work," unpublished report, 1988.

20. See M. Agar, "Stories, Background Knowledge and Themes," op. cit.; E. Bruner, *Text, Play and Story: The Construction and Reconstruction of Self and Society*, Washington D.C.: American Ethnological Society, 1990; C. Geertz, *The Interpretation of Culture, Local Knowledge—Further Essays in Interpretive Anthropology*, and "Local Knowledge and its Limits," both op. cit.; E.R. Leach, *Rethinking Anthropology*, London, 1961; B. Malinowski, *Argonauts of the Western Pacific*, New York: Dutton, 1961; M.N. Srinivas "Some Thoughts on the Study of One's Own Society," in *Social Change in Modern India*, Bombay: Allied Publishers, 1966, and "The Observer and the Observed in the Anthropological Understanding of Cultures," Singapore: National University of Singapore, Faculty Lecture 1, 1983.

21. M. di Leonardo (ed.), *Gender at the Crossroads of Knowledge—Feminist Anthropology in the Postmodern Era*, Berkeley: University of California Press, 1991; S. Gal, "Between Speech and Silence: The Problematics of Research in Language and Gender," in di Leonardo, *Gender at the Crossroads of Knowledge*, 1991; J. Stacey, "Can There Be a Feminist Ethnography?" op. cit.; M. Strathern, "An Awkward Relationship—The Case of Feminism and Anthropology," in *SIGNS* 12, no. 2 (Winter 1987); F. Mascia-Lees et al., "The Postmodernist Turn in Anthropology: Cautions from a Feminist Perspective," in *SIGNS* 15, no. 1 (1989).

22. M. Strathern, "An Awkward Relationship," op. cit.

23. S. Gal, "Between Speech and Silence," op. cit.; C. Geertz, *The Interpretation of Culture*, op. cit.; J. Goody, "Local Knowledge and Knowledge of Locality: The Desirability of Frames," in *Yale Journal of Criticism* 5, no. 2 (Spring 1992); D. Smith, "Sociological Theory: Methods of Writing Patriarchy," in R. Wallace (ed.), *Feminism and Sociological Theory*, Newbury Park: Sage, 1989.

24. This is discussed by T. Asad, *Anthropology and the Colonial*

Encounter, London: Ithaca Press, 1973; and Ngugi Wa Thiong'o, "Responses," in *Yale Journal of Criticism* 5, no. 2 (Spring 1992).

25. J. Goody, op. cit., 1992.

26. A. Coale et al., *Aspects of the Analysis of the Family*, Princeton: Princeton University Press, 1965; L. Csezh-Szombathy, "Modelling the Inter-Relation between Macro-Society and the Family," in *International Social Science Journal*, no. 126 (1990); and W. Kephart, *The Family, Society and the Individual*, Boston: Houghton Mifflin Company, 1961.

Aline K. Wong
Singapore

ALINE K. WONG (b.1941) is Associate Professor of Sociology at the National University of Singapore. She has been a Member of Parliament since 1984 and was appointed Minister of State for Health in November 1990. Dr. Wong specializes in urban sociology, population and development, and women's studies and has several publications to her credit. She is also chairperson of the Women's Wing of the People's Action Party, the ruling party in Singapore.

Feminism and Women's Studies

.·.·.·.·.·.·.·.·.

I t is a rare opportunity to pause from my daily work, sit down, and write a reflective piece on feminism and women's studies in Singapore, from the vantage point of a sociologist engaged in teaching and research, who at the same time has been involved in politics. The question is how to combine a perspective which is at once institutional and personal, academic and political. I shall begin with the personal, an approach that I have never taken before.

A sociologist and a woman

I did my graduate studies in sociology at the University of California, Berkeley, in the mid-1960s. I saw the beginnings of the student movement there, but I had left the States before the Civil Rights movement and the women's liberation movement really took shape. I never had the opportunity to take women's studies courses which became so popular in the second half of the 1970s. Being trained in functionalism and the liberal democratic tradition that it represented, I was naturally attracted to the "integration of women in development" perspective of the UN Decade for Women. Thus, at the start of my academic career, I began to look at gender inequalities as a development and stratification phenomenon. The Marxian perspective had not yet recognized the gender dimension of class, much less conceived of gender as a class. So I was comfortable with the UN Decade approach and the concomitant "basic needs" approach of the ILO. My studies of gender inequalities then were no more than a systematic documentation of the existence and size of the gender gap in Singapore. Along the lines laid down by Ester Boserup, I had set out to win recognition for women's contributions to the economy and other aspects of social life within the local context. I supervised students' theses, conducted surveys, and studied women's roles, values, and self-perceptions.[1] That was till the middle of the 1970s.

Between 1975 and 1981, Janet Salaff, from the University of Toronto, and I carried out a longitudinal study on a sample of women workers and traced changes in their lives during the period of Singapore's transition from an industrializing economy to a newly industrialized one. We learned how to do grounded theory, how to interpret individual life histories through references to changes in the societal context, and, conversely, how social change is felt and lived by social actors.[2] At the same time, I had kept up with contemporary feminist literature which, at the time, was still heavily focused on the anthropological and psychological debate on "anatomy is destiny."

Alongside my academic career, I had raised two children and experienced a working mother's guilt. In Singapore, middle-class families are still fortunate enough to afford domestic help. However, even with the help of a maid I could not fend off the feeling of guilt whenever I had to work late in the office, when a child fell sick, or when I went overseas to attend conferences. Those days, when my children were small, were hectic and anxious days. I did what was expected of every mother, taking care of the children's daily needs, driving them back and forth between home and school, taking them to music and painting lessons, supervising their homework, doing the grocery shopping, entertaining the occasional guests, and so on. Virtually all wives and mothers, whether working inside or outside the home, have to do these things anyway. In Singapore, as elsewhere, one can understand a woman's "double burden" better if it is examined against the particular socioeconomic, cultural, and political context. The relevant context in Singapore includes the high participation rate of the female labor force, the dearth of childcare facilities until recently, the predominant pattern of nuclear family living, the highly competitive educational system, which creates tremendous pressures for children and their parents, and the persistence of traditional values regarding gender roles, especially within the household.

By the early 1980s, I had carried out numerous studies on women, industrialization and family change, ethnicity and fertility, and public housing and urban life. My work on women workers in the electronics industry in particular drew on dependency theories that were current then. I had also come to appreciate the new feminist literature with a phenomenological approach. It was then I became fully conscious of what feminism is about: theory, research, advocacy.

A *woman politician*

In 1984 I entered politics. I was one of the three women candidates fielded for the general election by the ruling party, after a fourteen year period during which there was no woman representative in parliament. Since I had always advocated the integration of women in the nation's development efforts, and women's participation in decision-making at the highest level, I could not possibly decline the nomination. More importantly, politics is advocacy, and it posed a tremendous challenge. Just prior to entering politics, I had chaired a national taskforce on women in the labor force,[3] conducted a national survey on married women, which used life-cycle stages as an analytical framework for studying their needs and aspirations,[4] as well as chaired a committee of the national Advisory Council on Family and Community Life.[5] It would be an opportune time to press for the required changes identified by these various studies and committees.

As a woman parliamentarian, I was fully aware that a woman's constituency was part of my responsibilities. Together with the other two women who were members of Parliament (we were joined by a fourth in 1988), I pressed for equal medical benefits for female civil servants, citizenship rights of foreign spouses and children born abroad, childcare facilities, part-time work, flexible hours, the teaching of home economics to both boys and girls at school, changing women's media images, etc. Apart from my regular constituency work, I was chairperson of the Government Parliamentary Committee on Health. In 1989 I became chairperson of the newly formed Women's Wing of the ruling People's Action Party. During the first year of our work, we concentrated on building up a network of women's committees at the branch and district levels. We organized seminars to help raise women's political consciousness, and started leadership training and self-help programs for women. Meanwhile I continued lecturing full time in sociology at the National University, as members of Parliament in Singapore normally carry on with their own professions even while they serve as parliamentarians.

While I continue to work for the interest of women, I have faced nonetheless the dilemma that many women politicians in other countries have faced. Should we work exclusively on women's issues? Should we participate much more broadly in other areas so as to prove we are equally competent as men in such other areas? I must admit I have not concentrated exclusively on women's issues; instead, I have ranged over a rather broad arena. Perhaps this is one of the reasons why I have not encountered much stereotyping of myself as a "champion" of women's rights by my male colleagues. In fact, I have generally encountered very little male prejudice in the course of my work. At the constituency level, it may even be argued that being a woman provides me with some advantage during the MPs' weekly "meet-the-people sessions," which are similar to the "surgeries" of British M.P.s. These evening sessions are held to help resolve problems faced by constituents, for example, housing, employment, transport, etc. But sometimes the constituents would come with problems of a personal and family nature and women M.P.s are considered to be either more attentive or more inclined to deal with such problems. In addition to this perception, the tertiary educational background of all the four women M.P.s must have come into play, as we are not just perceived to be compassionate and helpful, but also professional and competent. My seven years of political experience also confirm that women M.P.s are particularly able to garner the support of women voters, irrespective of whether they are preceived as primarily champions of women's rights or not.

The state of women's studies

At the university, I continue to pursue my areas of specialization, namely, women's studies, family sociology, population, and urban sociology. Women's studies has not yet become a separate program at the National University of Singapore, the only university in Singapore at the moment.[6] For reasons I shall describe below, it is not likely to do so. However, staff and student interest has been on the rise over the past few years. Together with another colleague, Vivienne Wee, we started a course on Sociology of Gender in 1987. This may appear to be a late beginning, but our department has had to contend with a rigid degree structure, as well as some resistance from the older male professors at the faculty level. Of the two obstacles, the former was more formidable. The degree structure is such that the total number of elective courses (apart from compulsory courses) that a student can take within his/her two majors (e.g., sociology and economics) is very limited, and since they are year-long courses rather than semester courses, the number of courses that can be offered is also limited. While this type of degree structure, following as it does the British university model, provides depth rather than breadth of training, it does mean that multidisciplinary or loosely structured programs are difficult to initiate. It also means that, within the Department of Sociology, we are unlikely to be able to have more than one or two courses on women's studies.

As far as the course on Sociology of Gender is concerned, with hindsight, we could have started it a little earlier, because a critical mass of interest in women's issues was already forming. Several women faculty members in sociology, English literature, political science and law have been engaged in research on women for some years. In sociology alone, the rise in student interest started in 1985. This is seen by the increasing proportion of honors, masters, and doctoral theses written on gender issues. Topics range from housewives and women working in different occupations and industries, to gender and religion, marriage and singlehood, work, leisure and retirement, to ethnicity, politics of procreation, domestic violence, rape, and prostitution. Between 1986 and 1990, some thirty honors theses out of a total of 107 were devoted to gender, as compared to eight out of a total of ninety-two between 1981 and 1985. In addition, there were four masters and one Ph.D. theses on women's issues.

Why this sudden interest? Two major reasons were the arrival of some new staff members and the return of students from graduate studies overseas. These included both men and women who had been exposed to women's studies abroad, or had become interested because of the intellectual trends at those universities. For though I was somewhat of a pioneer in research on women in Singapore, I could not carry on the work alone. Hence the importance of a critical mass of staff and student interest.

There were also other reasons related to the history of the department. The Department of Sociology was established in the former University of Singapore in 1966 with a handful of expatriate staff. The first Singaporean joined the department in 1970. There was a great dearth of local teaching materials.

Thus, the early years were spent on empirical research on local society. In the early 1970s a great deal of research emphasis was put on population, family, public housing, inter-ethnic relations, and social stratification. Those were the pressing areas in which basic research was required. The spurt of family planning research in the mid-1970s was also fueled by available funding by various international population agencies. Thus, during this period, research on women, including my earlier efforts, was stimulated mainly by what was going on outside the university, in connection with women's organizations and unions that participated in the UN Decade for Women's activities. However, much of the research then was done by individuals on an ad hoc basis, such as for the purpose of presenting papers at conferences. There was very little concerted effort to explore the field of women's studies.

It was only toward the end of the UN Decade that some attempts at consolidation were made, such as the publication of bibliographies on women in Singapore by the National Library,[7] and by the former Ministry of Social Affairs[8] which also set up an information resource center on women in 1983. However, the resource center was short-lived. Meanwhile, several women's groups have become prominent on the scene. The Singapore Women Lawyers' Association (SAWL) and the Association of Women for Action and Research (AWARE) have published popular booklets on women's rights and status, organized symposia and exhibitions and have been vocal on women's issues, as has the Singapore Council of Women's Organizations. These associations distinguish themselves from the longer-established women's organizations, which, by and large, are social, charitable, or professional organizations. Fresh, energetic, outspoken, the new women's organizations have become women's voices. They are groups linked by a fair amount of overlapping memberships and by close personal friendships.

Is there now a new era in feminist research and activities in Singapore? If so, it has been brought about to a great extent by women's large-scale entry into the workforce, and rising education and changing social values. It has also been brought about by conflicting messages in the government's policies on women's economic and reproductive roles.[9] Although women in Singapore enjoy equal rights with men in many areas (such as education, occupation, pay, property rights, and legal rights in marriage and divorce), and in some areas have privileges available only to women (e.g., paid maternity leave, no military service obligations), they are nonetheless subjected to a range of pressures that are the result of rapid socioeconomic changes. There is a great need for family and social support services for women to play their multiple roles. There is an overall feeling of urgency, and a crying need for more women to enter politics.

New developments and concerns

In this brief account, I have tried to weave in my personal metamorphosis with the institutional and political factors that helped shape the development of feminism and women's studies in Singapore. I feel excited by the recent developments. At the same time, I have several concerns.

Local academic research on women seems to be hovering only on the level of empirical research, with the range of topics covered simply expanding. There is not much reference to broad conceptual frameworks, although concepts are taken from feminist literature and used to organize the data. The question about this type of empirical research is: Are we going to do more of the same, and so what? What if our research merely replicates what other scholars have done in other societies, and all that we can claim is to be doing no more than documenting women's lives here, adding one more place to the list of societies thus covered? Is this all we have to contribute?

In the field of women's studies itself, theorization seems to have reached a plateau, awaiting further breakthroughs. As a sociologist trained in the positivist tradition, I feel ill at ease with the new feminist fascination with ethnomethodology. Much of what goes for ethnography now seems to be the "anything goes" type of writing. But surely, sociology must be concerned with structures and systemic forces. Even though we are interested in individual subjective experiences and consciousness, we cannot escape addressing issues of the labor market, social class, ethnicity, power elite, and so on. Since resources are limited, we must establish some research priorities relevant to the times and the society under scrutiny.[10]

Feminism is action for women. However, action for women can be too narrowly focused as to become no more than an interest group or a political lobby. As a politician, I am constantly aware of the need for checks and balances among various interest groups. Equality for women, or, for that matter, for any other group, must not be simply a matter of rough justice.

If we were to arrive at a balance between self-interest, group interest, and national interest, there must be some give and take on the part of all involved. Thus, if feminism in Singapore appears to be conservative (and this need not be a contradiction in terms), we have no need to be apologetic about it.

Notes

1. Aline K. Wong, *Women in Modern Singapore*, Singapore: University Education Press, 1975.
2. Janet W. Salaff, *State and Family in Singapore*, Ithaca: Cornell University Press, 1988.
3. *Report of the Taskforce on Female Participation in the Labour Force*, Singapore: National Productivity Board, 1984.
4. *Report on National Survey on Married Women, their Role in the Family and Society,* Singapore: Ministry of Social Affairs, 1984.
5. *Report of the Advisory Council on Family and Community Life*, Singapore: Ministry of Community Development, 1989.
6. The Nanyang Technological Institute became a second university, known as Nanyang Technological University, in 1991.
7. *Women: A Booklist,* Singapore: National Library, 1985.
8. Marion Southerwood, *Information Resources on Women in Singapore: Survey and Bibliography*, Singapore: Ministry of Social Affairs, 1983.
9. Suzanne Goldberg, "Mixed Messages: Public Policy an Women in Singapore," *Commentary: Journal of the National University of Singapore Society,* Special Issue on Women's Choices, Women's Lives, 7, no. 2 & 3 (1987): 25–37.
10. Aline K. Wong, "Research Issues on Women and Development in Singapore in the 1980s," *Commentary* 7, no. 2 & 3, (1987): 13-18.

Aurora Javate De Dios
Philippines

AURORA JAVATE DE DIOS is a
teacher and researcher who has
been involved in the Philippines'
women's movement for many
years. A former political detain-
ee under the Marcos regime, de
Dios campaigned actively for the
rights of Filipina entertainers and
domestic helpers abroad, and
against U.S. bases and the debt
problem. She has served on various feminist and academic
bodies (such as KALAYAAN, a
feminist group) and is co-con-
venor of the Women's Studies
Consortium and the Freedom
from Debt Coalition. She has also
written and published widely on
women.

Triumphs and Travails:
Women's Studies in the Academy

•∧•∧•∧•∧•

It seems almost a refrain to a song, the questions that follow a discussion on women's issues. "Is it true that the women's movement is made up of frustrated, separated women who live unhappy lives?" "Does your husband approve of your opinions and ideas on women?"

Introducing women's issues in schools, among educators, students and other professionals in workshops, seminars, and the classroom, is as much a test of one's theoretical preparedness on the subject, as of one's patience. In many cases, I soon found out, it also entails laying bare one's personal life to give flesh and blood to what one is attempting to advocate. Women, too often glamorized and trivialized in the media, suddenly disturb and provoke as a serious subject.

In classrooms, boardrooms, and bedrooms, in congressional halls and in the parliament of the streets, intense discussion on women and women's rights still continues. Nearly a decade after Nairobi,[1] the ideal of women's equality and empowerment seems to be as distant as when it was first raised and acknowledged as an issue. And yet the perceptible, if at times wary, interest in consciousness raising—the slow and arduous process of transforming attitudes and thinking, as well as institutions—about women has at last begun.[2]

Introduction to feminism

My own introduction to feminism was not a formal one. Our family of six girls and one boy provided me with my first exposure to women's power as the daily affairs of the household were efficiently run by the women, without much help from the men. My father, a gentle person, came home only on weekends from work in another province, and seemed to leave everything to my mother. My grandmother, a strong-willed woman who excelled in the kitchen as she did in daily discourse with my grandfather, was as assertive as any modern-day feminist. While tending to her *botica* (drug store) and practicing her profession as a pharmacist,[3] my mother reared all seven of us as if it were the most natural thing to do. In those two women I saw qualities of resourcefulness, tenacity, self-reliance, and forbearance in the face of adversity, qualities that would later shape my own worldview of women. Yet my socialization, like anyone else's, was as traditional as studying home economics, with my *Lola* (grandmother) teaching me the rudiments of cooking at the age of ten, because this was indispensable to being a good wife.

I remember being admonished for being a *callahera*[4] when, as a child, I would play *tumbang preso*[5] with boys and girls my age. "Be home before dark," my Lola used to tell me and my sisters, though we never fully understood why. My mother and grandmother never spoke to me about assertiveness and feminism, phrases which they had probably never heard of anyway. Though they were bringing us up in the very traditional ways in which they were themselves reared as women by their mothers, the sheer strength of their characters, coupled with their resourcefulness, exemplified what, to me, were the qualities of latter-day feminists.

Activist involvement

The University of the Philippines was the seat of student activism in the 1970s[6] and, like most students, I was involved in the many mass actions to protest against the Vietnam war and the Philippines' role in a war not of our own making. My deepening political commitment caused my parents sleepless nights: they repeatedly attempted to dissuade me from joining street marches as much out of their concern for my personal safety as their own frustration in my taking up such an "unladylike" activity, which was not in line with my career path. I originally intended to be a diplomat and took up foreign service in college. Joining the mass movement at that time was like joining a social laboratory where students, professionals, and out-of-school youth from the middle class "integrated" with striking factory workers and joined the peasants in northern Philippines "to learn from the people."[7]

Among the many mass organizations that emerged in the intensely political atmosphere of the early 1970s was an all-woman organization that raised the issue of women's liberation. Malayang Kilusan ng Bagong Kababaihan, or MAKIBAKA[8] (League of New and Independent Women), was greeted with guarded enthusiasm by both male and female activists coming from the bigger mixed political organizations, alternately hailing it and warning of its divisive effects on the movement as a whole.

As early as the 1890s, Filipino women, especially those coming from the upper classes, began organizing in support of the independence movement against Spanish colonizers. A few exceptional women like Gabriela Silang even led troops in actual combat against the Spanish. Many more women, like Trinidad Tecson, Tandang Sora, and Teresa Magbanua, were to distinguish themselves as outstanding women during the revolution against Spain.[9]

The Americans succeeded in frustrating the Philippines' bid for independence in 1898 when they defeated the revolutionary forces led by General Aguinaldo. The American period saw the establishment of numerous women's organizations that campaigned for women's suffrage. The granting of voting rights to women in 1937 may be considered a high point in the development of the women's movement in the Philippines. Other women's organizations that emerged, especially after the postwar period (1940s and 1950s), mainly concentrated on civic and charity work for unwed mothers, prison reforms for female inmates, and so on, in short, reinforcing the domestic and auxiliary roles of women as wives and homemakers.[10]

MAKIBAKA emerged during a period of nationalist ferment, from 1968 to 1970, and began as a predominantly male-led activist movement for women's rights. Its beginnings may be traced to the women of Samahang Demokratikong Kabataan (SDK Movement of Democratic Youth), who saw the need to establish a separate group not only to mobilize women in political activities but also to raise their consciousness. Composed mainly of middle-class students, many coming from exclusive women's colleges in Manila, MAKIBAKA clarified in its manifestos that it is a distinct movement but integral to the national democratic struggle. Though its feminist orientation may be considered incipient, MAKIBAKA was by far the most political women's group in the 1970s. Its first mass action was a picket protesting the "commoditization of women" in the Miss Philippines contest. However, most of its activities re-volved around the issues of U.S. military bases, high prices which affect the masses, especially housewives, and childcare. Among its projects at the time was a childcare center catering to urban poor women and their children. The historical signif-icance of MAKIBAKA's founding was noted by Aida Santos:

> Locating the condition of women in the cultural superstructure, MAKIBAKA saw the need to integrate women's concerns into the broad national concerns of the movement. It tried to define the dynamics between class oppression and gender inequality. By es-tablishing an all-women group, the organization was really as-serting the need for their own cultural revolution, a battle that has to be fought in the arena of the male-dominated nationalist movement.[11]

I found myself instinctively supportive of this incipient feminist movement yet too preoccupied with the "larger" po-litical concerns of the day—U.S. imperialism as exemplified by the presence of its bases in the Philippines, feudalism, and bu-reaucratic capitalism—which the Movement for a Democratic Philippines (MDP), the organization to which I belonged, con-sistently pursued.[12]

Somehow a fourth "ism" did not quite fit into the political agenda of most progressive organizations, especially one that pried into the private sphere of relationships as an issue along-side other political issues. Even then I felt the unease and ten-sion that often surfaced in discussions on feminism among the activists.

MAKIBAKA, founded in 1971, managed to survive for about a year. In 1972, after staging fake ambushes of his cabi-net members, President Marcos used the widespread protest against his regime as an excuse to declare martial law in the country. Along with other mass organizations, MAKIBAKA was declared illegal and all its members went underground. Lorena Barros, an outstanding young, feminist poet who headed MAKIBAKA, later joined the New People's Army and died in an encounter in 1976. Nothing was heard of the organi-zation after martial law since many of its members were ei-ther detained or had joined other underground groups. How-ever, in the 1986 peace talks held between the Government of the Philippines, then headed by President Corazon Aquino and the National Democratic Front (NDF), MAKIBAKA re-emerged as one of the major organizations supporting the NDF.

Women under martial law: militarization and exploitation

Martial law was declared ostensibly to quell subversion and build a new society. But the fourteen years of the Marcos' dictatorship brought untold suffering to Filipinos, even as they enriched a few during the martial law years.[13] Marcos' regime was propped up by his coterie of "cronies," the military, and massive doses of U.S. aid. Despite the limited Philippine insurgency movement (no more than twenty thousand at the beginning of martial law in 1972), the military increased from a force of only 60,000 in 1972 to 3,00,000 in 1975, excluding the 221,000-strong paramilitary forces called the Civilian Home Defense Forces (CHDF), intelligence groups, and armed religious fanatics directly or indirectly supported by the military.[14]

Where military might is supreme, human rights abuses are bound to occur. The late Senator Jose W. Diokno noted that "if democracy rests on the premise that it is easier to count heads than to break them, militarism proceeds from the premise that it is easier to break heads than to change minds."[15] With the dismantling of democratic structures like the media and the legislature, all power was concentrated in the president, who transformed the government into a fascist dictatorship. Arbitrary arrests, search-and-destroy operations, and looting became commonplace. Being critical of the martial law in any form was an offense that merited imprisonment.

"Salvaging" acquired a new meaning under the Marcos regime—it meant extra-judicial killings. Torture of political prisoners was rampant. Women prisoners were subjected to rape, sexual assault, and harassment. A 1985 study conducted by GABRIELA noted that there were fifteen hundred recorded cases of women who suffered varying degrees of military harassment, ranging from arbitrary arrests to torture, rape, and salvaging.[16] Thousands more will never be known as the victims prefer to remain silent. Many wives, mothers, sisters, and daughters were casualties in strafing operations in the countryside. In areas where military operations were launched to flush out rebels, women became fair game to soldiers. Wives of suspected subversives were threatened with rape to force confessions. More than six hundred activists, many of them women, have disappeared since martial law.[17]

Female prisoners are the most frequent victims of sexual harassment, molestation, and rape. According to Tita Lubi, herself a victim of military abuse, even before a woman is brought to prison, she is molested by her captors in transit. She would be strip-searched, cajoled into submitting to the sexual advances of the military in exchange for freedom, or turned into a "girlfriend" with a promise of better treatment. To force them to divulge information, they were often threatened, if not actually subjected, to various acts of lasciviousness and rape.[18]

As a political activist during this period of repression, I was in constant fear for my life and the lives of my relatives and friends, many of whom died, disappeared, or were tortured. While in detention in 1978, I have known of personal accounts of torture suffered by my co-detainees which deeply affected and traumatized me. Accounts of Amnesty International and the Task Force Detainees in the Philippines have documented many cases of human rights abuses of women which show that, in fact, the most barbaric and gruesome crimes have been committed by men who are sworn to uphold the law.[19]

Despite the repression unleashed by the Marcos regime on democratic mass movements, underground urban- and rural-based resistance movements flourished. Women were part of the overall efforts to fight the dictatorship in both armed and unarmed spheres. Manifesto writing, underground network building, writing and distributing underground newspapers, and participating in lightning rallies, pickets, and prayer vigils were the main forms of resistance in the cities. Women acted as couriers and intelligence gatherers and many joined the armed struggle waged by the New People's Army. Sources also disclosed the formation of an all-women detachment of the New People's Army in the Cordilleras. In the NPA guerilla zones, the Barrio Organizing Committee always included a Women's Committee composed of peasant women.[20]

Except for MAKIBAKA, most of the prominent women's organizations were mainly civic- or charity-oriented in the early 1970s. Martial law allowed little room for fence-sitting. Many women's groups, previously uninvolved, were politicized. Women's religious organizations, in particular the Association of Major Religious Superiors and especially its Task Force Detainees, were at the forefront of the anti-dictatorship struggle. Women journalists, who organized under Women in Media

Now (WOMEN), dared to challenge the press censorship imposed by the military by publishing critical stories about militarization and, as a result, suffered surveillance and constant threats from the military. Concerned Women of the Philippines, an organization of daughters of former presidents and former cabinet officials, also exposed the torture of women political prisoners.[21]

It may be noted therefore, that although martial law had the effect of curtailing the nascent growth of the women's movement, it hastened the politicization of traditional or civic-oriented women's groups and contributed to the development of many women activists who later re-emerged in 1983.

The commodification of the Filipinas

After a few years of the World Bank-IMF dictated economic strategy of export-led industrialization, which the Marcos government had adopted since martial law, the country sank even deeper into economic crisis: this is evident in the massive unemployment, malnutrition, and militarization in the countryside. Young, poorly-paid women workers constituted 88.24 percent of the labor force in the Bataan export processing zone,[22] the showcase of the Marcos industrialization platform. Poorly-paid and mostly unorganized young women, coming especially from the countryside, became the backbone of the profitable electronics and garments industries, two emerging growth areas of the Philippine economy in the 1980s.

Meanwhile, using Filipinas as come-ons, the Ministry of Tourism mounted a sales blitz in a bid to increase tourist arrivals in the country. In just five years of active international promotion, tourist arrivals jumped from 166,431 in 1972 (the first year of martial law) to 1,008,159 in 1980.[23] To the hordes of Japanese male tourists, "sex tours" increasingly became associated with going to the Philippines. Only the determined opposition of women's groups in the Philippines and Japan temporarily put a stop to this trend. Because of the uproar the "sex tours" caused in the different Asian countries where Japanese tourists went, Japanese promoters imported "entertainers" from the Philippines, Thailand, and Taiwan. Known as *Japayukisan*, or Japan-bound women, these entertainers were employed as hostesses in the giant entertainment and prostitution industry in Japan.[24]

Filipino women also sought employment overseas as domestic helpers in the Middle East (Saudi Arabia, Kuwait, etc.), Europe (Spain, Great Britain, etc.), and Asia (Hong Kong, Singapore, etc.). It became clear that the export of labor was a major dollar-earning industry which benefitted the government. By the end of the Marcos term in 1986, the overseas labor industry was contributing more than a billion pesos in foreign exchange to the national coffers.[25] A clear trend had emerged by this time, the feminization of land-based overseas migration.

The search for greener pastures has taken another form for thousands of Filipinas who marry Australians, Germans, Japanese, and other foreigners via the mail-order bride trade, pen pal clubs, or through marriage brokers.[26] Whether as entertainers, domestic helpers, or "mail-order-brides," Filipinas are exposed to the risks and dangers of sexual abuse and exploitation such as contract substitution, rape, sexual harassment, trafficking for prostitution, and many others.[27]

The plight of the Filipina is succintly described by Aguilar:

> There is no denying that the blueprint for modernization that set into motion the process whereby the Philippines would join the "newly industrializing countries" also brought women into the sphere of public production or, to use a euphemism, "integrated women in development." The irony, as we have seen, is that this integration has worked in contradictory ways. Simultaneously pulling them into the realm of remunerated labour and pushing them off into the seedy margins of society, displacing them and drastically deforming their lives.[28]

The women's movement gains ground

The assassination of former Senator Benigno Aquino in August 1983 became the catalyst that mobilized thousands of Filipinos from complacency to political militancy. Not surprisingly, women became part of the surge of activism, asserting, as they never did, their right to overthrow an unjust regime. The formation in 1984 of GABRIELA, a coalition of women's organizations from the ranks of the grassroots women, the middle class, and some elements of the elite, was a watershed in the development of the women's movement.[29]

By the time Marcos declared a "snap election" in February 1986, women's groups were ready and organized to help run Corazon Aquino's campaign across the country, even while the more militant ones chose to boycott the elections. Cory's Crusaders sprouted all over in support of her candidacy. The dramatic turn of events in February 1986, sparked by a military revolt among former Marcos followers, paved the way for the eventual downfall of the dictatorship and the popular installation of Corazon Aquino as president, the first woman president of the country. There is no denying the pivotal role played by spontaneous people's power in this historic event, but one must view this also as a culmination of a long, drawn-out struggle of the Filipino people, in which women's groups played an important role.

The context of women's studies in the Philippines

Eventually the politicization of women's groups and the articulation of women's issues in the streets reverberated in the halls of academic institutions. At the outset it should be noted that the development of women's studies is inextricably linked with that of the broader movement for political and social change, of which the women's movement is an integral part. It can even be said that the academy is belatedly responding to the changing realities and the increased visibility of women in politics, in economic life, and in the professions.

Several considerations have to be taken into account in the way women's studies in the Philippines has been and is being shaped. First, women's studies arose from the concrete struggles of the women's movement in the anti-dictatorship struggle in the 1970s and 1980s. Thus women's studies necessarily reflects the democratic, nationalist, anti-feudal, and anti-imperialist character of the progressive movement as a whole. Continued feudal and imperialist domination impinges on the women's movement, and that is most evident in the still-strong colonial overlay in our national culture and the capitalist economy where cheap women's labor has become an important element. The importance of a feminist analytic framework in interrogating the contemporary problem of foreign political and economic domination is emphasized by Aguilar:

> In utilizing instruments of analysis that attempt to disentangle the intricate interweaving of gender, class and nation or ethnicity underpinning differential access to power, feminism has the capacity for broadening and deepening the movement for social reconstruction.[30]

Organized efforts to infuse education with a woman's perspective were initially undertaken separately, but almost simultaneously, by schools with a strong social orientation, such as the University of the Philippines College of Social Work, Maryknoll College, and St Scholastica's College.

The second factor that affects the substance of women's studies in the Philippines is the pervasive poverty of the majority of the Filipino women in the hovels of the urban slums and the militarized countryside. The methodologies and approaches of women's studies will have to be innovative and relevant to reach women who would normally not have any access to higher education. The role of popular education carried out not only by educational institutions but by women's groups, centers, and institutions is extremely crucial. The use of the national language (Filipino) in this effort at popularization is of extreme importance. As noted in a recent study:

> The colonial relationship between the U.S. and the Philippines demonstrates that language is power. With the imposition of English, the country became dependent on a borrowed language that carries with it the dominant political and economic interest of the U.S. . . . Conversely, the struggle of the Filipino people to emancipate themselves from foreign domination, including the value bias of the colonizers' concepts and postulates of reasoning, must also encompass the liberation of their national language. Linguistic nationalism is one of the weapons of the Filipinos against the growing U.S. economic and cultural domination.[31]

By utilizing our national language fully in the academy, as well as in our training programs, the women's movement is contributing to the narrowing of the great cultural divide between the English-speaking elite and the masses. In the process of utilizing indigenous dialects, we hope to fully explore and discover their potential for non-sexist linguistic usages.

Third, the interrelationship of the Philippine women's movement with those in other countries, as well as the linkage of international feminist scholarship with our own, are especially significant. Of particular importance here are the experiences of other Third World women's movements with whom we share common aspirations and issues. We need to understand religious fundamentalism and its repressive effects on women's liberation, militarization, economic underdevelopment, trafficking of women, reproductive rights, and sexual violence against women, which are but some of the issues that should be encompassed by women's studies in the Third World.

Fourth, the impact of women in development studies must also be investigated. Though the rationale for such studies was to generate benchmark information as the basis for national government policies on development in the early 1970s, the data proved to be useful to the women's movement in the long run. Despite its apparent inadequacy as a feminist approach in that it merely "integrates women in development" without a critical questioning of inherent gender and class inequalities in development, the WID studies are useful in two ways: first, women scholars who conducted such studies became feminists in the process; and second, new approaches evolved as a result of such research. These have further sharpened the academic circle's appreciation of the complexity of women's issues. These analytic tools have been used by women's groups in their advocacy of women's issues as well as in fine-tuning their own feminist approaches.[32]

Introducing women's studies to the academy

Research by feminist scholars has unravelled the ways in which traditional disciplines, from history to literature, sociology, and the natural sciences, have been gender biased in at least one of the following ways:

· Exclusion of women as subject matter.
· Distortion of the female image according to male perceptions.
· Denial of value to characteristics which society considers "feminine."

Only when women begin to consciously and critically reassess these assumptions within academic disciplines will the root causes of prejudice against women be addressed and redressed.

As a teacher, I have had to contend with my own gender blindness which, given my progressive background, I did not even realize was there. But my experiences and activist involvements, especially with feminists, helped to clarify my self-perception as a woman and reflect this in my teaching and lobbying work. My experience as a wife and a mother of three children helped sharpen my own understanding and appreciation of women's double burden. Along with other parents of my generation, we were keen to see that our children get a more enlightened, democratic, and gender-sensitive education. We found out that this was not going to happen unless we, in the profession, effect changes in the very content and substance of education. Many teacher organizations address the colonial and anti-democratic features of our educational system. I and other women's rights advocates in the academy choose to complement these efforts and address the gender dimension in education.

Miriam College (formerly Maryknoll College) was the institutional setting of the Women's Resource and Research Center (WRRC), which was established in 1987 to help in the empowerment of women through research, education, and advocacy. I was presented with a challenging opportunity when, as the women's studies director for two years, I was asked to introduce the women's perspective to our teachers in Maryknoll College. Though a core course on women has been offered since 1974, it was only in 1987 that the course was revised to reflect a more feminist approach.

The teaching of women's studies requires a style of pedagogy that encourages critical thinking, as well as classroom interaction, and participatory processes by tapping the wellspring of the students' personal experiences. Women's studies consciously links scholarship with activism. In our classes the lived experiences and insights of women activists and organizers from different sectors are integral to the curriculum. Since the establishment of the Women's Studies Consortium (WSC) in Metro Manila,[33] students often join seminars and symposia on women's issues such as sexual harassment, the condition of women workers, prostitution, and trafficking in women, all of which help to enrich the course itself.

Fieldwork, such as we had in the nightspots in and around the Clark Airbase in Angeles, Pampanga (where the U.S. Air Force base is located), helps students to become sensitive to the plight of women prostitutes who are often the same age as they are. A module on women and health helps clarify the students' own sexual and physical misconceptions. At the end of the semester, the students usually make a qualitative evaluation of the course. One student revealed that the subject helped her "to remove the blindfold from my eyes; it made me look closely at the real nature of women in society as oppressed, exploited, and deprived." Another student stated, "My consciousness was awakened to the kind of gender relationships that are going on in our family, within the community, and within society as a whole." Of late, my classes in women and society have included male students. Though terribly outnumbered, they have provided our class with useful insights on how men perceive the women's movement. Many of them admit to feeling "threatened" by feminism and initially perceive its influence on family relationships as "negative." One of my male students told the class that after reading a particularly critical piece, he felt as if he were a "criminal."

My classes often become a veritable battleground of ideas on male and female perceptions of issues such as marriage, relationships, prostitution, etc. As much as possible, I give full play to these debates and try to synthesize them at the end of the class. Grappling with their own feelings while deconstructing the very premises of their knowledge can unsettle the students' long-held beliefs. But given enough time to reflect and process their own ideas and inputs, both female and male students come out more enlightened about their own selves.

There is no doubt that women's studies has had a powerful impact on the students' consciousness and personal lives. Though not yet a degree course in many schools, the value of the woman's perspective is now better appreciated in such courses as psychology, sociology, and the communication arts. A number of faculty members in our school have begun "integrating" this perspective into their specific disciplines. "Integrating," or "mainstreaming," has very often meant including a module on women in a specialized course in history, literature, sociology, or psychology. Another approach utilized by the communication arts teachers at Miriam College has been to assign women-specific thesis topics to students. This has resulted in over one hundred studies on various aspects of women and communication. The introduction of courses such as "Women and Society" is just the beginning of many other women-specific courses being planned by different departments in our school.

The establishment of the WSC in 1987 gave a big boost to women's studies.[34] Each of the schools involved was at a different level of introducing women's studies in their respective schools, but the prime movers were united in their perception of the problems and challenges that the consortium faced. Teacher training was placed right on top of the agenda of the consortium.

By the summer of 1988, the WSC was able to hold a National Teacher Training Workshop with about one hundred faculty members from the participating provinces. An Elementary Teacher Training Seminar soon followed in November of the same year. In September 1989, the consortium conducted its own needs assessment to determine, among other things, the groups' long-range plans as they related to development in general.

The WSC is typical of most women's initiatives. Lacking funding support even from their own institutions, the consortium managed to sustain its activities mainly through voluntary work in the first two years of its existence. Meetings were held "round robin" style, with each school taking turns in hosting one. Resource persons and materials are also mutually shared. Decisions are always arrived at by consensus, yet each school is free to pursue its own initiatives in promoting women's studies nationwide. For instance, the WRRC had a series of "echo-seminars" in December 1987 to disseminate its various research findings and discussion papers in Visayas and Mindanao. St. Scholastica's Institute of Women's Studies regularly conducts an Intercultural Regional Workshop on women and society where women participants from the Asia Pacific region are invited. The College of Social Work and Community is the first institution in the country to offer a master's degree course in women and development for both men and women.

It can be said that a truly national women's studies network has begun with the activities of the Consortium. In January 1992, just as we all had envisioned, a formal national group, the Women's Studies Association of the Philippines, was organized.[35]

Possibilities and challenges ahead

Women's studies faces a bright future in the Philippines. The enthusiastic response of students to courses on women categorized as either women's studies or gender studies, as well as the endorsement of teachers all across the country, confirm its timeliness and relevance. Yet, we are also faced with many formidable problems that need to be addressed.

Institutionalization of women's studies at all levels in the private and public school systems is one of the main objectives of the Women's Studies Association of the Philippines. This means dealing with school bureaucrats who may be openly hostile or slow in recognizing the importance of gender issues in education. Lukewarm or token support and lack of financial support are some of the things that face women's studies programs. Women's studies has yet to make its mark as a distinct academic area in most colleges in the Philippines. The Department of Education and Sports, which formed a Focal Point Group to initiate gender training within the Department of Education, has a long way to go in fully introducing gender issues in its educational programs.

Where women's studies cannot as yet be introduced as a degree course, an independent subject, or a research program, the "mainstreaming" approach has been increasingly utilized. Mainstreaming entails, at the very least, a recognition of the need to correct sexist myths and notions at every level of the educational process in the different subject areas, especially in the social sciences.

Indigenization has been identified as one of the major concerns of the Women's Studies Association of the Philippines. Not only is women's studies viewed as a "trendy" area in the academic world, it is often viewed as too western. This is reinforced by the fact that many textbooks on women's studies are western. Acutely aware of this problem, the members of the Women's Studies Association have been active in producing textbooks and reference materials written by Filipinas in Filipino. Babaylan Publishing House of the Institute of Women's Studies in St. Scholastica's College, for instance, has already published a good number of herstories. WRRC and the University Center for Women's Studies at the University of the Philippines continue to grow every year. Many women's groups, among them KALAYAAN, to which I belong, and GABRIELA, continue to produce books on women.

Research on women conducted by the University in Los Banos, the University of the Philippines in the Visayas, the Philippine Women's University, and numerous training programs at the College of Social Work and Community Development and the University of the Philippines, has contributed to this effort at indigenization. Audio-visual materials, documentaries, and theses written by students at the graduate and undergraduate levels are likewise enriching the women's studies field.

Women's studies can be introduced, as it has been in the Philippines, through a variety of channels. According to a survey conducted by the Women's Studies Association in 50 schools in 1991, women's issues have been taken up by teachers in research, teaching, outreach, and extension programs, as well as in creative and literary writing. A wealth of material from different regions written in several local dialects is waiting to be discovered and organized. Particularly significant is the contribution of the grassroots-based women's groups in the field of non-formal education.

A personal note

I consider myself quite fortunate in that my experiences as a political activist, mother, wife, and academic all seem to converge and help clarify my goals in life. However, as part of the First Quarter Storm generation of the early 1970s, spanning several tumultous political periods, many of us feel rather unsure about the kind of legacy we have given our children. For those of us who experienced prolonged detentions and absence from mainstream political life, adjustment has been extremely difficult. People like myself who are in the teaching profession have managed to channel our idealism into education.

My recent involvement in feminism and, more specifically, in women's studies has broadened my own understanding of the fundamental causes of society's inequities and helped me to come to terms with issues I rarely confronted in my youth. In particular, the personal dimension of liberation that the women's movement espouses alongside the political was not highlighted, nor considered important, in the progressive movement of the past. A more holistic approach is now being increasingly accepted, which sees the interconnection between issues like political liberation, sustainable development, the peace movement, the environmental movement, and the women's movement in the process of social change.

My three children (one young man in college and two girls in the elementary grade) often ask me and my husband what it was like in our youth, and I tell them of the many trials we and our friends had to face. I tell them that many of the things that were wrong then are still wrong now, but that they, too, can do something about these issues in their own little ways. My girls are very active in promoting environmental issues in their school and my son likes to express his ideas in music. I would like to think that our generation has contributed something in making my children's lives better and more enlightened and giving them a sense of respect for human dignity (especially of women and children) and for nature. After all, in the end, their future is for them to shape.

Notes

1. The Philippine government, through the National Commission on the Role of the Filipino Women, then headed by the former First Lady, Imelda Marcos, actively participated in the Decade of Women and in the Nairobi conference. Several women's groups, however, presented an alternative report on women to counter the government position during the conference itself.

2. Among the earliest written materials on women in the Philippines were those written in 1928 and 1934, entitled *The Development and Progress of the Filipino Women*, by Ma. Paz Guanzon (1928) and *Filipino Women*, by Encarnacion Alzona (1934). Though much more research was done towards the end of the 1970s, the actual beginnings of women's studies as a specific academic stream dates from the mid-1980s.

3. In the 1950s pharmacists mixed medicines prescribed by doctors and sometimes even gave patients their injections.

4. *Callahera* means a girl who loves to roam the streets; this is considered inappropriate behavior for girls.

5. *Tumbang preso* is a local game played by two teams competing to strike arranged tin cans. This game is usually played in the middle of the street at night.

6. This period is otherwise known as the First Quarter Storm, as thousands of students held massive demonstrations against the corrupt regime of President Marcos, which was perceived to be a puppet government of the U.S. For more details on this period, see Pete Lacaba, *Days of Disquiet, Nights of Rage*, Manila: Salinlahi Publishing House, 1982.

7. "Learn from the People" drives were sponsored by the UP Student Council, where students from the University of the Philippines were encouraged to spend their summers with peasants in the provinces.

8. *Malayang Kilusan ng Bagong Kababaihan* (Movement for the Liberation of Women) was led by a UP scholar and writer, Lorena Barros. The organization was launched with a sensational picket staged to protest the Miss Philippines contest featuring Gemma Araneta, herself a former Miss Philippines and a Miss International titleholder.

9. A more detailed account of this period can be found in Aida Santos' article "Do Women Really Hold Up Half of the Sky?" in *Essays on Women*, Manila: St. Scholastica's College, 1987, p. 37.

10. Some feminists regard the suffragist movement as part of the overall pacification campaign of the Americans in the Philipines and, thus, an essentially reformist movement.

11. Aida Santos, "The Cultural Revolution and the Women's Movement," in *BAI* 2 (December 1988), p. 4.

12. The Movement for a Democratic Philippines (MDP) was one of the biggest coalitions of progressive student, labor, and peasant groups in the early 1970s, which challenged the declaration of martial law by President Marcos.

13. See Aurora Javate de Dios, et. al., (eds.), *Dictatorship and Revolution*, Quezon City: Conspectus Foundation, 1988.
14. Ibid.
15. Ibid.
16. Aurora Javate de Dios, "Participation of Women's Groups in the Anti-Dictatorship Struggle," paper read at the National Women's Studies Association, Atlanta, Georgia, 1987.
17. Task Force Detainees and KAPATID (meaning brother or sister) were established during martial law to monitor human rights abuses and to assist families of victims of torture, detention, and involuntary disappearance. It has been in existence during the Marcos years, the Aquino administration, and the government of President Fidel Ramos, elected in the May 1992 elections.
18. Elisa Tita Lubi, "From Inside Prison Walls," in *And She Said No,* Quezon City: National Council of Churches in the Philippines Program Unit on Human Rights, 1990.
19. Accounts of Amnesty International and Task Force Detainees, from 1974 onwards, increasingly showed this pattern. Many of the notorious military torturers later figured prominently in the February 1986 revolt that toppled the Marcos dictatorship and paved the way for the popular Aquino administration.
20. Aurora Javate de Dios, "Participation of Women's Groups in the Anti-Dictatorship Struggle,"op. cit.
21. Ibid.
22. For an extended discussion on women in the export-oriented industries see R. Pineda, "Domestic Outwork for Export Oriented Industries," in Amaryllis Torres (ed.), *The Filipino Women in Focus,* Bangkok: UNESCO, 1989.
23. Japanese group tours in the early 1980s were promoted abroad as sex tours until Filipino and Japanese women's groups, among them the Japan Christian Temperance Union and the Third World Movement Against the Exploitation of Women, pressured the Japanese government to stop this outrage.
24. There were an estimated eighty thousand Filipina entertainers in Japan in 1992, half of them undocumented workers. Because of the high-risk nature of their jobs, which are mainly controlled by the dreaded Yakuza, there have been numerous reports of mysterious deaths, beatings, torture, and enforced prostitution of Filipinas in Japan. See Senate Committee Report No. 1033, *On the Plight of Filipinas Working Overseas,* 6 April 1990, and Senate Committee Report No. 1681, *On the Death of Maricris Sioson and the Plight of the Filipina Entertainers in Japan,* 12 December 1991, Manila, Senate of the Republic of the Philippines.
25. The earnings of the overseas contract workers, half of whom are women numbering more than five hundred million, contribute an estimated U.S. $1 billion in foreign exchange to the national economy. It is the third largest dollar-earning industry of the Philippines, next to garments and electronics.
26. In recent years there has been a dramatic increase in Filipinas mar-

rying foreigners through third-party channels and marriage brokers. Increasingly too, pornographic materials in the West feature Filipinas as wives. *Asiatinnen*, an erotic magazine in Germany, regularly features Filipinas for marriage.

27. In the recent Gulf War, Filipina domestic helpers in Kuwait were raped by some Kuwaitis and Iraqui soldiers. Some Filipinas who were abused by their employers were driven to commit murders. An increasing number of psychiatric cases have also been noted by service centers assisting overseas contract workers.

28. Delia Aguilar, "Women in the Political Economy in the Philippines," in *The Feminist Challenge*, Manila: Asian Social Institute, 1988.

29. GABRIELA (named after the nationalist woman warrior, Gabriela Silang), an alliance of women's organizations, initially constituted a "rainbow coalition." Later the alliance was dominated by the militant women's groups and is now composed of over 100 organizations nationwide, most of them grassroots women's groups.

30. Aguilar, op. cit., p. 16.

31. Torres, op. cit.

32. Class evaluation of Women and Society classes, 1988–1989, Miriam College, 1989.

33. The Women's Studies Consortium is composed of representatives from St. Scholastica's College, University of the Philippines, College of Social Work, De La Salle University, Miriam College-WRRC, Philippine Women's University, Ateneo de Manila Gender Studies Committee, and the Philippine Normal College.

34. The Women's Studies Association of the Philippines was formalized as a national organization of women's studies advocates and teachers in January 1992.

Cho Hyoung
Korea

CHO HYOUNG (b. 1943) has studied at the universities of Harvard and Seoul. At present she is Professor of Sociology, Ehwa Women's University, and has held several other academic posts in both Korea and the U.S. She is also a member of the Korean Association of Women's Studies and has many publications and translations to her credit.

To Grow with Women's Studies

The turning point

Life is a continuous affair, but one often faces moments of drastic change. The year 1975 was very special in my life. To begin with, that spring I began teaching at Ewha Women's University, my first fully committed job after my doctoral work. In addition, two separate events provided a critical momentum for my subsequent involvement in women's studies.

One was research on women factory workers that I conducted in the Seoul metropolitan area. It was on a small scale, but valuable for me in that it was my first exposure to non-middle-class women and, more importantly, to women's struggle for survival. This was followed by a series of research studies on rural and urban women over a span of seven years.

The other was a series of workshops held on the Ewha campus, where I was one of about twenty faculty from various fields, including philosophy, literature, history, law, sociology, psychology, education, and physiology. The aim of the workshops was to develop an experimental course in women's studies for Ewha undergraduates. During the workshops we had the opportunity to learn about developments in women's studies in the U.S. and in Europe, to compare the status of women in those countries with women in Korea, and to exchange ideas on basic issues in women's studies. Rather hot debates took place on certain questions. To illustrate a few:

Biological determinism/cultural determinism: Even though everyone could accept the feminist claim that so-called feminine and masculine characters were, to a large extent, formulated culturally through the socialization process, biological difference also seemed to be significant. What determines

53

gender and how it has been and is reproduced remained arguable theoretical problems.

The specificity of Korean women's studies: The oppression of women was understood as a universal and ubiquitous aspect of human history. However, it seemed necessary to discover varied patterns and associated factors before it could adequately be understood and explained. In this regard, what are the specific features of women's situation in Korea? Are Korean women unique? If so, what makes them unique? How does one relate the unique with the universal? A debate over the choice between "women's studies in Korea" and "Korean women's studies" reflected these questions.

Women's studies as an independent discipline: Participants at this workshop unanimously agreed on the necessity of women's studies as an elective general education course for young women and also agreed that a multi-disciplinary approach would be the most feasible form. However, there was skepticism concerning the feasibility and usefulness of women's studies as an independent discipline/department. (This attitude persisted for some time within the group, until members were persuaded by the popularity of the course.)

Integrating a gender perspective into existing courses: It was hoped that a feminist perspective would somehow be integrated into every single course offered on the Ewha campus. Most of the participants recognized that the sciences have developed in non-gender-sensitive ways. Although it was also realized that it would not be easy both technically and emotionally—indeed, there was, and still is, some resistance to women's studies on the campus—it was the direction that we hoped would develop.

On the whole the workshops were quite productive. They resulted in the compilation of two textbooks; in addition a pool of lecturers was formed for a women's studies course. The course was first offered in the fall of 1977 and has become increasingly popular. The workshop participants also acted as core members in establishing a research center, the Korea Women's Institute, in 1977 and the first master's degree program in women's studies was introduced in 1982. I am proud to have been a part of these developments.

"A promising sociologist" turned feminist

My involvement in the studies on women during the 1970s was not only exciting in itself but quite important for my academic and personal life. The whole process accelerated the growth of my inner self; but the process was gradual, until a dramatic moment made me realize it.

It was at a seminar in the Soknisan resort area, toward the end of 1979, where I presented a research proposal on poor urban women, that the turning point came. The group of participants was predominantly male and prominent sociologists and economists were present. Commenting on my proposal, a senior sociologist made a provocative remark: "Why should a promising young sociologist like you spend so much time and energy on such trivial matters as women and poverty?" In a sense he was trying to show affection and concern for a junior colleague. Whatever he meant, his comment sounded rude, arrogant, and even nasty. At that moment I had no stomach for an open retort; (Why? To be polite and feminine, to conform to the expectations of the participants...) but I said to myself quite firmly, "Hey, dear colleague, what constitutes important issues in your kind of sociology is not comparable to women and poverty for me. I admit that I have begun to take interest in a sociology qualitatively different from yours, and it is for the cause of equality and human liberation. From this moment I wouldn't mind not being recognized as "a promising sociologist" by you or your friends. I would be ashamed to be part of your world. Goodbye!" How free I felt after this private declaration!

At the same time I gradually became grateful to this man who had unintentionally prepared me to face the anti-feminist world. I cannot enumerate how many verbal and non-verbal comments I have encountered which meant the same thing as what he had said to me at the seminar. Comments such as the following have become quite familiar to me: "Yes, it is true that women in Korea are more disadvantaged than most men. But isn't it also true that it is partly the responsibility of the women themselves? Women are unprepared to compete with men, so whenever they try to, it only instigates chaos," or, "We agree that women's issues are important, but only secondary to serious class issues. Women can improve their status when the problems of the working class and farmers are solved. Until then women had better assist and support our movement."

My reaction to these has not been uniform. I tried to persuade my male listeners to recognize women's liberation as the companion of men's liberation. To women I propagated separatism: I still believe that Korean women ought to work towards freedom by themselves, rather than through cooperation with men, at least for some time, until Korean men become willing to fight against the social structures that have benefitted them, while keeping women imprisoned and oppressed.

I have to confess that my earlier academic concern was to expose myself as a Korean sociologist to the lives of Korean people in different strata, and that the nature of the studies remained plain fact-finding, so-called "scientific," empirical research. I took it for granted that sociology was a scientific endeavor and that science was exactly what I was doing. I was a well-disciplined student in the great tradition of U.S. structural-functionalism and empiricism. I had not imagined that I would lead a feminist revolt against conventional sociologists. However, by the time I came to writing the second paper based on my field research, I had begun to be increasingly bothered by feelings of guilt toward the objects of my research: I had been exploiting already disadvantaged women on whom I was producing articles to add to my professional credits.

There was another research project that helped to widen my latent feminist vision. It was on the role of women in the Korean national family planning policy and was sponsored by a feminist group within UNDP. As is well known, Korea was one of the countries that successfully lowered fertility during the decade of the mid-1960s to the mid-1970s. To find out what women did to achieve this success was the main concern of my research. Two groups of women were investigated: local family planning workers at the forefront of the implementation of the policy and the women in reproductive ages who were clients of the policy. Since the government emphasized female sterilization and female contraception, the family planning workers had to be women. We learned that the workers, who were temporary employees of the government, worked hard to meet the required number of acceptors of sterilization or contraception. On the clients' side, virtually all women of childbearing ages became the "targets" of these workers. Being persuaded by government agents (the government being the "authority" to many less-educated women) and believing incorrectly that male sterilization might cause permanent impotency and fragility, several women became "voluntary beneficiaries." To me many of them seemed to be "involuntary victims" of the policy. To be sterilized was perceived as a duty of a virtuous wife to her husband and thus to his ancestors. A majority of the women suffered side-effects, which had not been fairly reflected in the previous and subsequent research by researchers and planners, mostly male. Having become aware of all this, I could not help thinking of family planning in terms of a male conspiracy, manipulating women as agents and targets of the policy. It was no more than a project typical of the patriarchal system around the business of human reproduction, involving the family, the community, the government, and society as a whole. There was no room at all to allow the concept of "a woman's right to control her own body" to enter in the whole process of the planning and execution of the policy.

Around that time there came a turning point in my personal life. In the summer of 1979 my husband and I were formally separated despite my parents' strong objections. This was again a thing that had never been dreamed of before by a girl who had aspired to be a successful career woman, combining a profession and a happy marriage. I used to be a good child to my parents who treated my brother and me fairly equally. Brought up by a middle-class, well-educated couple and receiving an elite education, it seems to have been natural for me to identify my future self with a "superwoman." It was not a feminist identification, but a somewhat elitist one. I simply believed that a democratic society could not discriminate against outstanding women and that a woman's life becomes complete only with marriage and children.

I married a man of my choice while I was in graduate school. He was a thoughtful person who knew how to help out his student wife. We had a child after I had passed my qualifying exams. Our marriage seemed to go all right until after three years of involuntary separation—he was completing his doctoral dissertation in the U.S. and I was going through the resocialization process in Korea I have described above. When he came back to Korea, I suddenly found that he was a typical Korean man; a demanding and domineering husband and father of his child. He was happy to have a working wife, particularly in such a prominent job as that of a university professor, but he hated to see her preoccupied with outside activities and especially with the women's movement, women's studies, or anything in that line. He was even hostile to that sort of "unwomanly" activity.

While I was becoming more and more critical of the dictatorial, patriarchal, and vulgar capitalistic arrangement of Korean society, he was entering into it as a conformist. At home it meant not only two marriages, but two different worlds, espousing contradictory perspectives. The gulf was widening and becoming unbridgeable.

The late 1970s was certainly a difficult time for me. But I found myself containing the pain well, a sign of personal growth. I even congratulated myself for choosing to become "a notorious critical sociologist and a terrible feminist," and giving up a promising career as a conventional sociologist along with the pretense of being a happily married working housewife.

And the 1980s

The decade of the 1980s was a period of institutionalization of women's studies and of reorientation of the women's movement in Korea. These were consequences of the rise of women's consciousness during the previous decade. I participated in these processes as a self-declared feminist.

At Ewha I was an active member of the planning committee of the Korean Women's Institute. KWI undertook various research and action programs on women and coordinated women's studies courses on the campus. It was also the womb for the creation of the Department of Women's Studies in 1982. It was the only advanced degree program in Asia, as well as in Korea, until the spring of 1990 when two other universities introduced similar degrees. This program has been so popular that it recruits only outstanding students. What is more exciting about it to a teaching faculty is that by introducing feminist discourse, the classroom became an ideal setting for higher education. Both lecturers and students are frequently involved in debates through which both learn more than through reading.

Soon women's studies developed enough to gain popularity outside Ewha as well. More than twenty colleges and universities offered similar and related courses. In 1984 a new academic community was formed, the Korean Association of Women's Studies. Essentially a multi-disciplinary group, it became a target for the critics of women's studies. However, as a founding member I was happy to see those interested in women's studies develop and have a forum of their own to strengthen their identity. The academic standard of the association is outstanding, and the papers presented at the annual symposia are excellent by any international standards. Involving myself in all these activities, I felt obliged to take a certain responsibility for the future development of women's studies. No one forced me or gave me the authority to do this; I simply felt that way. It seems that watching and steering women's studies in the right direction will be one of my life-long assignments.

My academic concern with women's studies does not stop here. As a trained sociologist, it is quite tempting to incorporate feminism and the outcome of women's studies into sociology. To put it more strongly, I would very much like to contribute to a paradigmatic shift in the entire discipline of sociology. Women's studies, being inspired by the scientific consciousness that women's oppression and gender inequality are interlocked with the system of knowledge and education, rejects the one-sidedness of the mainstream sciences. The feminist charge against the validity, reliability, and justifiability of the existing knowledge system and "scientific" methods is sound and of relevance to sociology. Thus I feel obliged to take part in the correction of my field, starting with a reorganization of courses. I began to include women as an important section in conventional sociology courses and plan to move toward restructuring them into feminist sociological courses.

I have also been involved in the feminist movement outside academics, mainly through two organizations, Women for Equality and Peace (1984–86) and Alternative Culture (1984 to the present). WEP was organized by a dozen young Ewha graduates who had wanted to form a progressive women's organization to work for the masses. Though their disciplines varied, they were unanimous in hoping to have an organization that was quite different from the existing non-governmental women's organizations. Their criticisms of existing organizations were that these were no more than closed networks of members who pursued their own interests; that their social functions were negligible and philanthropic in nature; that the organizations were undemocratic, each being dominated by one autocratic and charismatic leader; and that they often functioned as political machines for dictatorial regimes. Unlike these organizations, WEP was open to the masses, worked for and with them, and was democratically organized, securing equal participation from its members. And most of all, the purpose of WEP was to struggle against every establishment in patriarchal capitalist society through political campaigns and consciousness-raising programs for working-class women. I was elected one of three co-representatives. Unfortunately, soon after the organization had begun work, a fierce debate took place between quasi-revolutionary Marxists and progressive socialist feminists. In 1986 the latter, including myself, had to leave WEP.

It was a painful experience. However, this unfortunate division within the progressive women's movement was considered an inevitable stage. The more radical group was comprised of younger members who had just graduated from college and were ardent leaders of the student movement. They were anxious, and even impatient, to see society change into a classless one without any sort of exploitation. On the other hand, the older group (the average age then was not over thirty-two) was a little more experienced and, therefore, had a more realistic view. They were also for an egalitarian society and believed that this could be realized by many-sided measures for liberation from both class and patriarchal oppressions. They were more patient than the former group who criticized them as cowardly *petites bourgeoises.* At any rate, the split was in the cards, and the debate itself was unproductive. Finally the older group, including most of the founding members, decided to leave WEP to their juniors. Later, somehow WEP shrank in size and in vigor until it merged into the newly organized Women for Democracy in 1987.

Alternative Culture (AC), which was organized at about the same time as WEP, was different in many ways. It is a loosely organized group, open to everyone eighteen and above. It boasts of more than two hundred members, including about twenty men, of various occupational and educational backgrounds. It is a group for a cultural movement, working toward a gradual change of society through change in consciousness and in the way of life. It aspires to a world community in which individuals, women and men, adults and children, participate as equals and as autonomous beings. It searches for alternatives, emphasizing reconstruction more than deconstruction, although the former should be based on the latter. Major projects of AC aim at developing personal autonomy and freedom and at changing social conditions. Books, publications, children's camps, reorientation camps for college freshmen, and annual cultural events sponsored by AC are all experiments toward the "rebirth" of individuals.

Most decisions are made at weekly meetings and the general conference where everyone is welcome to participate. There is no president or formal representative. Everything is handled on the basis of voluntary participation and on unanimous agreement among the participants. In effect, a core group has emerged. It is composed of those who regularly participate in the weekly meetings and in the major activities of AC. Women are the majority in the core group and many of them are connected with universities as teachers or as students. The formation of a core group ensures control over size and quality of input: because of its character, most activities tend to be academically-oriented and isolated from other action groups, while, for the same reason, AC can concentrate on the members' expertise, for example, in research, education, and writing. With regard to the impact of AC on society at large, we find that it is in general positive: we notice that those children who have participated in our camps are freer and more creative than others and that our writings are quoted by many people with various perspectives, even though frequently without acknowledgement. We are also encouraged by many thoughtful parents who like our way of handling children in camps and who agree with our philosophical stand on child education.

Personally I have found it very challenging and fulfilling to participate in AC. I like the people I meet there: I find they are free, creative, and mature and feel most comfortable working with them. I also like the way the organization is run. It is a genuine experiment in democracy in an undemocratic society. I feel as if I am growing, becoming more positive, loving children more than before, and caring about the future of the world more seriously. I may sound too self-indulgent and self-satisfied. However, it is my true feeling that, in the past decade and a half, I have grown because of my involvement with women's studies and with feminist groups. My only wish is that I should continue to grow in this way.

All this does not amount to a conclusion that our future is all that bright. Society outside the small circle in which I work still remains either indifferent or hostile to the women's movement. There are many of the Soknisan brand of sociologists among intellectuals, politicians, and other elite groups. This category may seem rational in masculine terms and, at times, even sympathetic to the most disadvantaged women. However, they are highly opportunistic, can easily be adversely influential, and are therefore potentially a dangerous group. There are others who are openly chauvinistic and, unfortunately, this group is larger. How about ordinary men and women? Most of them, being trapped in the capitalist-patriarchal structure, compete with one another in the search for an opportunity to maximize comfort and status and to minimize costs. Each of these individuals finds his or her own ways at work and at home to cope with the given conditions of life and usually ends up with short-sighted means and tactics. This competition takes place among women, among workers, within the family, within firms, and, as a consequence, society looks as if it is minutely divided and segregated by invisible walls.

My hope lies not with the established elite, nor with the revolutionaries, but with ordinary visionaries scattered around a gray world, who are critical about the way of life in which most men and women (including themselves) are trapped. I perceive my current task as one aimed at locating these scattered visionaries and developing a true sisterhood. I look forward to the day when I will work in a larger community of practicing visionaries, whom I view as the building blocks of a new feminist society. "How?" is my current area of research.

Fanny M. Cheung
Hong Kong

FANNY M. CHEUNG studied at the universities of California and Minnesota. Currently she is a Senior Lecturer in the Department of Psychology at the Chinese University of Hong Kong; Course Coordinator, M.S.Sc. Program in Clinical Psychology in the Department of Psychology and Psychiatry; and Coordinator, Research Programme on Gender Studies in a Changing World at the Hong Kong Institute of Asia Pacific Studies.

Promoting Women's Development

How I became a feminist

I may be considered a "feminist" in Hong Kong. But then, anyone who actively promotes women's concerns here would be labeled a feminist. My feminist orientation grew out of a personal evolution which bore little direct relationship to my own academic training in Western psychology. When I was a student in the United States from 1966 to 1975, I did not feel any strong identification with the feminist movement. From the little contact I had, I found the feminist approach too simplistic, rhetorical, antagonistic, and militant. I remember an article on women's liberation in my college yearbook at the University of California at Berkeley which declared that given the choice, nobody would enjoy the drudgery of housework. Although I did not care for housework myself, I could not deny some homemakers might derive satisfaction from their vocation. Nor did I agree with the thesis that all women were oppressed by capitalist society and by men. Such a militant approach did not fit with my own personal style.

It is possible that simply because I wanted to study for a higher degree, I may have carried within me the spirit of a feminist who chooses to achieve goals on the basis of her potential as a person, rather than go by the social norm of what a woman is "supposed" to be. And I did not heed the warnings that my overqualification would jeopardize my "mission" in life, which was to get married. Any woman's mission should be much more than that. My reaction was a determination to prove to myself that being a Ph.D. and a woman were not mutually exclusive.

I grew up in a traditional extended Chinese family at a

65

time when most other families in Hong Kong were becoming nuclear units. We lived with our uncles, aunts, and cousins in one big house. There were six girls and eight boys at home, all around my age. We were socialized in traditional gender roles and order, the only exception being the emphasis on education. Regardless of gender, academic achievement was rewarded. At the end of the school year, my father, as the patriarch of the family, would line up all the children and award medals to those who had gotten good results on their report cards. Although there was no active guidance from my parents, who had little formal education, we were all supported financially through college. I was taught to behave like a girl, but, clearly, I did not have to limit my academic pursuits because I was a girl.

Throughout my childhood I was always a "good" girl at home and in school: diligent, intelligent, quiet, obedient, and tidy. My only foray into misconduct was during Primary 6 when I led the girls in my class in a scuffle with the boys. It started when my cousin came home complaining that the boys in her class were bullying the girls during recess. After a few weeks of fighting, our form teacher found out and called some of the students in to investigate. Some of them were reprimanded. I thought for sure I would lose my honor roll that term because of my bad behavior. To my surprise, I still got an A for conduct. In the column on comments in my report card, my teacher wrote "righteous and courageous." I still hold this teacher in great respect for her fair-minded handling of the case. My active involvement with women's issues began when I returned to work as a psychologist in a general hospital in a working-class neighborhood of urban Hong Kong. The year 1975 was the beginning of the United Nations Decade for Women. The general consciousness about women's issues was still low, especially among local women. Although legislation was passed in the early 1970s to enforce monogamy in marriage and to equalize pay for equal work in the public sector, many areas of inequality still remained. Women's social roles were still bound by cultural traditions and women were still perceived in stereotypical roles of being weak and inferior. In response to the Decade for Women, some women's groups had begun to publicize their concerns about the situation of women in Hong Kong, such as the need for separate tax returns for husbands and wives, and women's health needs. The problems of rape victims, too, were raised in this context.

In my clinical work I became aware of the large number of unreported cases of rape and sexual assault among my patients who suffered life-long trauma and self-deprecation from the experience. Through long-term psychotherapy, I helped such patients to accept themselves and to rebuild their social lives. With an orientation toward prevention, I reviewed the problems these rape victims had endured before they became afflicted with mental illness. In my protected early life I had only learned about rape from movies or novels. Even during my training the topic was studied only in academic terms. The face-to-face encounter with victims and the phenomenology of their trauma had a profound impact on me. I was further bothered by the fact that my patients did not receive any help at the time of the incidents and had to carry the burden of shame and guilt for so many years before their psychological disturbance surfaced in the form of psychiatric symptoms. This reflected the lack of social support and resources for rape victims. I began to advocate more social awareness of the traumatic aftermath for rape victims, which could be as disastrous as the rape itself. I raised these issues from the perspective of a psychologist. Members of the Hong Kong Council of Women invited me to join forces with them. We aligned with other social service agencies to launch the War-on-Rape Campaign. The campaign set up aftercare services for rape victims; ran training programs for nurses, social workers, and volunteers; got the police to work out a standardized procedure to respond to victims sympathetically; and suggested a standard medical protocol for doctors at casualty departments to examine victims. Public talks and workshops were organized to correct myths about rape and to promote community understanding of rape victims. Influenced by the publicity and community concerns generated from these activities, the Legislative Council passed laws to protect the anonymity of rape victims and ruled out the use of a victim's previous sexual history as evidence in court.

Soon, from the needs of rape victims, I began to identify the broader needs of women in general, and became more involved in the promotion of women's development. I was interested not only in the prevention of rape and aftercare for victims. In these advocacy activities, I have adopted a community psychology approach instead of the female-versus-male confrontational approach presented in some feminist literature on rape. By defining rape as a concern for the whole community and emphasizing that both women and men should work together to prevent rape, I was able to enlist the support of professionals and social service agencies, in addition to women's groups, for the campaign. Similarly, in promoting women's development, I found more receptive reaction and cooperation from the public when these issues were addressed in the context of the whole community and not as the plight of women who are being oppressed by men.[1] Instead, women are presented as valuable resources for the community and it is clarified that the women's movement is necessitated by the changing socioeconomic conditions in which traditional roles for women are no longer adequate to accommodate these changes.

When I moved into academia I did not find a particularly enlightened environment for women. I joined the university in late 1970s, and women constituted only about 10 percent of the faculty of around 250. There was only one woman who held the rank of a senior lecturer. Women had won the battle for equal pay with men just five years earlier, after an extended campaign by the few female legislators and senior female civil servants in the government. Fringe benefits, such as a housing allowance and educational allowance for children, were not yet extended to married women. The explanation I gathered from my male colleagues was that men, as heads of the households, had the responsibility for taking care of the family. Single or divorced women might be provided housing on compassionate grounds. By 1989 the fringe benefits for male and female staff had been standardized. However, the percentage of female faculty was only marginally improved—13 percent out of a total of 570 faculty members (492 male and 78 female). Although the number of female senior lecturers had increased to 15 compared to 190 males, in the rank of senior lecturer and above, no woman was promoted beyond that rank. The ratio of male to female staff at the lecturer rank and below is 4.8 to 1; that for senior lecturer and above is 12.7 to 1. By 1992 only three women had been promoted to the rank of reader. With women in the minority and the lower ranks, there were implicit stereotypes in existence about women, such as the lack of dedication to work, especially after marriage and childbirth. In the consideration of female applicants, concern about turnover was expressed by referring to the few previous cases of female colleagues who resigned to take care of their families.

Even in recent years prejudice is reflected in statements such as "the sex ratio has worsened," referring to the reversed gender trend in undergraduate admission into some faculties of the university due to a new selection scheme. By introducing a new admission scheme, whereby students would be offered provisional admission based on their Form 5 (grade 10) public examination results, more girls were able to get into the university due to their earlier maturation. As a result, the gender ratio of the students became more equal, as opposed to the 2 to 1 ratio in favor of boys previously. Some faculty members were worried that female graduates would not contribute as much to the labor force or get ahead as much as male graduates. The concern was serious enough to warrant a special item on the agenda of one of the faculty's Admissions Committee meetings, although it was finally decided that no action should be taken to reverse the new scheme. Some of these concerns may well be relevant. Despite their achievements, female students are often still tradition-bound and have poorer self-appraisal and lower aspirations, as indicated in a recent survey of Chinese university graduates after their first year of employment.[2] However, little has been done to confront this problem by building up the confidence and motivation of the female students.

Promotion of gender development
At the Chinese University of Hong Kong my promotional activities have included student extra-curricular interests, research, and teaching. With more women graduating from the university, women and men face new challenges in their social roles. Without readjustments and changes in attitudes, highly educated women face the uphill struggle of being career women in traditional male-dominated settings. As reported by a number of surveys conducted by local social service agencies, the dual responsibility of career women and housewives has added more pressure than benefits to women.[3]

An important opportunity for the review of gender stereotypes and resocialization of the complementary roles of the two genders exists at university. University students are likely to be more open to liberal attitudes of equality. Both female and male students could benefit from more enlightened views on relationships, which could be carried to their future work and family life. In 1984, when I was the chairperson of the Student Life Committee of Chung Chi College, I initiated an extracurricular program called Gender Relationships. It took the form of an informal discussion group involving both students and staff on topics ranging from gender stereotypes and gender barriers at work, to love, courtship, marriage, and sex. Although the number of students who participated each year was limited to less than twenty, their involvement was active. Students took turns to prepare for the seminars and meet with speakers. The lively discussions provided an opportunity for the men and women students, and even staff, to challenge one another's viewpoints. Given the voluntary nature of these activities, students who joined these groups would have been more open to new ideas about gender relationships in the first place. Nonetheless, the candid discussions among faculty members and students encouraged both male and female students to re-examine their former beliefs and question traditional stereotypes.

In addition to the discussion group, topics on gender-related issues have been incorporated into other series of talks organized for student activities, such as women's self-protection and problems in heterosexual relationships. The objective is to raise students' awareness of these issues in a nondidactic context. With the increasing proportion of female students in the university, we included in our extracurricular activities programs that would prepare our future graduates for a changing world of gender relationships in their professional careers, as well as in their family and social life.

To gain a solid ground for discussion on gender issues, a strong knowledge base has to be established. It is particularly important that this knowledge base be relevant to the local historical, cultural, and socioeconomic context. Scholars in western humanities and social sciences have pointed to the extent to which women's perspectives have been left out of these disciplines. Women's studies programs promoting research and teaching have been established in many major universities in North America. While their perspectives and methodologies are important references, the content needs to be indigenous. Thus, to develop a good teaching program, research on local gender issues needs to be built up. For example, given the historical perspectives on the role and status of Chinese women in the Confucian tradition and in an agrarian society, how much have urban Chinese women in Hong Kong changed? What are the social, economic, political, and psychological factors promoting and impeding these changes? What conflicts do Chinese women experience in the face of contradictions between traditional values regarding women and the family on the one hand, and modern westernized ideals of equality and independence on the other?

As the associate director of the Center for Hong Kong Studies of the Chinese University from 1984 to 1990, I initiated the establishment of the Gender Role Research Program. The center's task was to support and initiate social science research at the university by providing opportunities for intellectual exchange, as well as seed money for small research projects. So I was able to enlist an interdisciplinary team of colleagues from different faculties and departments, including business administration, education, English, Chinese, history, religion, economics, psychology, sociology, social work, and community medicine. Although the majority of the researchers were female faculty members, we were able to recruit a few male members. I chose the title of gender role research, rather than women's studies, so as to broaden the perspective of gender issues which are not confined to women only. Although many of the studies undertaken are related to women's concerns, we viewed these issues as being embedded in the social context of women in their relations with men.

The first task I undertook to promote gender research in Hong Kong was to take stock of what had been done so far and to provide researchers with an updated bibliography on the local literature. The first volume covered studies conducted during the UN Decade for Women (1975-1985). An expanded bibliography extending from 1945 to the present day was published in 1991. In addition to bibliographies, the Center for Hong Kong Studies also collected local documents, publications, and newspaper clippings in order to build up a database on gender issues in Hong Kong. These reference materials have been useful background information for researchers, teachers, and students.

With the support of colleagues from different faculties and departments, our research interests included gender biases in the educational context, such as educational aspirations, gender and class, gender role portrayal in advertisements, Chinese women and Christianity, self-perception and values of women, health and mental health, and continuity and change in women's status. My own research has covered gender stereotypes, attitudes toward rape, and women's social participation. Regular meetings are held to exchange research ideas and share preliminary findings. Some of the completed studies have been published in the form of occasional papers of the Center for Hong Kong Studies. An international conference on Women's Studies in Chinese Societies was held in November 1989, during which scholars from mainland China, Taiwan, and other parts of the world were invited to share their research experiences and theoretical perspectives.

In the reorganization of the Institute of Social Studies at the university in 1990, the Gender Role Research Programme has been chosen as one of the seven strategic research programs in the new Hong Kong Institute of Asia-Pacific Studies. Although the program has generated active interdisciplinary participation, it continues to face queries about its academic relevance and significance. An important consideration for the development of the research program is how to promote interdisciplinary collaboration despite differences in theoretical and methodological orientation among the various disciplines. Furthermore, the study of gender issues within individual disciplines has often been limited to the use of gender as one of a set of variables in data analysis. While there has been increasing participation from colleagues, it has remained, by and large, a side interest of female academics, most of whom had to spend more time on mainline research within their own disciplines in order to gain recognition for their scholarship. To the older male administrators of the university, gender studies is considered an esoteric sideline which is based more on polemics than on scientific rigor. While individual academics in some fields have admitted their neglect of women in their former models, most disciplines have not addressed the patriarchical nature of their constructions. Given the small number of women academics and faculty members with gender consciousness, how can we integrate gender issues into the mainstream of our own disciplines? Clearly, in the long run, we believe that gender studies should be accorded recognition as a fundamental area of research and not be considered as a potpourri of polemic interests for feminist academics alone. Again, I have adopted an evolutionary, rather than revolutionary, approach here. Our strategy is to build up a team of female, as well as male, faculty members doing quality research in gender studies so that the discipline, as well as the researchers, will gain respect and visibility.

A number of individual teachers have incorporated women's studies as a major or minor subject. However, the two universities in Hong Kong have remained very conventional in their curriculum development. The establishment of an independent department of gender studies is very remote, but individual teachers have, on their own initiative, incorporated their theoretical and research interests on gender in their own coursework. For example, I have included the topics of gender stereotyping in my course on personality, gender differences in the manifestation of psychopathology and in the help-seeking process in abnormal psychology, and women's development and movements in community psychology.

There have been some discussions among colleagues in the Gender Role Research Programme about the feasibility of a women's or gender studies department, but we concurred that at this stage of the university's development we are unlikely to get resources for such a formal establishment. To justify the establishment of a major new department, we have to convince the university, as well as the founders and the University and Polytechnic Grants Committee of the government, of the academic and pragmatic bases for the program of studies. In addition, the administrators would be concerned about the marketability of the graduates of this major subject.

We decided that instead of aiming for a full-fledged program, we would propose new courses within existing departments, for example, sociology of women in the Department of Sociology, and women in theology in the Department of Religion. Another interdisciplinary course on women's studies has been developed under the auspices of the General Education Program in which all students have to choose from a range of courses on general knowledge. Such a course may be able to attract a cross section of students from different disciplines. The addition of more courses on gender within the university will help to build up the core of a future department or a graduate program.

Gender research in the community

Many of the members of the Gender Role Research Program are actively involved in the women's movement in Hong

Kong. To some feminists, being close to the praxis of women's activism is decisive in informing feminist scholarship. The program is seen as a vital catalyst of both academic and social change. Although I did not begin my active involvement with the women's movement to legitimize my scholarship, my advocacy work for women's development in the community continued as a natural extension of my academic work. Community experiences provide the raw materials to stimulate my academic pursuits. In return, my theoretical knowledge and empirical studies can be extended into practice. Being a community-oriented psychologist, there are fertile grounds for me to integrate research and practice on women's affairs in Hong Kong. While I have promoted gender studies at the university, I have adopted a slightly different strategy in the community. Instead of promoting awareness on gender issues in general, I have focused on women as the target group. I believe that there are many more issues that women in the community have to address on their own before men can be enlisted into joining with them. An important issue for women in the community is that, unlike women in the university who would have achieved superior status and greater competence, working-class women and housewives often lack the awareness of, and access to, resources and information.

Cheung and Yuen[4] found that there were many social barriers against working-class women's participation in community affairs. They often lacked self-confidence and misjudged their own competence. There was generally little assistance from their husbands. Unless alternative support could be obtained from other family members or neighbors, women were not able to become socially involved. On the other hand, those who had become active in community affairs found rewards in a greater sense of accomplishment and affiliation.

My involvement in the promotion of women's development in the community began with my campaign on behalf of rape victims. During the course of the campaign, we recognized the need for a place where women could come for understanding, support, and direct services. It became obvious that a rape crisis center would not appeal to women because of the stigma attached to it. Instead, a women's center, which catered to the needs and development of women in general, would be more acceptable.[5] The concept of the Women's Center took into account the cultural and psychological contexts in which local Chinese women live, and sought to expand their range of choices.

The Women's Center started in 1981 with a telephone inquiry service to provide information and act as a referral center for women. Since its inception, it has been run entirely by volunteers who donated their time and money to keep up the service. Although we received strong support from the Federation of Women Lawyers and individual doctors who provided free advice to our clients, it was difficult to generate financial support from the local community. There was skepticism among local charity organizations that women in Hong Kong needed support for their development. Many argued that women in Hong Kong fare well and enjoy western-style chivalry from men. Only women in distress, such as battered wives and rape victims, would be given pity and considered as possible targets for social welfare. Even as welfare targets, they were seen as less needy than orphans or the handicapped, who are more popular with donors. We also had to contend with the question of why we did not set up a men's center or a people's center.

Our initial attempts to procure international funding were also frustrating. We tried to apply for the UN Decade for Women grants as a non-government organization. It took about a year to go through the government bureaucracy to be recognized as such because no government department at the time wanted to be identified with the project for fear that they would have to pick up the tab after the external grants had run out. Despite encouragement and support from the Asian regional office, our proposal was turned down by the UN headquarters because Hong Kong was no longer considered a developing territory for funding purposes. Our members were patient and persevering. We tried many other contacts and prepared and sent many proposals. In 1986 we finally received funding from a European church organization to support an office space and full-time staff. Through the sympathetic support of a senior official in the Social Welfare Department, our request for concessionary rent for a unit in a low-cost public housing estate was approved without long delay.

In addition to the telephone service, the center now houses a resource library of over two thousand books, magazines, and reports related to women's interests and concerns. It also runs educational programs on topics ranging from language to health care, self-awareness, and civic education. There are over two hundred members and subscribers of the center, including about thirty dedicated volunteers who continue to staff the telephone service. A member's group has also been formed among local housewives to develop their own interests and to enhance their abilities.

In order to provide a stable financial foundation for the Women's Center, more long-term local funding clearly has to be procured. Through my own professional network in the community, the work of the Women's Center has become more recognized and proposals for funding receive a better hearing. In 1989 we began to receive large-scale local funding to support the running costs of the center. In addition, special projects have been developed for specific funding. One such project is the Self-Help Resources for Women.

In this technological age, when the flow of information is so rapid and access to information can be a form of power, women at the grassroots often lag behind fast-moving social developments. At the Women's Center, the idea of Self-help Resources for Women was formulated and, in 1988, a donation was received from a charity organization to develop the computer database for this project. The Self-Help Resources consists of information and directories of services related to women's concerns. Ten general areas of common concern have been identified, including health, mental health, education, social services, law, finance, etc. Questions which women frequently ask in these areas are addressed and clarified by leading the user through options and alternatives before providing them with a list of available resources. Professionals and academics have been recruited to serve as expert consultants and provide information for the database. When completed, the Self-Help Resources will be a useful reference for researchers, frontline workers who are helping female clients, and women in general. The database is designed in a "user-friendly" format so that women will be encouraged to try out the computer and help themselves to accurate information and resources.

Integration

My experiences and awareness as a woman have directed my efforts both at the university and in the community. In turn, these efforts have facilitated my own growth as a woman.

One of the rewards of coming back to work in Hong Kong was the opportunity to try out my ideas and start something from scratch in my own community. When I returned to Hong

Kong, little had been done for women's development, as no institution had taken up that responsibility. It was through the persistent efforts of individual women that community awareness was raised. Back in the 1970s, most of the feminists in Hong Kong were expatriate women. Not being Chinese isolated them from the larger community. Some of them also adopted more confrontational approaches which pitched women against men. Such approaches alienated men as well as many women in the Chinese community.

Gradual changes are less likely to receive opposition in Chinese societies. When changes are based on knowledge and are shown to be useful, they will be more readily accepted. I believe in this approach and have found it advantageous in my own promotion of women's development in Hong Kong. I may be confident, diligent, and persistent, but I do not like to be pushy. Although my western education has trained me to speak up, my traditional Chinese upbringing still inclines me towards modesty and moderation. Of course, my style is not the only model for the promotion of women's concerns; it may be considered by some to be too conservative or elitist. However, I believe there is room for pluralistic approaches to feminism. In the past five years, other local women's groups have been founded to promote feminism. Some of them have adopted more rhetorical and polemical approaches. Diversity may offer more options for women of different backgrounds and styles to identify with various orientations.

Being a promoter of women's development has thrown me into a limelight that I personally dislike. One of the conflicts I often face has to do with the exposure to publicity. I understand the importance of publicity to the promotion of women's causes in Hong Kong; however, there is a simplistic association of importance in the mind of the public when someone appears regularly in the newspaper or on television. In turn, the mass media tend to turn the few academic or professionals who are willing to speak out publicly into instant experts on a variety of topics. The image of a celebrity does not always fit my identity as a scholar. I am keenly aware of the danger that a high-profile image may lower the credibility of a professional. Throughout my years of experience in working with the press, I have learned to hold onto my principle of talking entirely about issues and not about myself. I also prefer to speak only from knowledge and experience rather than from opinion. Although a high profile may bring about more attention to women's issues, I have chosen to maintain my integrity.

Many people have asked me how I could do so much at the same time. I am generally busy, but I always manage to find time for important things. The truth is that I do not think I am giving enough attention to every involvement I have because I am spreading myself too thinly. I am more capable of initiating ideas, bringing people together, and raising awareness. With insufficient time, I am not always able to follow up on the details of the implementation, but have to depend on other colleagues. One of the tasks I have been concerned with in recent years is to build up systems that will replace me. Having started various programs, I would like to see them continue and be improved by other interested persons who could take over from me.

A true sense of women's development lies in active participation by women. Unfortunately, the continuation of these programs still depends on the efforts of individuals. At times I feel that I may be losing my stamina. However, I derive strength from the fact that there is still much to be done. The reward I gain is a sense of communality with a sector of the population with whom I share an identity, and the awareness that whatever little I have done, I am contributing to the advancement of women.

Notes

1. F.M. Cheung, "The Women's Center: A Community Approach to Feminism in Hong Kong," *American Journal of Community Psychology* 17 (1989): 99; also, F.M. Cheung, "Changing Attitudes: the War on Rape Campaign," *Bulletin of the Hong Kong Psychological Society* 19/20, (1988): 41–48.
2. G. Chow, "Report on a Study of the Career Aspirations of 1987 Graduates with Special Regard to Their Entrepreneurial Inclinations," unpublished report of the Office of Student Affairs, Hong Kong: Chinese University of Hong Kong, 1988.
3. Hong Kong Young Women's Christian Association and Hong Kong Shue Yan College, *Report on Working Mothers in Family Functioning*, Hong Kong: YWCA, 1982.
4. F.M. Cheung and R. Yuen, "Psychological and Social Characteristics Related to Social Participation among Working Class Housewives in Hong Kong," Occasional Paper No. 22, Centre for Hong Kong Studies; Hong Kong: Chinese University of Hong Kong, 1987.
5. F.M. Cheung, "The Women's Center: A Community Approach to Feminism in Hong Kong," op. cit.

Fareeha Zafar
Pakistan

FAREEHA ZAFAR was educated at the universities of Lahore and London. She has been involved in both activism and academics in Pakistan and is a founding member of the Women's Action Forum (WAF) in Lahore. At present she is Assistant Professor of Geography, University of Punjab, Lahore, and has been nominated as Director, Centre of Excellence for Women's Studies at the same university.

A Feminist Activist

Early influences

My awareness of gender inequalities began in early childhood. Perhaps that is the reason why I became a "tomboy." In upper-class patriarchal societies such as the one I grew up in, it is possible for a girl to be allowed greater freedom of action and movement if she is able to suppress her femininity and has no male siblings to contend with. Education was given a significantly high priority in our family. My maternal grandmother, who had wanted to study medicine and become a doctor, was married at the age of fifteen and spent the next eighteen years of her life in producing one child every two years. But her desire for education found another outlet: she saw to it that her five daughters were educated. This was rare in the Punjab in the first quarter of this century. Consequently, my mother, a graduate herself, wanted her daughters to be highly educated as well. In this she was supported by my father, a government servant and engineer by profession who later become an educationist. He was not only supportive of women's education, but also of their emancipation and took the practical step of making my mother discard her *burqa* (veil) on the day of their marriage.

The 1930s and 1940s was the period of struggle by the Muslims of the subcontinent for an identity and a better economic deal in a country free from colonial domination. There were few educated Muslim families. Earlier, Sir Syed Ahmad Khan's identification of the backwardness of Muslims with their lack of education, combined with the biased attitude of the British toward educated Muslims and the fall of the Khilafat in Turkey, helped to create a class of conscious, pro-

81

gressive Muslims in India. During the 1940s and after the partition of the subcontinent, Fatima Jinnah, Jehanara Shahnawaz, and other women who had participated in the movement for Pakistan became role models for the women of educated families in Pakistan. The poetry of Iqbal and Hali, which urged the Muslims to develop themselves and play a historic role, took the place of nursery rhymes for the children of educated Muslims. Consequently I grew up hearing stories of bravery, courage, hard work, and sacrifice of both men and women.

In 1947 the All-Pakistan Women's Association (APWA) was formed and it soon emerged as the premier social welfare organization for women. It played a major role in rehabilitating shelterless women by teaching them basic skills in order to make them economically independent. APWA's role in setting up industrial homes, adult education centers, and providing shelter to women was followed by other welfare-oriented organizations that focused on teaching skills in handicrafts, embroidery, sewing, and knitting. The women's issue, at this stage, was seen as one which required the social uplift of women and attracted housewives as well as working women. Prominent among these were some who had participated in the movement for Pakistan.

For urban educated women the 1950s and 1960s were promising decades—society appeared to be moving toward a modern, progressive future. Despite the declaration of martial law in 1958, General Mohammad Ayub Khan presented a liberal, modernist front when his daughter accompanied him, unencumbered by the veil, at home and abroad. Ayub Khan abhorred religious orthodoxy and had an aversion to reactionary elements. In such an environment there were no obstacles placed in the way of women's education and work.[1] One of the few progressive and significant pieces of legislation affecting women, the Family Laws Ordinance (1961), was enacted during this time. The catalyst for APWA's agitation, which began in 1955, was the second marriage of Prime Minister Mohammad Ali Bogra, since the Family Laws Ordinance places (among other stipulations) certain regulations on polygamy and divorce. It was also in the 1960s that the opposition to Ayub Khan was led by Fatima Jinnah (sister of the founder of Pakistan), and when elections were announced, expediency forced the *mullahs* (traditional clergy) to support her candidacy for the position of head of state.

My own career was shaped by a number of sexist biases in

our education system and in society in general. Science was taught in few girls' schools and I happened to be schooled at the Convent of Jesus & Mary in Lahore, where science subjects had not yet been introduced, but where the daughters of most government officials tended to study. The University of Engineering and Technology was not open to women, with the result that, after completing school, I was left with no option but to pursue a course of studies in the humanities. There were few career opportunities open to women at this time, and teaching and medicine were considered the two most "respectable" professions for women. These factors, combined with my own inclination toward education, resulted in my joining the University of the Punjab, Lahore, as a lecturer in the Department of Geography in 1969. It was clear to me that freedom of action was related to economic independence and, despite what is generally voiced, if a woman is economically self-sufficient her family and society are forced to recognize and acknowledge both her individuality and contribution.

It is important to mention, however, that while my family had given me all the support and encouragement to study up to Masters level in Pakistan and take up a job, they were not prepared to let me go abroad for higher studies on my own. The priority given to marriage, especially for girls, became an obstacle at this stage in my life. For my mother it continued to be a major problem until it was resolved several years later when I married and went to the University of London for postgraduate studies.

A period of politicization
The post-independence politicization of Pakistan's people can be traced back to the long years of suppression under a military regime, the emergence of the Pakistan Peoples's Party (PPP) on the national scene, and the Tashkent Declaration (an agreement arrived at between Pakistan and India following the 1965 war). Educational institutions reopened in April 1969 after having been shut for several months following massive street demonstrations by students and agitation by other sections of society, including women, against Ayub Khan signing the Tashkent Declaration. The movement culminated in the overthrow of Ayub Khan, who was replaced by General Mohammad Yahya Khan as the Martial Law Administrator. Elections were guaranteed within three months and the restoration of political activity after almost eleven years created an

Fareeba Zafar

atmosphere of intense political fervor. Zulfiqar Ali Bhutto, Ayub Khan's charismatic foreign minister, launched the PPP, whose slogan of "*roti, kapra, makan*" (justice and equality for all), attracted the poor, the working class, peasants, intellectuals, and women. The election campaign of the PPP was marked by mammoth rallies and meetings in which women participated in large numbers. This process of collective struggle included many of us from the universities and colleges, where a clear cut polarization between the right and left began to emerge. The participation of men and women in the political process created a new sense of awareness among women. In the 1970 election, the right to vote was used by them, often against the wishes of their male family members.

Apart from playing a progressive role within and outside the university in organizing female teachers and students, I was also motivated, along with a group of friends, to organize women working in factories and in the informal sector. Women were beginning to be employed in factories and, with the acceleration of trade union activity, we were encouraged to set up the first women's trade union in Lahore in the early 1970s. This was followed by the formation of an association of domestic women workers who lived in *katchi abadis* (slums). Although the main issues at this time were related to economic benefits, better pay and the like, the issues of discrimination against women in skilled jobs, the lower wages offered to them in comparison to men, and harassment of female workers by managements, etc., were also raised. These issues gained more importance with the increasing militancy of the trade union movement, when the management of certain types of factories, such as pharmaceuticals, biscuit making, light packaging, etc., began to replace male labor with female labor, as women were considered to be more docile and vulnerable.

From 1971 to 1977, I worked with groups of women from low income neighborhoods, motivating and conscientizing them to organize and solve their problems on the basis of self-help. We held weekly meetings in several *katchi abadis* to create core groups in each area, and through collective action succeeded in developing a code for domestic women workers, whereby no woman would agree to work for lower wages and cause the displacement of a fellow co-worker. We did manage to get some benefits—such as a weekly holiday—from employers. The male members of the community readily lent their support in implementing strikes and other action.

84

Our group was part of a larger organization working among different sections of the urban and rural communities. Strategies and tactics were worked out collectively, but as time went by our women's group found that we were being asked to report to a hierarchically higher all-male group and that the informal reciprocal relationship had transformed into a formal one-sided linkage. The tendency to give orders and expect compliance grew until we were forced to dissociate ourselves and express our autonomy. This break occurred not only in our group, but in the student, labor, and peasant groups as well. Those members of our group whose husbands were part of the bigger group felt bound to side with them out of personal loyalty, while those of us who had no such familial bonds were in a position to make our own decisions to go it alone and take the support of other groups whenever there was need for it. All such class-based activity came to an abrupt end with the enforcement of martial law in July 1977.

Feminist activism

When I left in September 1977 for the University of London to study for a doctorate in geography, it had already become apparent that, under the changed political situation in Pakistan, we would have to develop alternative ways of mobilization and of creating awareness. Although I did not work with any women's groups in England, I had opportunities to learn from their experiences. As an outsider it was possible for me to assess how effective the various feminist groups were in motivating women and in eliciting a sensitive and sympathetic response to their problems and needs. What came across very clearly was that, despite outward expressions of freedom and liberty, which are a reflection of Western culture rather than the success of feminism per se, there exist common impediments to the development of women both in the personal and public spheres. Patriarchal values and thinking persist whether we are looking at tribal, feudal, capitalist, or socialist societies.

Three events during 1979 served to give a direction to educated Pakistani women at home and abroad to begin thinking in terms of specific feminist issues. First, the Iranian Revolution and the clamping down by the clergy on progressive forces and women in Iran. Second, the execution of deposed Prime Minister Zulfiqar Ali Bhutto in Pakistan, which revealed the barbaric face of the military regime and its denunciation of freedom of thought, speech, and action under a state-sponsored reactionary program of the "Islamization" of society. Third, the promulgation of the infamous Hadood Ordinance, which authorized the award of *hadd* punishment (flogging, stoning to death, cutting of limbs, etc.) for certain crimes. In its application to women, this ordinance equated adultery with rape, because the admission of rape on the part of a woman was taken as confession and proof of adultery in the event the rape was not proved—which was usually what happened since proving rape required four Muslim men as witnesses. For most of us who had not until then developed a feminist perspective, these expressions of fascism helped crystallize the issue of the specific and universal dimensions of women's problems.

The growth of semi-autonomous and autonomous women's groups had already begun during the latter half of the 1970s. While the semi-autonomous groups were the women's wings of political organizations, the autonomous groups consisted of new women's organizations, as well as the breakaway segments of larger sociopolitical organizations.

In 1981, in accordance with the procedures laid down by the Hadood Ordinance of 1979, a Sessions judge accorded the punishment of death by stoning and one hundred lashes to a man and woman respectively. This case, Fehmeeda and Allah Bux versus the State, acted as a catalyst for the formation of a women's pressure group in which women came together individually, as well as in women's associations and organizations. A broad-based forum of women, the Khawateen Mahaz-e-Amal (Women's Action Forum), or WAF, as it is commonly referred to, was first formed in Karachi. A month later a meeting of about twenty-five women was organized in Lahore in which I participated, and the Lahore chapter of WAF was formed.

For me the Women's Action Forum was a culmination of the struggle I had taken up more than a decade ago. The status of women in Pakistan is that of second-class citizens, no different from that of other oppressed sections of society, and this is sufficient reason for joining in the struggle for women's rights. Moreover, being part of WAF did not restrict one from working with any of the other groups at the same time. I continued to be part of another semi-autonomous women's group whose focus was on the working class and women from the lower-middle class.

Under the repressive policies of the military regime, reactionary and fundamentalist religious elements were encouraged to interfere in the private and public lives of individuals, particularly women. This forced most activists to focus on two issues, the question of democracy and the rights and freedom of women. As women, we saw the two issues as being inseparable. Restrictions on the movement of women, their employment, participation in spectator sports, access to education, and a prescribed dress code were accompanied by legislation introduced in the form of martial law ordinances under the garb of the Islamization process.

As a member of the working committee of WAF, Lahore, from 1981 to 1985, I was involved in both policy making and the organization of the forum. Sub-committees were set up to focus on specific areas, such as the research committee of which I was the convenor. When the military government put forward the proposal for a women's university, our committee wrote a research paper based on the views of girl students, working women, and housewives.[2] The overwhelming response was that a separate women's university was not needed and that coeducation creates greater confidence in women. The proposal for a separate women's university has been consistently opposed by WAF, as it would reinforce existing patterns of segregation and has the added danger of "ghettoizing" whatever higher education is available at present for women.

Essentially WAF's program has been to take up issues of injustice and crimes of violence against women, as reported in the media or brought to it by individuals. Its activities have included the holding of seminars, workshops, meetings, *jalsas* (happenings or meetings that include song, dance, discussion, plays, etc.), and other programs to conscientize women, mobilize them for action, and to create awareness about women, their roles and status. Demonstrations have been organized on several occasions: the twelve February, 1983 demonstration was against the proposed Law of Evidence, which equated the evidence of one man with two women. It was also the first demonstration by any group or organization against the military regime, and it set the pace for other groups to openly express their views. To gather support against reactionary legislative measures, WAF has conducted signature campaigns, published leaflets and posters, given out press statements, and held press conferences. As a consequence of the hectic activity of WAF members in the first few years of its formation, the issue of women was placed squarely on the agenda of every people's organization, political party, and the government.

Since 1985, WAF has also lobbied government officials and members of parliament to promote the cause of women and to delay retrogressive legislation.

Recent years have seen our struggle largely directed against the Shariat Bill, passed in May 1991, which was another attempt on the part of fundamentalist religious elements to impose their interpretation of Islam on the people. Since the passage of the bill affects all sections of society, WAF initiated the formation of a Joint Action Committee, comprising several organizations, to fight against the Bill.

Academic feminism

In August 1985, I went to UC Berkeley as a Fulbright Scholar for one year to follow up my work in regional planning and development. This was one of the low periods for the women's studies program at Berkeley, but I was invited to address a colloquium, "Women and Development in Pakistan," at the Department of Sociology, Hayward State University. This was the beginning of my involvement with the academic side of the women's question. Participation at a conference in Delhi in 1986 extended the focus of my interests to women and education in particular.[3] The appallingly low level of female literacy (16 percent) in Pakistan is clearly an obstacle to the development of women, especially in the rural areas where female literacy levels are as low as 7.3 percent. Official statistics have proved to be unreliable at both ends of the spectrum. Literacy levels are much lower than generally stated and, at the same time, economic participation of women measured in terms of the labor force is several times higher than the official figure of 4.8 percent.[4]

In 1983, some of us from the university and others interested in education outside the formal system set up a Society for the Advancement of Education (SAHE). Here we work informally with students from existing colleges, and women's issues have formed part of the program we offer to students. Our work has also included the development of a course on social studies for private girls' high schools and this course, too, includes a component on women. A SAHE team undertook research, then wrote and organized the filming of a series of programs in collaboration with Pakistan Television on the relationship between society and education. The series included two programs on attitudes toward women's education.

A Feminist Activist

During the 1980s a number of women's resource centers were set up, some by women activists, to collect information on women, conduct relevant research, and facilitate projects of income generation, skill development, training, and consciousness raising for women in which foreign donor agencies were willing to cooperate. Many of their initial research studies, however, were sponsored by the Women's Division established by the government in 1979. The combined efforts of WAF and the women's resource centers have induced the government to include WID issues in the national Five-Year Plans and in government training programs.

At an individual level I have been involved with some of the women's resource centers as a resource person. It is only recently that a formal women's studies program has been initiated. In 1989, the Women's Division—now a full-fledged Ministry of Women's Development—prepared a proposal for the establishment of women's studies centers at five universities. I was nominated as the director of the Centre of Excellence for Women's Studies at the University of the Punjab, Lahore. We are still at the early stages of developing relevant programs and courses. A consensus has emerged about initially designing a one-year diploma program, and a series of workshops has been organized to prepare the outline for courses and reading materials.[5]

As is always the case, it is very exciting and challenging to be associated with a project in its initial stages. For me this opportunity has come at a time when, having been an activist and a teacher for over twenty years, and part of the women's movement for more than a decade, I can contribute to a women's studies orientation that has grown out of a social movement and whose grassroots links must continue. By being actively involved in the development of this program at this stage, it may be possible to strengthen the link between academic work and the women's movement so that women's studies, whether it emerges as a separate discipline or a subject, will not become irrelevant or useless, as have most of the courses in other disciplines at the degree and post-graduate levels.

Notes
1. K. Mumtaz and F. Shaheed, *Women of Pakistan, Two Steps Forward, One Step Back?* Lahore: Vanguard Books (Pvt.) Ltd., 1987, p. 57.

89

2. K. Mumtaz and F. Zafar, "Women and Higher Education," *Muslim,* (July 1982).
3. F. Zafar, "Islamization, Development and the Role of Women in Pakistan," Unesco (publication pending), 1986.
4. *Census of Population,* Government of Pakistan, 1981.
5. F. Zafar (ed.), *Towards a New Beginning: Women of Pakistan, a Book of Readings,* Unesco (publication pending), 1990.

Konta Intan Damanik
Indonesia

KONTA INTAN DAMANIK (b. 1944) is Professor of Economics in the Faculty of Economics at Satya Wacana Christian University in Indonesia. She has worked for several years in the fields of economics and women's studies and, from 1989 to 1993 was Coordinator, Women's Studies and Roles, Wacana Christian University, Salatga, Indonesia.

A Decade in Women's Studies
1979-1989

The third daughter

I was born in 1944, a year before the independence of the Republic of Indonesia. I was my parents' third daughter. We are eight daughters and two sons born between 1940 and 1959. At that time the size of our family would not have been considered big, as no population policy had been introduced or implemented. My father, the only breadwinner in the family, was a government official in the local agricultural office. We were of a solid middle-class background. In spite of my parents' heavy responsibilities in raising their children, we were all given equal treatment as far as education was concerned. All of us were sent to college and are now professionals in our respective fields.

Even though I am in my forties, I am not yet married. This is by choice; however, I readily admit I have not made my last and final decision. Things may and can change in the future.

After graduating from the Faculty of Economics, North Sumatra University, Indonesia, in 1967, I took a job as a teacher at my alma mater. At that time I had never thought that the job would be my career. When an opportunity came for me to pursue further studies, I left the country with the full support of my family. My major, monetary economics, did not provide me with the background to encourage me to examine issues related to women and, in fact, I did not develop any interest in this area. Rather, I concentrated on a theoretical framework and the application of policies from a macro point of view.

Later, when I returned to Indonesia, I decided to continue teaching at the university. I gladly accepted an offer to teach in Satya Wacana Christian University, Salatiga, Indonesia. Satya

Wacana is a private Christian university located in a small hill town in Central Java. I started my teaching assignment in early 1979 with the expectation that teaching would be a challenging and rewarding profession. It was at this university that I became involved with women's studies.

How it started

I accepted a request to be a speaker at a panel discussion, held on 21 April 1979, to celebrate Kartini's Day, an annual commemorative occasion to honor Indonesia's heroine, Raden Ajeng Kartini (1879–1904). The topic was "The Role of Indonesian Women in Society" and the discussion was jointly organized by the students' organization and the women's group on the campus. This was just a couple of months after I had joined the university and I was introduced as a scholar who had been studying abroad and had worked temporarily in Jakarta. Aware of my background, the organizing committee felt I would be able to expound on the subject from a broader perspective.

Having given my work to the committee, I started feeling uneasy because of my lack of experience or involvement in women's issues. I gathered the courage to take advice from my colleagues, spent long hours in the library, and informally expressed my ideas. In this manner, I gained many insights on the topic I was supposed to present. I allocated most of my time to this assignment; I treated this very first challenge and initial involvement in a brand new field as a real test of my abilities. Ultimately I was able to write my very first paper on women's issues.

In the paper I highlighted that, quantitatively, women outnumbered men. This fact can be a potential power and asset to the development process as far as the labor force is concerned. However, qualitatively, disparities exist where men receive priority treatment; this, to a large extent, is due to the patriarchal system in our society. Secondly, although Indonesia has a rather fast-growing literacy rate, the rate for women is far below that of men. The educational system and structure in Indonesia seem to be unable to remove barriers that block women's access to education. Indeed, while quite a number of women enter the highest level of education, those left out are still numerous.

Meanwhile, with improving health conditions, the infant mortality rate has shown a significant decline. The availability of several government-financed health programs that percolate down to the villages all over the country has been the main reason for health improvement in Indonesia. Life expectancy at birth is always higher for female than for male children. An increasing number of women reach higher managerial positions in both the public and in the private sectors, indicating their ability to fight for higher positions and their self-esteem. Although the percentage is relatively low, it still tells the truth that women are capable of doing what is supposedly men's business.

In spite of impressive changes in the profile of Indonesian women, discriminatory treatment toward them is still practiced. Legally sanctioned differential remuneration schemes have been implemented by various business entities. Improper employment security for the female labor force, and more requirements for women applying for a particular job, and restrictions for women in occupations that are not similarly restricted to men are just a few examples of this discrimination. This discrimination is not new or peculiar to the Indonesian context; but in our country they have been ingrained in the social fabric and it would be hard to pull them out without creating chaos. Nevertheless, they should not be maintained, and changes should be made. In my talk I reiterated Kartini's thought that women should be given the same education as men, otherwise they are perpetually second-class citizens. This thought made good sense, since my own family, in microcosm, had proven it true.

Other panelists at the discussion also brought out that women's issues in Indonesia are crucial and should be properly examined for the benefit of society as a whole. I was greatly impressed that, in the discussion, women's issues were treated as issues of major societal and national importance. Furthermore, we reached something like a consensus that the university faculty should further examine and deal with women's issues, and that activities should not be limited to panel discussions or the like.

I was also excited that my paper was strongly commented upon and criticized. I was even accused of opening a new door for confrontation as far as the role of women is concerned. A major line of attack against my paper was that it contained provocative thoughts on how women should change established norms and values. In other words, part of my paper clearly indicated that women are treated inequitably by society because of society's view that they are less deserving than men. I strongly opposed this view and I had clearly stated that there was no basis for such an assumption.

Comments came especially from men who thought and believed that women should not think as men do or expect to be treated as men are. Women are born to be different from men. There was a shocking comment that women should always serve men, and that women tend to utilize their "charm" for their benefit. I retaliated confidently, although even today I do not know how I turned out to be that firm. Wonderful, I told myself; silently, deep down in my heart, I started building up commitment to work further to prove my views. When I left the discussion hall, my mind was filled with a strong conviction that women's issues could draw our faculty's attention, be brought up for examination, and, perhaps, something concrete could be done institutionally. I had a feeling that more than a handful of faculty and students, both men and women, were concerned about women's issues. Each of their contributions could be an asset. The immediate question that emerged was how could this potential strength be mobilized and who would do the mobilizing? Since I was a newcomer, I was not in a position to talk to the policy-making body of the university. Confused, I felt powerless; yet the desire to do something preoccupied me for quite some time.

In between my teaching assignments, I used all my spare time to think of formative ideas on women's issues, but I could not foresee any opportunity, in my present condition, to implement my ideas. Fortunately, the old saying, where there is a will there is a way, turned out to be true.

Toward the end of 1979 I was approached by a male faculty member with an interest in women's issues. He asked me to consider a joint project on women's issues with another institution in a nearby city. I responded positively to the offer. A team of four faculty members (I was the only woman) was appointed and a working agenda was planned. Within my limited capacities, I tried to contribute to the shaping of the joint project. Admittedly, the work was tough and complex. We decided to base the project on the effort to realize the three-pronged principles of higher learning institutions in Indonesia: teaching, research, and community outreach. A seminar on women's studies, as the teaching part of the project, would be carried out as an initial activity. On the basis of this seminar, research would be carried out and recommendations for a community service program initiated.

The first effort was to conduct a seminar on women's condition in the present era in a broader perspective. The proposed seminar was not to be a repetition of the one conducted earlier that year, but was to go more deeply into the subject matter. Three topics were to be discussed: first, an overview of the available selected literature on Indonesian women; second, the condition of women in the rural areas, particularly in the agricultural sector; and third, the position of women from the Biblical point of view. The latter point was intentionally included because the two universities had the same religious background.

The work now had to be assigned to available faculty with an interest in the project and a willingness to take part. Knowing that I had presented a paper on the role of women in society, the first topic was entrusted to me. The second and third aspects were assigned to faculty from appropriate fields. What I was expected to do was to review what various authors had said and draw conclusions from their findings. In order to do so, I had to carefully and thoroughly read selected literature which I had not looked at earlier. What should I do to fulfil my responsibility?

Learning from my first experience, I devoted most of my spare time to reading this literature. The work seemed endless and the weight unbearable; but I persevered and finally produced my paper. My most striking finding was the different attitude toward the involvement of women in trade or business; while in some areas that particular type of work was not supposed to be done by women, in other parts women were very involved. The comments from faculty and student participants from both institutions enriched my understanding of women's issues. This made me feel happy. However, what I appreciated most was that more points were added to the set of issues I had produced in my earlier presentation. Later I learned that many people began using the paper as a reference. For me, my critical reading helped to broaden my views and prepared me for my involvement in many seminars and workshops.

Research involvement

The seminar came out with a number of recommendations, one of which was that research should be carried out on the socioeconomic conditions of women in rural areas. Our team developed a joint proposal with the counterpart institution.

This research was the very first on the topic done by our university. Designing the questionnaires was extremely exciting because the farther we went, the more questions we wanted to ask. Which questions should be retained and which ones were to be discarded required long and tiring deliberations; none of us in the team would easily agree with the others. To my disappointment, there was no other alternative but to trim down the questionnaires in a way that barely sufficed to meet our goals. After pretesting, we realized that the research areas—namely employment, educational attainment, sources of income, expenditure, housing conditions, religious practice, and the socialization process—were not adequate to uncover the real conditions of women in everyday life. Revising the questionnaire was as difficult as designing it in the beginning, although the insights and inputs from the pretest allowed us to make some improvements.

Training enumerators and conducting interviews were exciting as well; I really enjoyed the fieldwork. My encounter with respondents, many of whom were illiterate, opened my eyes to the fact that women's problems are societal problems. In spite of their poverty, I was touched by the attitude and expectation of many women respondents who felt that if there were alternatives, they would take them up immediately so as to survive. Some of these women showed that they no longer believed that they had to accept whatever happened to them (*nrimo*—full surrender); on the contrary, they had to fight for improvements and progress in their lives. Many of them, especially those who had been to school, thought that society and the family had been unfair to them because they were women.

When the analysis was being done on the data collected, we found that some concepts were overlooked and others were overemphasized. In spite of this, our research objectives were largely met, which meant that further planned activities could be implemented. Our enthusiasm in the writing of the report indicated our commitment and eagerness to complete this stage and move onto the next. Our research indicated that the women in the village under observation were very much in need of productive ways to reduce the pressures of poverty. On the other hand, health conditions were not that bad, since government programs were available. This finding was critical for determining the focus of our community outreach activities.

The experience I gained from this research was invaluable, for, several years later, I was involved in another research project on women's issues conducted by our Faculty of Economics. Our research was on the process of decision making in the production and marketing of small ruminants, such as sheep and goats, and how far and to what extent women were involved. It was interesting to see that women were playing an active role in production as far as food collection and feeding animals was concerned. When it came to marketing, women become inactive and men would dominate in the decision making. Our findings revealed that women were not usually consulted in financial matters, but were expected to support whatever decision was taken by the men. Likewise in the allocation of resources, women were generally not actively involved. In other words, financial decision making was almost out of the women's reach. This finding was in keeping with the values of Javanese culture, which stresses that women's place is in the home, while men must handle non-household affairs. While this finding inspired us to think of more work in the area, several years have passed without any follow-up.

Community outreach programs

We felt that the best possible way to deal with women's issues, especially those in rural areas, was to set up some community outreach programs with stress on women's problems. Through these programs we could participate and contribute directly to the possible solutions of various problems and shortcomings faced by women in particular, and rural society in general. It was perceived, at least by our research team, that the time had come for us in the university to start doing things together with women in the rural areas. Therefore we approached the university administration for support.

To set up the outreach program we worked more carefully. As we did not want to create a suspicion that the Christian University was trying to convert people through our program (a sensitive matter in our society), we approached the village head, through whose influence we could ensure support from the villagers. The government had already established the Family Welfare Education program for the improvement of family life in the village. Knowing that our programs were in harmony with the one introduced by the government, the village head allowed us to make the government program the entry point for our work. In a sense, we worked within a formal institution. Our outreach programs took different forms.

Simple tailoring courses, credit cooperatives to provide additional working capital for informal sector activities, tending rabbits, and planting a back garden were attractive activities enthusiastically adopted by both men and women. Social acceptance for our program was actually quite high since we did not create a financial burden for the villagers. Instead, we introduced productive ways to help alleviate financial pressures. Women in our program were treated as the "other door" to improve the family's economic condition.

Despite our frequent contact and communication with the village, the response from the villagers was not always positive. Negative responses usually came from the older generation who firmly believed that women should take care of the family and that their place should be at home. Any attempt to question this value, not to say to change it, was seen as a betrayal of the values of the forefathers. Indeed, although only a handful of people retain these beliefs, they were influential persons whose words and deeds were heeded. The younger generation, on the contrary, particularly those who had to give up schooling because of lack of finances, were very enthusiastic about our program. When we introduced a short, simple course on tailoring, quite a number of young men and women joined up. They were in need of any skill that would help them seek employment outside the agricultural sector.

This conflict between the older and the younger generation, if not carefully handled, could burst into hatred and revenge directed at us. So in order to avoid any unnecessary and unwanted confrontation, we kept a low profile and were careful about every single move. I was particularly cautious, especially because I am not Javanese and might be accused of trying to impose my own values and norms on these people. That could be dangerous! Nevertheless, I did not want to withdraw from the program. Surprisingly, however, we were always given a warm welcome by the villagers and received much cooperation from the informal leaders, which strengthened our commitment to the project.

Determining what sort of programs would be suitable for women in the village was not an easy undertaking. In order to reach our goals, programs were implemented by the women themselves, which allowed them to be more creative and innovative in their own way. This also gave them confidence. Our team acted more like consultants, as programs were determined in consultation with the village head and informal leaders. Sufficient supporting funds were made available by the university as working capital, which had to be repaid after five years. Regular meetings were held in the village every thirty-five days to discuss progress and problems and to plan further action. The programs met with ups and downs, and, frankly, as the chairperson of the team, I often did not have enough time to attend to the needs of the programs because of my other engagements. Sometimes I felt guilty about being ignorant about a project.

By now the villagers themselves have taken over the programs, while we are in a process of withdrawing from the project. We are thinking of other programs on the basis of the evaluations we have recently conducted. We hope that in the near future better programs can be designed and implemented, not only in this village, but in other villages which are in need of our services.

My research and community outreach activities have provided me with inputs that enrich my teaching, particularly in the area of economic development. Even if no specific course is offered on women's studies at our university, some courses, in general education and social sciences, include women's issues (though these, too, are not explicitly contained in the syllabus). Women in literature, for example, was once offered for students in the English Department, but has been discontinued. With my interest in women's studies I find it stimulating to expose students to women's issues. The first-hand data I give my students in class have increased their understanding of the real situation regarding women and stimulated some of them to write papers on this subject. Our university is coeducational, with more men students then women. However, students who wrote papers on women's issues were all women. The work of students on women's issues was critically received, at least by other teachers who happened to examine them orally. Meanwhile, in some of the official rhetoric, feelings of dissatisfaction and a need to overhaul values are becoming quite obvious. This clearly demonstrates that women's issues are not regarded as trivial or as something to be taken for granted. Today young people feel that some drastic action, for example on employment guarantees and the remuneration system, should be developed to improve labor relations. I feel that the voice of the younger generation should also be heard and considered.

Further involvement

In 1983 I was appointed Dean of the Faculty of Economics for a three-year term. I was the first woman dean the faculty had had in its twenty years of existence. Male faculty outnumbered female faculty, and not all of them seemed happy with me as the dean. I wondered whether they did not support me because of my style of leadership or because I was a woman. If the former was the reason, it did not matter a lot to me, since no one can expect to please everybody in an organization. However, if it were the latter, then the problem was different! I prepared myself to face opposition for both reasons and, until the end of my term, I strove to create and maintain a climate within and outside the campus that showed that a woman can be as good as, if not better than, a male dean. Often I succeeded, but at times of failure I could not help feeling upset, frustrated, and powerless.

In 1984, during my tenure as dean, the university cosponsored a nationwide seminar on "The Development of the Potency of Women's Horizon in Indonesian National Development." The coordination of the seminar was entrusted to me. I dared not refuse the responsibility for I knew it would enhance my understanding of women's issues and enable me to share my limited knowledge on the subject. A steering commitee was set up consisting of representatives of the sponsoring agency, a particular non-government organization, and myself. We decided that the seminar would deal with education, health, and employment as the core themes, after which participants could draft a program on women's issues for their respective institutions. In the beginning it was quite difficult to get a response from the thirteen Christian universities invited. Long correspondence and frequent reminders gradually generated positive responses for participation. The most difficult part of the work was to get the confirmation of the proposed speakers because of their previous commitments. The lack of women's centers in the participating universities was one likely explanation for the late responses. Eventually more than enough participants joined the seminar. Some were already equipped with an understanding of the themes; others just came to listen and learn. Most were enthusiastic during the discussions in plenary as well as in group sessions.

One of the sessions was on designing a program that could be beneficial to an institution as well as to society as a whole.

Acting as the moderator, I become more aware of the lack of a theoretical and methodological frame of thinking among the participants. Admittedly, those participants were new to women's issues and some of them were hearing about them for the first time. This was not surprising, since the subject was only just being introduced in higher education. Consequently, no theory or methodology had yet developed for the specific context of Indonesian women.

Not long after the seminar, another opportunity to work in the area of women's studies came my way. This was an "interfaith" research project jointly carried out by four different private universities: a Muslim, a Catholic, and two Protestant universities. I was the chairperson. The research was at its first stage in collecting authentic data from in-depth case studies done by each university on a particular women's issue. There were seven areas of focus: women and entrepreneurship; women as domestic servants; multiple roles of women; women and crime; women and architecture; women's involvement in traditional customs and practices; and women as middle-level managers. At the second stage, a group of experts would be commissioned to write case studies on the basis of the data collected, and the third stage would be the preparation of teaching modules from the case studies. The idea behind this project sprang from the awareness that it is difficult, if not impossible, to find teaching modules using women's issues in the Indonesian context.

In August 1989, almost three years after the work started, the research stage was somewhat near completion. I learned a very important lesson from the work: big and ambitious ideas are definitely needed, but transforming those ideas into reality is something that requires expertise, personnel, funds, and time. But despite the fact that the second and third stages would not materialize within a short period, research reports from the other three universities would add to the available material on women's studies in Indonesia.

Looking at the first draft of the report, I have become more convinced that women are not weak, but capable of determining what they believe is best for their own lives. They are hardworking and possess a vision for the future. These qualities were found among the women domestic helpers and entrepreneurs who were the respondents in our study. They simply lack better opportunities and the chances for mobility available to men. These women combine their domestic chores and earning money outside the home. They carry the proverbial double burden. Although writing up the planned teaching modules is still far from a reality, I am sure the case studies will eventually become, useful academic references.

Roads to other activities

In a situation like ours, where formal recognition and acceptance are crucial to any activity, efforts must be made to develop and institutionalize women's issues. Work on women's studies in various forms has been carried out by our university in a sporadic manner, coordinated by a particular unit in the university. If there is an opportunity created by the university or there is a request from outside institutions, usually a team consisting of faculty from various disciplines would be set up to handle the work, and they would report directly to the president of the university. This approach has been beneficial to me because in most of the projects on women's issues my involvement is assumed. To a large extent, I have somehow become an informal resource as well as contact person for those who would like to inquire about women's studies at my university.

At times I feel I am not able to satisfy those who come with myriad queries. After discussing the growing interest with people in authority, as well as with some women teachers who gave further insights, initial steps have been taken to consider formalizing our efforts in women's studies.

A task force of six women faculty from various disciplines (coordinated by myself) has been appointed to review the program and strengthen its foundation. The faculty involved are from different backgrounds and levels of understanding and experience in women's studies. Willingness to get involved, despite their hectic schedules, availability for consultations, and commitment to the nature of the work are essential to the continuation of the task force. Anxiety about women's issues and other related matters is the basic rationale behind our task force's activities.

We began by gathering materials on women's studies, scattered in three university libraries, and compiling them in a useful way. The compilation process is still going on and about sixteen topics are already listed. These include women and employment, psychology of women, women and health, women in journalism, women in politics, women in theology, and women in the business sector. A corner is provided in our central library for women's studies materials. We are also prepared to face faculty or staff who appear to be opposed to this kind of work; they interpret women's studies as an instrument to hide women's weaknesses and to help them freely meet their personal and subjective goals. The question they always ask when women's issues are brought up is, "Why should we wake a sleeping tiger?" To them, women in general are already satisfied with their present conditions. Since they do not argue and there is no protest, they seem to readily accept their fate. In seminars, panel discussions, and public lectures I attended, questions were raised that indicated that some people still doubt, and probably hesitate to accept, the objectives of women's studies. My reaction to this ticklish problem may seem somewhat soft. In my opinion, the situations and conditions in society have made many women accept whatever is given to them. I also agree that some women actively maintain a status quo that allows them a passive role. They do not ask for more freedom, opportunity, and appreciation because they are blinded and deafened by the status quo. However, while collecting data and putting together our resource material, we were struck by the variety and diversity of problems with which women are confronted. It illustrated the complexities of women's issues in Indonesia and the importance of exposing the reality of women's experience. The bibliography we developed is meant for teachers, students, and other interested people.

Initially my involvement in women's issues was academic. Recently I accepted the position as the chairperson of Women's Communion in Satya Wacana, an organization of all women teachers and staff, together with wives of male faculty and staff. It functions as a forum for sharing ideas, problems, plans, and concerns of women in Satya Wacana and is largely directed toward social and family affairs. One of its aims is to mobilize women toward social activities on the campus. As chairperson I took responsibility for improving social relationships. Members of this group are diverse in educational achievement, values, socioeconomic background, and family structure. This diversity makes instruction quite difficult as many members consider themselves unfit to take on the responsibility of handling projects. This feeling of inferiority becomes a hindrance to change and I am eager to subdue this kind of feeling. One of my male colleagues once teased me by saying that the biggest enemy of women is women, not men or society, and that if women could conquer women, they could conquer the world. Often this joke bothers me and I start thinking about the truth of it.

A decision was made recently to include women's studies within the Institute of Community Service of our university and I was appointed the coordinator for two years. This appointment is an acknowledgement of the importance and relevance of women's issues. I planned to make the best out of this appointment by realistically devising programs to promote women's studies in the academic setting. Assuming that the syllabi of various courses can be changed, then the provision of bibliographies of relevant articles or other publications, the availability of more accurate and reliable data on women's issues, and women activists and a forum for action can lead to an integration of women's issues in various subjects, especially in the social sciences.

I believe that the personal touch, honesty in appearance and actions, and thoughtful and fruitful policy implementation are effective approaches. I feel that any action I make in the future will reflect my understanding of women's studies as part of knowledge required to bring forth peace, prosperity, and harmony in a world created for all. I am well aware that the position I hold is not an easy one. It can be a heavy burden, particularly if I am alone in pursuing these objectives. I need support from the system and the people in the university to make my work enjoyable and fruitful. Long and rough roads are ahead for me, and others like me, to travel.

Li Xiaojiang
China

LI XIAOJIANG was born in Jiujiang city, Jiangxi Province and studied for her master's degree at Henan University, Kaifeng, Henan Province. A European literature major, she is currently Associate Professor in the Department of Chinese Language and Literature at Zhengzhou University and also Director, Center for Women's Studies.

My Path to Womanhood

A youthful fantasy

Thirty years ago I was full of fantasy and budding idealism. But my ideas had nothing to do with women. In fact, I was quite blind to the connotations of the word "womanhood." Most of my childhood and adolescence was spent within the confines of various campuses. While at school I was a boarder, and during the vacations I used to go home to my parents. My parents were often transferred from one university to another: Jiujiang City, Nanchang, Shanghai, Changchun, Shenyang, Beijing, and, finally, Zhengzhou, the end of their journey. By accompanying them on a migratory journey that traversed almost the entire length of China, I had the opportunity to see many beautiful places across the country and form friendships with a lot of interesting people. However, my early years were so confined to university campuses that I felt quite isolated. Thanks to the tranquil environment of campus life in China and a political climate characterized by a national *esprit de corps* emphasizing class struggle, neither I nor my four sisters experienced discrimination as girls or labored under any of the humiliations women are traditionally destined to suffer. Despite the fact that China's women were still victims of social biases, because of which my parents continued to want a male heir, we were raised in relative freedom.

In my opinion, the experiences of contemporary Chinese women are quite different from the conventional pattern. Women enjoy almost full equity as circumstances and social conditions allow it. Contemporary Chinese women have shared equally with men in all the weal and woe that befell the country. For the duration of at least a certain historical period, conventions and traditions receded before the onrush of the revolution. While repelling the bourgeoisie energetically, the proletariat also stamped out many manifestations of feudalism. The term *feudalism* in Chinese distinctly connotes an involvement with the norms governing the relationship between the sexes. *Feudalism* does not refer to anything political in nature, and *feudal* is used as an epithet for a person who holds a conservative stance on gender relationships. All contemporary Chinese women, urban or rural, engaged in physical or intellectual labor, were subject to a political environment that propelled them into a new pattern of life, a pattern labelled "the age of liberation."

Though four decades have elapsed, and much of our lifestyle has reverted to what it was like four decades ago, the life of the present-day Chinese woman has not really deteriorated. What my father once said concerning the status of contemporary Chinese women still seems appropriate: "Thanks to the four decades of 'liberation', the social strata in China that have undergone the greatest change in terms of status are women, actors and actresses." Living in a social community marked by a sense of equality makes it rather difficult to identify one's own "gender status." Of course I did, and do, know my own gender, but I confess I had no idea of the quality that might distinguish one gender from the other. I was quite ignorant about what distinguishes a woman from a "human being" or from a man. Indeed, in my younger years, I might have even turned out to be an opponent of women's studies!

In my childhood I behaved more wildly than is normal even for a boy; I liked to climb trees, scale walls, and shoot pebbles from a catapult. I hated wearing shoes and was against having my hair combed. I was fond of sports, singing, and romping, but was reluctant to be involved in an athletic contest where I had to abide by rules or in a performance that called for make-up. I was not deliberately imitating the behavior of a young boy; rather, I was striving for the common human desire for freedom and the need to be free of restraint. While for three decades I have trudged the long path typical of the contemporary Chinese woman, the desire for freedom and the propensity to be rid of any restraint remain with me.

Femininity and sexuality

My awakening to my femininity was synchronous with my sexuality. My reaction was drastic. I had extreme contempt for femininity and longed for a way to rid myself of any trait that could be termed feminine. In the years between my awakening and now, I have come across a great many women who had mental experiences similar to mine. These feelings have led me to try to understand the experience of today's Chinese women. The evening pending my graduation from primary school, two girl students in my class, who were both a bit older than the rest of our classmates, flatly said that they were not interested in going ahead with their secondary education. They were determined to begin work in a textile factory. Their determination made me feel very sad, but they remained quite unperturbed. One of them even came to comfort me, saying, "Come, come! Don't feel sad for me. I've been bored to death by life at school. It isn't a girl's fate to become a scholar. She's bound to get married in due course and give birth to children. And as for struggling with men for a career, she's up against more than her match there!"

I remember that evening as one that was lit by faint moonlight. Seven or eight girls in the graduating class sat on a carousel in the playground of our primary school. After the two older girls had announced their determination to forsake their pursuit of a secondary education, the rest of us turned mute. A funereal silence reigned over us. At that juncture, I would have shouted back at the two girls, words such as, "I won't believe in fate!" But actually I felt gagged. I just bit my upper lip so hard that it bled. Inwardly I took an oath: I swear that I shall surpass all my male classmates in the pursuit of a brilliant career; I am going to convince you of the falsehood of your blind trust in fate. To this day I can feel afresh the salty and rancid savor of blood oozing from my lip.

During the course of my secondary education, most of the girls in my class began to menstruate. Girl students had a nickname for menstruation: ill luck. When a girl student was in her ill luck, she was exempt from attending hours of PE and from doing manual labor. Boys jealously complained of girls' privileges. On the occasion of choosing a model student, boys, more often than not, would reject girl candidates on the ground that they were too self-indulgent when it came to physical exertion. At that time, I was on the side of the boys rejecting girls, on the same ground. I thought a girl should have the guts to strive to be a boy's equal in everything and ought not to offer such a feeble pretext as "having the menses." Some of my female classmates retorted, "Since you have not met your *ill luck* yet, you can afford to be smug."

I regard the day of my first menstruation as monstrously ominous. It was during the early stage of the Cultural Revolution. On that day my father was hauled out to parade in the streets and lanes by red guards; he was in disgrace. He was dragged along tied with a rope; a placard with humiliating and abusive words hung from his neck and dangled on his chest, and an ugly fool's cap was crushed on his head. I walked stealthily in the midst of a throng on the sidewalk as I had on several previous occasions, following my father at a distance as he completed his mortifying march. Abruptly he came to a standstill for no apparent reason and was instantly shouted at and shoved along by some of the red guards following him. One of them poured a big bottle of ink on his head. My heart shrank at such a grim sight and, driven by impulse, I was at the point of rushing to his rescue when I felt a drastic twinge in the lower part of my abdomen. A flow of hot liquid trickled down the inner sides of my thigh ... suddenly it dawned on me what the flow meant. Tears began to run down my cheeks. It was an instant of bewilderment; the ink that was poured on my father's head, my menstrual discharge, and my tears churning like a whirlpool. I seemed to be engulfed. I felt a deep sense of humiliation in my status as a woman and as a daughter. In those days I was disgusted with myself for being female.

Rejecting womanhood

As I matured physically, I developed a craving to become more and more like a boy. I tried to read all the biographies of great men I could find and strove to strengthen my willpower. I deliberately sought to torment myself in the same way as Laharmeitov (a character in *What To Do?*, a novel by Chernishievski, a Russian writer). When a roaring gust of wind rose, I would stay for hours on end where it blew the strongest. I would expose myself to the sun during the hottest days of summer. I would swim in the river during the coldest spell in winter. Years later, when I was assigned to settle down in a rural area, I continued to torment myself so as to harden my willpower. Though I had never before worked in the field, when I was sent to live in the countryside I insisted that the executive chief of the village production brigade give me the most strenuous farm work, assigned as a rule only to men. Consequently, I volunteered to handle almost all the heaviest and most tiring

farm chores in the village, carrying on my shoulders a pole
with two big bales of reaped paddy hanging from it, climbing
to the top of an immense stack of paddy in the sheaf in order
to make the stack conical, handling a primitive instrument
(called *jiang* in Chinese) for sowing wheat seeds, and other terrible, physically exacting farm chores that have been left un-
touched by the average village woman for millenia. In the
freezing days of winter, I carried water in pails suspended
from a pole on my shoulders, going uphill, with a total load of
more than seventy-five kilos. Only God knows how many
times I fell on the slippery ground with my waterload, and
only God knows how many times I rolled, with my pails full
of water, down hills crusted with snow and ice. I was often totally soaked with spilt water, with shoulders first bruised and
then broken by my poles. Even then I almost never shed tears.

I was challenging my own fate and my "gender status." I
chanced upon Irving Stone's *A Sailor on Horseback*. I read it
and then forced myself to follow the example of Jack London.
I applied myself assiduously to reading books for increasing
my own stock of knowledge. My self-imposed discipline continued beyond the days I lived in the countryside and had to
work in the fields from dawn to dusk, to those when I was assigned as a factory worker and had to work in the daytime and
take part in sports matches in the evening. As an amateur
sportswoman, I persevered for more than a dozen years in this
strenuous self-education. In those years, I slept for only five or
six hours each night. During the dozen or so years of such arduous self-education, which many men found unbearable, I
never flinched; and I finally emerged victorious. Together
with other resolutely enterprising people of my generation, I
struggled to successfully shake off the yoke of our hostile fate
and succeeded in tiding over a decade in which our nation was
on the verge of total collapse.

University years

In 1979 I enrolled at Henan University as a graduate student. At
that time I had had only eight years of schooling. In Chinese society it is permissible for a woman to strive as strenuously as a
man to carve out a career for herself. So long as she works hard
to build her career, there is every likelihood that her achievement will be as much as a man's. After the decade of turmoil
had ended, life in China gradually returned to normal and be-

came stable and peaceful. Both in the days when I was pursuing my postgraduate studies and when I became a teacher, I did not experience, and have not since experienced, any major discrimination because of my gender.

After my postgraduate career, I was designated an instructor and taught on the campus of a university. Before long I was promoted, before my originally scheduled time, to the rank of associate professor by a special order from the university authorities. I had surpassed my male colleagues in the competition. During my postgraduate career I was trained in the natural sciences. At that time I devoted all my zeal and time to studies on women, which, as a branch of knowledge, was completely neglected by academic circles in China. I plunged into it quite alone and have been pushing ahead energetically in this field of study ever since.

After I married, I soon discovered that I was hindered in every direction when I sought to think and act in keeping with the willpower, independence, values, and conduct of my unmarried days. My husband, my son, family chores, and my family's social connections all could turn out to be one sort of obstruction or another if I persisted in following my earlier path. They tended to take up almost all my time and energy and foiled my attempts to pursue my plans independently and without restraint. On the other hand, it would have been like a death sentence had I been forced to part with my husband and family: I acted the way a traditional woman would have acted in the matter of indulgently giving and receiving love; I have been extremely indulgent in selfishly drinking in conjugal love and selflessly bestowing maternal love—I believe it is my own fate that has preordained me to behave like this. And my own fate is typical of the lot of many Asian women. As long as I was unwilling to part with my husband and family, I had to assume all the consequences that stemmed from this unwillingness. And no sooner had I volunteered to assume all the consequences, then I realized I had been lured into another trap. I was forced to play two roles at the same time, to carry a load which would be twice as much as that usually carried by a man.

All modern women are doomed to fall into such a trap. Most are now wallowing in it silently and in a docile manner. It is not that someone has necessarily endeavored to entice a woman into such a situation. The existence of this trap, and of the trapped, seems to be quite a "natural," occurrence that simply happens with time. But it is actually not all that natural; in the long run I came to realize that the dual role women are obliged to play in everyday life entails dual philosophies of life. Such a duality splits a woman as a social entity and deprives her of the capacity to present herself as the perfect "ego" in either family or social life. But the question baffles me: Why are women alone made to suffer in this manner?

I believe that nobody will come forth with a ready answer to this question. For, in modern society, only men are entitled to come forth with answers to social problems—but men know precious little about women, especially contemporary women. And women, instead of finding an answer to this question, either evade it or curse their own lot aimlessly and wantonly. Perhaps we are haunted by the fear that men will look down upon us if we confess to the truth of this question. But then, I feel that women, too, are ignorant, devoid of answers. I have arrived at this conclusion only after reading for many sleepless nights. My conclusion troubles me, but in ways which have roused me to become enterprising and single-minded in the pursuit of women's studies. Women are a complete enigma to me. The role they have played in history, society, and the cultural development of humanity is an enigma, one which has oppressed us, fooled us, degraded our status, and made our lot more unbearable.

I hope to discover why women have been so tormented and full of disgrace. In an age that boasts equality between the sexes, why do women lead a painfully laborious and depressing life? My own experience has already shown me that differences do exist between the sexes; still, I want to understand the real causes of the view that men are irreversibly superior to women. As a woman who has had to go through much, I believe all women ought to be brave and enterprising. Despite the fact that women's inherent status and value have been completely obliterated by the writers of history and society, I harbor the hope that my academic studies may contribute to the rediscovery of that status and value. And only by making such an appraisal can I become fully independent, confident, and competent as a woman scholar and exert myself to dive into a study of humanity.

A hard path to womanhood

When I first aspired to study womanhood in my own capacity as a woman and expected that other women and the academic community would lend a hand, I never anticipated that these very groups would deliberately block and hinder my pursuit. The only legitimate women's organization in China is the All-China Women's Federation. I expected the federation to help me and answer some of my questions by supplying me with relevant data to facilitate my study. Therefore I wrote to ask them for materials I needed urgently. I also wrote to some acclaimed women leaders for their support in developing women's studies. I have not received a single response to these appeals and, by the time my first paper on women was published, women leaders were so upset that my work was drowned under a sea of disapproving voices.

Academic polemics in present-day China are generally tied to a particular political orientation. Some authorities or officials seem to want to use their power to reshape truth. Owing to the fact that the All-China Women's Federation was largely a political facade and scorned by people from all walks of life, my pursuit of women's studies was likely to have only a slim chance of survival. Then, as luck would have it, the leadership of the federation changed and brought in fresh, new elements. Women intellectuals in the prime of their lives were promoted to the rank of leading officials to fill the posts of editor or reporter. And they were determined to be of use to women. These women have now become my true friends and help in publicizing my efforts by providing financial and moral support.

Another hindrance to my efforts in women's studies came from the academy, which chose to remain silent. Their silence was a contemptuous defiance of women and women's studies. Scholars, in their twenties, thirties, and forties, especially those who had taken the lead in developing reforms in their disciplines, responded to women's issues as "little whines" uttered by the weak, who were still mentally enslaved by feudal tradition. This was because they were obsessed with complications existing in the macrocosm, major fields of knowledge, the world community, and *man*. I have been tempted to feel sorry for contemporary men. It is widely known that in the 1917 May Fourth Movement almost all advanced male thinkers addressed themselves to the liberation of women: Lu Xun, Shen Yanbing, Chen Duxiu, and Li Dazhao, to mention but a few, were exemplary in that regard. But the leading reformists of our day have chosen to shun the study of women. It was not until 1986 that any periodical or institution dedicated to women's studies came into existence in mainland China. Nor was there a university or college that would take the lead in offering academic degrees or faculty positions in women's studies.

The pretext used to camouflage this lack of attention was simple: as long as women are a part of humanity, any study related to them ought to be placed within the category of human studies. It was deemed redundant, therefore, to establish an independent branch of knowledge or speciality. I recall a symposium on literature, when a rather celebrated professor taunted me, saying: "Literature bears no gender, you know. It would sound absurd for it to split into two departments, one for men, and the other for women. Literature is not a latrine which can be dedicated to one sex only." Implicit in his words was his opinion that I intended to rouse our academic circles in a futile endeavor. There was another pretext also: since women have special problems, women's studies ought to be favored with exclusive treatment. It should be placed in a special niche in the edifice of sciences and receive exclusive treatment. At a scholar's salon in Beijing, after I had finished a lecture on women's studies, a fairly renowned philosopher immediately protested: "I've hardly ever heard of this so-called 'women's studies.' As far as I know, in Chinese history there has scarcely been any woman philosopher. And a great many philosophers in our history remained single all their lives. It seems that no woman in Chinese history has ever played a significant role in the field of philosophy." His protest suggested that developing women's studies was like building castles in the air.

Today hindrances or obstructions such as these have largely disappeared. Although some influential elements in the leading stratum of the All-China Women's Federation still have a grudge against me, and I face contempt from major portions of the academy, the development of women's studies in China is no longer held in check. The people who have devoted themselves to the study of China's women have formed an organized contingent and built their own stronghold. In some disciplines women's studies components are already included in collegiate curricula. They are warmly welcomed by the majority of our women intellectuals and highly appreciated by far-sighted male scholars. No matter what the political situation in China may become, a number of persevering researchers have now vowed lifelong devotion to the cause of women's studies in China. They are working extremely hard to trace the history and the current condition of China's women.

A lifelong commitment

In my postgraduate career I majored in Western European literature. It was a great leap forward from the status of a high school student assigned to live permanently in the countryside, or to be an amateur basketball player and fitter in a factory. Many reporters have asked me to write about my life. They want a story about a self-taught woman. I shunned them all as if I were fleeing a disaster. I hated the intrusion upon my privacy (and I would also avoid involving myself in other's private affairs). Besides, I did not want the mass media to present me as a stereotyped portrait of the self-taught woman. My work and studies are motivated by a conscientious craving to realize my own worth. In my opinion, when one decides on an option in matters related to a career or private life, one is either motivated by a penchant to explore or dictated by a desire to survive. The desire to survive, however, could become a constraint in that it hinders a personal zeal to keep on exploring.

For me, women's studies is neither the starting point nor the termination of my career. Our generation has now been pushed forward to the threshold of a new century and is confronted with innumerable *terrae incognitae*. I aspire to penetrate more and more *terrae incognitae* and earnestly hope that I can set about my research right away so that I can soon solve many enigmas that are now puzzling me, my fellow countrymen, and contemporary humanity. But it is also very difficult for me to give up my deep commitment to women's studies, and I have found that I need to leave all my previous hobbies, interests, and theoretical explorations in order to concentrate on women's studies. At times it seems as if I am being dragged along on an invisible rope and cannot tear myself away from this field of study.

For me, developing women's studies is the fulfillment of a kind of duty. Such a duty may be regarded as an absurd obligation by Westerners. There is a Chinese saying, "Beginning is the most arduous part of any undertaking." Therefore, whoever is charged with the duty of making a beginning ought to make the beginning successful. And one ought not to give up the undertaking of which one has made a beginning. Over a period of time, I have come to realize more and more deeply that I have become one of the pioneers of women's studies in China. And I must function dutifully as one of the cornerstones to the edifice of women's studies. I am obliged to do so. My paper, "Progress of Mankind and Liberation of Womanhood," was published in 1983. It was the first treatise on women published in China since 1949 and immediately caused a commotion. Some people howled vehemently for its suppression and labelled it an "anti-Marxist gospel." It is because of this treatise that scholars ,who later became the core of the "women's studies contingent," rallied to form a front. In 1984 my paper, "China's Womanhood's Road to Liberation and its Characteristics," was published. I put forward the argument that all the progress that has so far been made by the movement for women's liberation in China is an outcome of legislation too advanced for the political awareness of the populace of its age. In the paper I argued that the liberation of women in China has so far been only an outcome of a social revolution, rather than an outcome of a feminist movement. These two arguments and others I have made constitute the watershed between the "new" and the "old" school of research on women's studies. My arguments drew much crossfire from conservatives in the women's liberation movement in China and were regarded as heresies. Yet they also attracted honest and kind friends and a group of women intellectuals who involved themselves with me at that time.

The year 1985 saw the initial success of our tentative efforts to form some sort of organization and offer women's studies as an independent course for college students. In the spring of that year the Society of Women's Studies was founded. The Henan Provincial Futuristic Research Society sponsored the foundation ceremony. It is the first women's research institution in China and is not financed by government. In August of that year, the Society of Women's Studies organized China's first women's symposium in Zhengzhou. Higher educational institutions and research units in eight provinces in mainland China sent their representatives to the symposium. The representatives were, for the most part, young women scholars, the majority of whom had master's degrees. They came from more than a dozen disciplines.

In May and June of that year, under the auspices of Wang Li-Huan, president of Henan Provincial Institute for Women

Cadres, a household management course was started. The course is the first of its kind in China; its participants were initiated into the topic of "Recognizing Our Womanhood" during the course. The course was first regarded as an eyesore by some conservatives. But it has won support and trust from the vast majority of women in Henan Province. Liang Jun, herself an undergraduate studying at Beijing Normal University and majoring in world history, volunteered to abandon her original major and take up women's studies as her life career after attending the course. From then on, she has run courses, given many lectures on radio and television, and travelled through dozens of cities and provinces to deliver about a thousand lectures on the subject of women's liberation. She has been doing her utmost to alert our women to their predicament and has won the hearts of the women of China.

In September of that year, I began to offer a course on women's literature to the students of the Department of Chinese Literature and Language of Zhengzhou University. This was also the first of its kind offered at a university in mainland China and was a success because of the support of the Academic Affairs Committee of my department and the students who took the course. In a 1986 essay in the magazine *Women of China*, I put forward a synoptic proposal for the establishment of a curriculum at a college or university for women's studies. A proposal of this kind had never been put forward in mainland China before. Since then, disapprovals have been voiced. Some people have defiantly argued against establishing women's studies as an independent field of knowledge, while others have advanced their own views and proposals. It is quite natural that people's approaches to a new field will vary considerably, and that is not a bad thing. In my opinion, my proposal has induced other people to take women's concerns seriously. From the polemics surrounding the establishing of women's studies as an independent branch of knowledge, I was able to gather information regarding categories and topics, which I will include in *Serial Books on Women's Studies*, a multi-volume publication I have been editing.

In 1987 I applied to the leadership of Zhengzhou University for the establishment of a university center for women's studies and my application was soon approved. The establishment of this center was a significant event. It was the first research unit dedicated to the study of women established on a campus. In the last two years, the Center for Women's Studies of Zhengzhou University succeeded in rallying women's studies researchers at dozens of higher educational and research institutions in different parts of China to coordinate efforts. Now the center has become the general base for women's studies in China. Its work arouses intense academic interest for those who work to focus on women as an exclusive target of study and touches on topics related to more than a dozen branches of the humanities. It provides comprehensive comparisons between women and men. The materials supply more than enough background information and knowledge for substantiating a full curriculum for a major in women's studies at a college. With financing from the Fund for China's Reform and Opening to the Outside World, we are planning to publish a periodical, *Women Intellectuals*. China's women intellectuals are among the most advanced in society and ought, with perfect self-assurance and courage, to call upon the whole of the country's womanhood to rally together. Such intellectuals can now act as the core force in the movement for women's liberation.

This is but a rough description of the journey my comrades and I have taken in promoting the growth of women's studies in mainland China. We still remain pioneers in this field. And we are yet at the initial stage of our pilgrimage. One consolation is that we have, after all, made women's studies sprout from the barren soil of China's land. What will women's studies be like in the future? Our projects will develop on the basis of the successes of previous projects. It is probable that our future journey will be easier than our past. Perhaps unjustifiable pressures will be less often applied, and opprobrium will no longer be so profusely heaped on us. Still I do not think I can be too optimistic. In my opinion, for a considerably long period in the future, women's studies will still be in its academic infancy and the development of its theoretical foundations will be shaky.

Although we may expect that more and more scholars, especially women, will work in the field, our society and our women can hardly be expected to respond very enthusiastically to our call for a vigorous development of the women's cause. This lack of response can be accounted for by two factors. One of them is the political climate in China; the other our financial difficulty. As long as China is beset with political and economic disaster, its women and women's studies will find it difficult to develop and expand.

Still, we can hope that the progress we have already made not be wiped out and our development not be given up easily. Whether circumstances are favorable or unfavorable, I know there will always be women who will stand by me, shoulder to shoulder, through thick and thin, and that is enough! On our pilgrimage to the shrine of freedom, they cannot dispense with me or my work. With such mutual understanding, nothing in the world can constitute a permanent hindrance to women's progress.

Liang Jun
China

LIANG JUN (b. 1945) was born in Yi Yang country, Henan Province, and graduated from the History Department of Beijing Normal University in 1968. She now works as a senior teacher in Henan Women Cadres School.

A Serious Mission

Self-consciousness

I started my "real" life at the age of forty. Since then, whatever I have done is clear in my mind and unforgettable. But my life before forty is another story. I was born into a family of intellectuals; my father is an engineer and my mother a doctor. I was the only girl among six children. Like their peers, my parents are traditional, although they have accepted some new ideas. As a result, in my education new demands often competed with old concepts: my parents required me to do as well as my brothers; at the same time, they restricted my behavior to conform to the traditional virtues of the "Oriental" woman. Consequently, I was taught to be tender-hearted and obedient as well as eager to do well and to be successful.

While I was growing up, people with a family background such as mine were discriminated against. In most cases, those who faced such discrimination looked on the world with cold resentment and even hopelessness. Or they go along with the social norms and strive to mold themselves in a way that will make them acceptable. Being obedient, but unwilling to be "backward" and out of step with the times, I naturally chose the latter method of adjustment, one that was easy to choose but extremely hard to conform to. As a young woman born into an intellectual bourgeois family, I felt I needed to relate to workers and peasants; as a woman who was growing up during the era of "equality of men and women," I needed to fit into the standards created for men. While I regarded these as my lofty goals, I was apprehensive: I did not know what would happen to me. At that time I only knew that I should seek, strive, and exert the utmost strength.

When I took part in voluntary labor, in spite of my menses, I stood with boy students in the water above my knees, scooping up sludge from the river or transplanting rice seedlings in water. When the "four clean-up" movement was carried out in the countryside, I fetched water during the drought and carried manure to spread in the field with male peasants during the day; at night, alone, I crossed the mountain passes, haunted by wolves, to call on and learn about the poor and lower middle-class peasants.

When I graduated I was disdainful of the male students who asked for an ideal assignment; I transferred without hesitation to Tibet, which is known as a place where "no grass grows on the mountains but stones move when the wind blows." There I lived in a tent with holes on all sides, used my hand to eat the half-cooked mutton with the herdsmen, and rode horses to keep sheep and cattle within bounds. I fell off my horse once and suffered a moderate cerebral concussion, but I did not stop my work. I also climbed a five-thousand-meter-high mountain, talking cheerfully and humorously in spite of a terrible headache; this gained me increasing respect from my male companions. At the time I did everything with great enthusiasm and did not feel tired. Illness did not deter me and I did not regret my choice. I only thought that the dream that "women would live like men" had come to pass at last in my generation.

However, I am a woman, after all, with traditional roots. I planned to marry and bear children. I fantasized about having a warm and sweet family. So, like most Chinese women, I got married and had a baby boy the following year. I became busier and experienced great happiness. Nonetheless, I soon started feeling overburdened with work at home and outside. "I will not give birth any more," I said to my husband, and I sent my son to kindergarten when he was three years old. But not long after that I whispered to my husband, "Should we have one more child?" I soon had another baby boy.

It seemed natural, but I was no longer the person I had been earlier. From the "modern heroine" I had turned into a professional person and a housewife, whose life was confined to working at the office and doing housework at home. All day long I was in a desperate hurry and felt exhausted. Gradually, the brave "pledge to compete with men" was abandoned as an illusion. I came to believe that a marital relationship could not remain balanced. Like a seesaw, one end rises and the other end falls. "So long as you are successful in your achievements, I am willing to do everything for you," I said to my husband. If I delayed doing housework because of official business, I would feel ashamed and guilty, as though I had done something scandalous. My husband was sincere, simple, and kindhearted.

But in my innermost self, I wished to develop myself. It was hard for me to live this way, tied down by my double burden. Sometimes, when my husband did more work, I blamed myself for lacking in enthusiasm. Sometimes, when I had to do more housework, I complained that my husband and children hindered me in my professional work. Because of my own emotional instability, there was often a grim atmosphere at home, and a "cold war" started between me and my husband. I shouldered the heavy load of work and life, unable to bear it, and yet unwilling to abandon it. Day and night I was worried, depressed, and resentful. My enterprising spirit was subdued and I felt prematurely old. I began to look for a less demanding profession so that I could have more time to help my husband at home. Around this time I was transferred from Henan Financial and Economic College to Henan Women Cadres School.

I never expected that the new job would become a new beginning for me. Li Xiaojiang, an extraordinary woman, led me into another life. At the end of the spring of 1985, Li Xiaojiang, an associate professor of Chinese language and literature at the Zheng Zhou University and Henan Women Cadres School, jointly organized the first national Women's Household Management Class. Since I had just come to the school I knew nothing about Professor Li, or about the class. It was only out of curiosity and thirst for knowledge that I went to Li's lecture.

What a vivid lesson on "self-consciousness of women!" Professor Li stood on the platform, graceful and confident, without being overbearing. What were riddles for contemporary women were explained and clarified by her flowing words: the differences in physiology and psychology and in the historical process of evolution between men and women; the inequality of men and women at the present time; the damaging interruption of women's lives because of women's reproductive activity; the historical inevitability of tension arising out of the dual roles of women; the unbending pursuit of spiritual life among women, and so on. She pointed out boldly that equality between men and women is not the final yardstick of women's emancipation. All the problems of women cannot be solved by the founding of the socialist system. However, the formal recognition of the "equality of men and women," although according to the norms of men in the 1950s, provided a starting point for Chinese women to assert their identity. Women live a hard and burdened life. Well, since we are born women, we should squarely face our existence and value, she said, and accept the challenge.

The audience was overwhelmed by her sharp words, penetrating analysis, and original point of view. I still remember someone shouting in class "You are right!" One of the women, who was more than fifty years old, said weeping: "Teacher Li, why didn't you tell us all this earlier?" At that time, I did not express my feelings, because I suffered from a sense of inferiority. But I was greatly affected; it was as if I had seen a lighthouse on the dark sea. The depression sitting heavy in my heart for so long dissolved at once. I was eager to start my new life. I thought I should tell all women who were depressed like me what I had heard from Professor Li.

I soon became acquainted with Professor Li and, as we saw more of each other, became good friends. All the same, I look up to her as my teacher and spiritual guide, even though she is six years younger than I. Reading Professor Li's works and talking to her are exciting experiences. She has opened up a new world for me—a new sphere of learning and a new realm of thought.

Certainly I underwent an arduous process before I became aware of myself and of my womanhood. It is a common failing of the Chinese woman, and a remnant of history, to rely on her husband and child at home, or to depend excessively on the social environment for self-realization. In the practice of women's studies and education, I learned that women's emancipation is dependent upon women themselves. I did not dream or wait for a miracle any more, but sought a path forward. I would not change my faith, no matter what the political climate was, or how policies changed.

I give the impression of being a strong woman to those who meet me for the first time. In fact, I am quite traditional. I am turned off by the cold and negative portrayal of strong women in the newspapers. I am unwilling to sacrifice sweet domestic happiness for my cause. So I try to be a woman devoted to both work and family life. I believe active understanding is better than passive acceptance. The dual roles of women are essentially beneficial to the progress of women, given the social and material constraints of China. Further, the tension of the dual roles is an inevitable reality at this stage of history. Since we cannot get rid of the load, we may as well accept it of our own accord. Our generation of women has to pay the price for the emancipation of women in the future.

Soon I rearranged my household work on the principle that both my husband and I should bear the responsibilities of the family. Our children also did what they could for the family, which enabled me to increase their sense of responsibility and independence. I am grateful that my husband and sons are doing well. Now, in our family, when anyone has an urgent task, the others will do the housework voluntarily, without complaint.

One day both my husband and elder son were away from home. My younger son was with me. I was so busy writing the draft of a lecture for that night that I had no time to cook. Quietly, my younger son prepared rice and fried eggs. When I left, he saw me off at the door, waving his little hand, "Good luck, Mummy." As I heard those words, my eyes brimmed with tears. That night, my lecture went especially well.

In March 1990 a discussion on social participation and development of Chinese women, organized by Li Xiaojiang, was held in Zheng Zhou. As I was in charge of over 150 representatives, I was too busy to take care of the family. My husband was still preoccupied with his work. In his spare time, he came to help me, sometimes staying until midnight. At the meeting, my husband was much admired by the women from Taiwan and Hong Kong. I complain no more; men are not unchangeable. It is possible to change them just as we change ourselves from passivity to strength.

In recent years I have become more active and more work is given to me. But I do not feel overloaded. On the contrary, I am happier. Old friends who now meet me say they can hardly recognize me. Through the process of learning about feminism I have recreated myself. I counted my fortieth birthday as a new start to my life. That year, I devoted myself to the cause of women's education.

Awakening sisters

My awareness of feminism is accompanied by my growing understanding of women's issues in China. In 1985, when reform of the urban economic structure was launched in the country, various women's issues came to the surface and intensified with the developing reforms. Women, convinced that they would gradually achieve the same position as men in Chinese society, now heard worried reports from all sides. Eighty-four percent of women broke away from social production and returned home to be housewives in Da Qu Zhuang village of Jing Hai country in Tianjin; many women workers were retrenched from establishments and awaited relocation in various enterprises; several women cadres lost pitifully in elections at all levels of government organizations; women students who were once regarded as the lucky ones were rejected by employers; the numbers of women intellectuals promoted to higher ranks decreased in scientific research institutions and universities. Why did this happen? The state becomes more progressive while women appear to be under increasing pressure! Why?

Puzzled and worried, women turned for support to their own organization—the Women's Federation. But the Women's Federation too was puzzled by the new policies. For some time, Chinese women felt perplexed: they questioned what was happening and wanted reasonable answers to their questions.

Just then, Li Xiaojiang held up the banner of Chinese women's studies. She organized academic discussions and gathered a contingent of theoretical scholars. She was the chief editor of the *Women Studies Series,* which was the first publication of its kind in China. Her other publications were *Exploration of Eve, Women's Way,* and scores of essays, which evoked nationwide response, especially from women. Nevertheless, the oppressed status of Chinese women is such that her theories must be popularized before they can be absorbed by the mass of women. This was a task I felt confident to take on. I decided to give up my specialization in world history and devote myself to women's education—rousing educated women to realize themselves.

When I began my work, I found myself treading new ground. Chinese women enjoy the same rights to education as men, enter schools or universities at the same time, and receive the same education. Before the 1960s there were several girls and women's schools. During the Cultural Revolution women's schools were combined with schools for boys to ensure an equal social environment and equal educational opportunities for both sexes. But there were no special organizations for women's education, nor were there schools offering a course on women's education. After the Cultural Revolution, however, some women's schools were restored or rebuilt. In these schools, all the students come from the Women's Federation. The party's principal tasks and policies are taught there, but education for ordinary women is ignored. Under such circumstances I had to break the traditional patterns of education to directly contact millions of women from diverse backgrounds. As for women's education, it was extremely difficult for a few educationists to accomplish such a task because of the variations that existed in educational levels. Fortunately, various women's organizations helped me out.

The Women's Federation gave me much help. It is the only organization of women with establishments at all levels across the country. Before the reform, the Women's Federation worked mainly for rural women and the urban unemployed. Under the pressure of reform there was a growth in awareness. Breaking the structure of closed organizations, the Women's Federation strengthened ties with a range of women. When I became involved in women's education, the Women's Federation helped me to reach vast audiences. Women's sections of labor (present in most institutions and organizations) also helped me a great deal. In the past, women's sections only existed in the labor union of enterprises that employed mostly women workers. With an increase in the number of women's issues during the economic reform, it became routine to establish women's sections in all unions. Without the help of these sections, I could not have met a range of women to carry on the cause of women's education.

Student unions also played an important role. In China the students are basically separated from society as they form a community of their own. By and large, women students are indifferent to the mass of women. This psychological distance reduces their adaptability after graduation. Through the women's section of student unions I was able to give numerous lectures with good results. Besides, many working women's groups, such as the Women Technical Workers' Association, Women Cadres' Association, Women Teachers' Association, Women Medical Workers' Association, etc., sprung up during the reform. These associations provided me with a platform where I could address women from a variety of professions.

Since 1985, with the help of various bodies, I have gone to government organizations, hospitals, oil fields, railway departments, factories, and villages in the provinces of Henan, Jiang Xi, Guang Dong, Guang Xi, Tianjin, and Inner Mongolia, to report on different subjects that I have been researching. Some of these were issues such as women's self-realization, the dual roles of professional women, the consciousness of female students, and "When You Grow into a Young Girl." It is astonishing how unclear the notion of womanhood is for most women, worn out as they are by the pressures of their daily lives.

Sitting face to face with them, I had a strong sense of responsibility and mission. I knew that I wanted to help them resolve the complexities of their lives. One of the women cadres said, "Having listened to your lectures, we became conscious that we had not known ourselves as women, though we had done women's work for some decades!" Some others said, "We are accustomed to our present condition and do not make the effort to change anything anymore. What you said will inspire us to strive for a better life. We will have a foothold in society as women." Many rural women related: "We are thought to be light-hearted and happy so long as we are rich. That is not so. We hope more people like you will be concerned with our cultural and social existence." Women students said, "We are lucky to have listened to your lectures before graduation." An interpreter said: "Having listened to your lecture, I am proud to be a woman."

Each of my lectures received warm applause, which reflected the urgent demand of women for education and awareness raising. Once I visited the ethnic minority by way of He Chi City in the Guang Xi autonomous region. I was "kidnapped" by the cordial mayoress and made to lecture there for an entire day. Looking at the faces in the audience, I felt excited and stimulated. Now my mission in education over the past twenty years has extended into a new and vast field. How vast is our country! Travelling up and down this land day and night is an important part of my life. I have frequently lectured in one place and left for another at night for a lecture the next day. On the way to a meeting I was once held up on the Yellow River Bridge at night, shivering with cold; but it did not affect my enthusiasm for work. My strong adaptability resulted from frequent encounters with the unknown: I became used to any vehicles and to all kinds of hotels. No matter how tired I was, I would be full of life and enthusiasm whenever I walked onto the platform.

Of course it is impossible for a few educationists to achieve the expected results by only giving lectures. The mass media are ideal educational tools. Consequently, I offered on television and over the radio lecture courses entitled "The Road for Today's Women," "The New Woman of the 80s," and "Women, Goal and Family." This was well received. Many intellectual women wrote that they hoped to join the contingent and to make their contributions to enhancing the quality of life of Chinese women. Wang Haiyan, a college teacher, suffering from cancer, wrote to me: "So long as I live, I will try my best for women's education. As a woman, I am fortunate to be able to do something for women." How great is the awakening of Chinese women!

Looking back, we have made some spectacular progress in the pursuit of women's education; thinking ahead, we are beset with difficulties. Women's education has not really established itself to the extent desired. All levels of women's schools need to be strengthened and reformed. It seems that women's education has not been "aligned" with the national educational policy-making body. Without establishing a system with an ongoing policy, the pace of women's education might slow down soon after its initial momentum. It is necessary for women to work and strive for themselves. It is a great pity that, with intermittent political struggles, the development of women's education suffers a setback every now and again. I realize that I shoulder a heavy and serious mission and I shall face countless difficulties. In spite of this, I am willing to persevere in the hope that these small sparks will start a prairie fire one day.

Malavika Karlekar
India

MALAVIKA KARLEKAR (b. 1945) is a Senior Fellow at the Centre for Women's Development Studies, New Delhi. She is the author of *Poverty and Women's Work* (1982) and *Voices from Within: Early Personal Narratives of Bengali Women* (1992).

A Fieldworker in Women's Studies

A civil servant's daughter

When my children were born in the seventies, I was clear that I would send them to a coeducational school. My husband and I had been to single-sex missionary and convent schools and felt that it was much more "healthy" for boys and girls to mix freely together from an early age. We have never regretted the decision. Interestingly, though our son occasionally says that he wished he had spent a few years in that bastion of male privilege, an exclusive public school, I don't think he's terribly serious. Our daughter feels that she has gained much from being in a mixed school, and I think she's right.

As the daughter of a civil servant, I have lived most of my life in Delhi. When I was growing up, my parents felt that a girls' school, and later college, were *de riguer*. Strangely enough, my elder sister had been sent to a mixed school. I did not question parental judgment, though I had once or twice rather half-heartedly said that I would much rather have studied at an on-campus women's college. A coeducational institution was never mentioned. My wish was rejected out of hand; I was never given a reason, but I suspect in part it was the proximity to men's colleges which deterred my parents. The very same parents who, three years later, were delighted when I got admitted to the University of Oxford! Clearly the chance of an education in one of the best universities in the world took precedence over doubts regarding the safety of the environment; and, of course, one could not rule out the influence of the colonial legacy and parental pride that one's child had made it to where the best in the empire were educated.

I greatly enjoyed my two years at Oxford and the freedom

they brought. The freedom to make choices and to be responsible for one's decisions. It was an exciting time to be a student in England, as one's friends came from different backgrounds and many countries. The foundation of the Radical Student Alliance, activism over Vietnam and Rhodesia, did not really affect me; while the famous sit-in at the London School of Economics in February 1967 was soon a topic of heated conversation, it was too close to the Final Schools examination for us to do much else. Of course, Tariq Ali (a well-known leftist activist) was around off and on, delivering fiery speeches, and I used to attend debates at the Oxford Union fairly regularly. But I cannot say that I was "politically conscious" or terribly sensitive to the questions of inequality, poverty, and injustice. A twenty-one year old from a sheltered home well over two decades ago was indeed an innocent compared to her successors of today!

In those days, whether one should come home or not was not much of an issue, at least not for me. The euphoria of the Nehruvian era lingered on, and there was no reason to believe that India would not have a place for me, particularly with an Oxford degree safely in hand. By the end of the sixties, the "brain drain" was increasingly being talked about; it was a cause of growing concern in technical and medical institutions as the brightest started leaving for the West. But it did not concern me, nor ideas about my future. I got myself a job at a magazine where I wrote about the exodus as well as marvelled at the growing numbers of middle-class working women, the need for family planning, violence in West Bengal politics, and so on.

Soon I was tired with journalism as I found it too superficial. The choices in those days were not many, nor was risk taking looked upon too favorably. In 1968, then, I enrolled for an M.Litt. degree at the Department of Sociology, Delhi School of Economics. I spent considerable time training myself in research methods; my degree in philosophy, politics, and economics, with two special papers in sociology, did not have much on methodology and research techniques. My specialization in the sociology of education oriented me toward a research area that reflected my interest. In those days there was growing interest—and a substantial body of literature—on the sociology of professions, the school as an institution, socialization processes, education as an agent of mobility, and so on. I read Mydral and Klein[1] on working women and their dual roles and, in keeping with the current emphasis on role theory, decided to study women school teachers and their commitment to a profession and professionalism.[2] Based on a study of fifty-six teachers in both government and private schools in Delhi I concluded that "more than 30 percent of the sample had chosen teaching because they perceived it as a respectable occupation for educated women."[3] Thus, social respectability, which meant working in the safe environment of the school, mostly with women colleagues, going to work by school or chartered buses, and limited working hours, were important factors in determining choice of a profession.

I found that the economic motive was very important for over a third of the sample. While a quarter spent their entire income on household expenses, a majority of the rest said that the extra earnings helped improve the general standard of living of their families. As over 90 percent were first generation women earners, I analyzed, in some detail, the social change brought about by growing female employment. My thesis was an analysis of increasing paid work among middle-class women, contrasts between government and private employment, and motivations for working outside the home. The emphasis was primarily on *professionalism*, and then on *women*, as a category of analysis. Thus, I concluded, women in private schools who did not need to work for a wage were more professionally committed and involved with their students. Most of those in government schools, on the other hand, did not think that being a teacher meant a special responsibility; in fact, as students often came from underprivileged sections of society, middle-class school teachers were keen to keep a social distance from them. A few also articulated that a lower-caste background meant limited capacity to learn.

What I did not do was to question things too closely or enter into heated discussions on any issue, be it determinants of student capabilities, parental roles, or relations with the school administration. Nevertheless, I observed interaction with students, parents, and the administration and discussed these in the thesis. I did not question respondents on role sharing at home—what is now known as the sexual division of labor—or whether they found the dual, if not triple, burden situation onerous. I remember myself as an eager young woman, anxious to succeed and to please. But I also remember being aware of my privileged position: I had a good education, a secure and well-placed family background, and, above all, the freedom to make choices and ask questions of myself and of my family. I was acutely conscious of these factors, which I'm sure also held me back from questioning those with few choices too intensely. On the other hand, I listened carefully to the teachers' observations and value judgments and noted them down almost verbatim. These were then included as long quotations in the text. The women's voices came through clearly here and in the case studies of eight teachers.

The beginnings of fieldwork

In 1969 I was at the stage of writing my thesis when I got married and moved to Calcutta. I decided to marry a man from a well-known intellectual and cultured Bengali family, with a tradition of strong, highly educated women. Yet my in-laws were not Westernized, nor had they much experience of official Delhi where I had been born and brought up. Living in a nuclear unit helped us adjust to each other and me to come to terms with a new and, at times, intimidating environment. My ever-affectionate aunts and cousins were a welcome buffer; they showed me the ropes in housekeeping, managing domestic servants, and coping with that all-pervasive mass of humanity and contradictions that is Calcutta. My husband's parents, in particular my father-in-law, spoiled me and felt that I needed protecting.

This was not really true, though at times I did long for a familiar environment, my parents, and my friends. During my two years in Calcutta I was introduced to several different social milieus. While writing my dissertation, I briefly taught at a women's college. It was far too reminiscent of the convent school I had hated so much and I left in a couple of months. Another reason, of course, was that I wanted to prepare a synopsis for my Ph.D. One day in the teachers' common room, when I told my colleagues that I was to leave, one of them burst out, "Of course, you are lucky enough to have the option. Your salary is like a speck of dust on your palm—you can flick it off and more will come!" I remember not knowing how to react. I also remember thinking of some of my school teacher respondents: maybe this woman shared a similar background, a common grievance, I thought, with them. This was one of my early, first-hand encounters with inequalities among women and what they can do to human relationships.

When I enrolled for a Ph.D., I did not think of expanding

my M.Litt. dissertation, which was a common option for many doctoral theses. In part, my decision was governed by the fact that marriage had taken me to Calcutta and a different social and political world. Also, clearly, I was not sufficiently interested in women teachers or professionalism among women to pursue the theme in West Bengal. Work on my thesis took me into a completely different life situation, that of *realpolitik*, violence, and coping strategies, both fair and foul. I studied the Chhatra Parishad, a student association affiliated with the Congress party, and its role in the party's resuscitation between 1970 and 1972. At that time, my husband, a journalist who had been active in student politics, had excellent contacts with the congress. He introduced me to several congressmen and Chhatra Parishad leaders.

Fieldwork for my Ph.D. had taken me to secret hideouts stacked with arms caches, and rundown homes and offices. As I did the rounds of yet another small alleyway, I began thinking more and more about privilege and the lack of it, power, motivations for success, and the pain and sorrow at failure.... For many of my respondents, politics was an avenue for social, as well as political, mobility. They had little else to fall back upon. I empathized with them, but only up to a point. Again, as for my M.Litt., I included the respondents' voices in the text: I was acutely aware then, as also now, of the problems of representing the Other and felt that by using their words wherever possible I would, in part, take care of this problem. Of course this was years before postmodernism, deconstruction, and the decentred self.

I remember wondering why the Chhatra Parishad did not have more women cadre or leaders. In fact, of my eighty-one respondents, only two were women. While one of these women was included as a case study, and hence interviewed in detail, I was more concerned with her political socialization than with her role as a woman in a male-dominated movement. I did not ask her any questions on whether she felt discriminated against in the organization or if she was trying to get other women friends to join the Chhatra Parishad. In other words, as with my M.Litt. dissertation, my interest was with social change and mobility. While the M.Litt. concentrated on women, the emphasis was on the growth of a profession. For my Ph.D., I was fascinated by the evolution of a movement, the creation of first generation leaders and their socialization. Both theses then straddled contemporary interests in agents of mobility, change, and political development. The collective processes were of greater importance than individual dilemmas.

By the time I had finished with fieldwork and Calcutta, I was the mother of a son. I soon faced the perennial maternal dilemma of leaving a young child to go to work. In those days, however, domestic help was fairly easily available and little children had started going to nursery school by the time they were two and three. A fellowship enabled me to stay at home to write my thesis; I felt then that I could understand better the problems of my school teacher respondents.

In 1974, when I was nearing the end of my fellowship and my doctoral work, the *Report of the Committee on the Status of Women in India: Towards Equality,*[4] was published. Its many startling findings indicated the need for much greater investigation into the issues before women. Accordingly, the Indian Council of Social Science Research (ICSSR) funded several studies, many of which were available in mimeo form by the end of the decade. A few years earlier, after my Ph.D., I had worked briefly in a private research institute on the mobility patterns of successful members of the scheduled castes. I was deeply moved by many stories of oppression, the struggle against caste hierarchies, and the quest for education. Thus, when in 1975 Vina Mazumdar, who was in charge of the ICSSR Unit on Women's Studies, sugggested that I should combine my growing interest in caste and gender-based inequalities with my basic commitment to the sociology of education by studying a segment of urban scheduled caste women, I readily agreed. I applied for a fellowship to work on the socioeconomic status of Balmiki women, a subcaste of the North Indian caste of Bhangis, or sweepers and scavengers, in a West Delhi tenement colony.

I was by then gradually "getting into" women's studies: *Towards Equality* and Ester Boserup's *Woman's Role in Economic Development*[5] provided plenty of material for reflection and anxiety. And, of course, days in the field brought home dramatically the lived reality of the written word. I combined an open-ended interview schedule with in-depth interviews from a selected number of the total sample of eighty. Not unexpectedly, many theoretical premises were tested and discarded: in particular, I found that, in the field situation at least, it was a myth to assume that mechanization and development would deprive women of employment; at the subsistence level, women would work at anything.

At the end of my fieldwork, I felt that I had enough material for a study of a section of working-class women. My book, *Poverty and Women's Work—A Study of Sweeper Women in Delhi*,[6] based on an initial report, was published a few years later. What did not come through in my published work, however, was the dilemma I faced while in the field and the consequent mental and conceptual adjustments I had to hastily perform. Problems arose primarily because of my construction of a different reality on the basis of certain presuppositions; though I had pretested my interview schedule, obviously what I considered relevant and important were not always similarly viewed by my respondents.

I learned much from the women I interviewed. I knew soon that poverty led women to work for a wage anywhere and at any time. I also had to accept that town planners and well-intentioned researchers like myself knew little about urban congestion, or of how families are bound to shacks and huts in what the middle class considers to be abject squalor. The proximity of jobs, kin, and friendship networks become of vital importance, leading individuals and groups to resist relocation. I also did not know that women could not use public latrines after dark: it would never have crossed my mind that these are the chosen venues for rape and molestation. I did not ask questions on domestic violence, alcoholism, or family planning. In part, I was told not to ask about the recent, much-hated sterilization drive. But also, I did not know how to ask many questions. Above all, I did not know in 1975 that wife beating and abuse are part of daily family life in large segments of the population. I had to wait till 1990 to hear first hand about this horror of women's lives.

When, at the end of fieldwork, I told my respondents that they had been of considerable help to me, Shanta, who had become quite a friend, said, "*Bibiji, aap to apni kitab likhenge, pur hamara kya hoga?*" (Respected lady, you will write your book, but what will happen to us?) I had no honest answer to give her, just as I had not really been able to deal with the persistent question of many women, "*Bibiji, hamey issey kya milega?*" (Bibiji, what will we get out of this?) My dilemma is, of course, not something unique: many a fieldworker is faced with similar situations where questions of one's role keep cropping up. Such questions inevitably set up a chain of thought, a process of introspection: is one in fact exploiting one's respondents by taking up their time? Does not the process of questioning sooner or later sow the seeds of doubt in the minds of one's informants? For instance, how did my constant harping on the issue of how much work men actually did within the home affect women who had internalized exploitation as their fate? Or, for that matter, was I justified in asking probing questions on relationships with the natal home and how often women visited their families? Was I right in asking those at the subsistence level what consumer goods they owned?

When I sat down to write my report, many images continued to flit through my mind. I saw Bimla's anguish and Mayavati's cynicism, as well as little Sharada's excitement as she prepared for a longed-for day in school. I was not always sure of what I should write about the lives of the women I had spent days with: while I knew that any act of telling is interpretive in nature, I was nonetheless anxious to be as true to my respondents' reality as possible. Here again, I used the women's own words whenever possible. I also knew that when those one is studying are physically and mentally subjugated by society and by men, the moral overtones of a fieldworker's intervention and probing have implications of a different order. Inadvertently one may be initiating a process of self-analysis, of consciousness-raising, among a group who have little hope of escaping from the bondage of their lives. The resultant frustration and anger are, in this case, the direct responsibility of the fieldworker, who becomes an agent of exploitation. I don't think that I have ever been able to answer my own doubts on this sensitive issue of relationships across social classes. As already described, my intellectual apparatus, be it categories of analysis, vocabulary, or questions I regarded as important, was, in many cases, not relevant. Consequently, my pre-fieldwork construction of what a typical oppressed Balmiki woman was like had to be constantly amended: I realized soon that a conversion of experience into expression is never easy.

Teaching and research: 1977-1986

Shortly after the completion of fieldwork, I became a research associate at the Delhi School of Economics: this was a time when there was an incipient—though growing—awareness of differences in social attitudes toward men and women. I can now look back quite dispassionately on the ten years between 1977 and 1986 when I taught master's, as well as research, students courses in the sociology of education and supervised their term papers and dissertations; I have mixed feelings on how I negotiated my way as a relatively young woman teacher in the Delhi School of Economics, where I had been a student. It was not always easy to accept the views of one's former teachers; at the same time, no clear alternatives had crystallized. While the course I taught had been developed by my M.Litt. thesis supervisor, I was free to innovate a little. Nonetheless, my attempts at convincing students (both boys and girls) that they could work meaningfully in women's studies were more covert, subterranean. By the end of the seventies I was talking about the problems faced by certain categories of students, in particular girls. A few students were disaggregating educational data by sex while looking at enrollment and retention rates. Together with a colleague from the Department of History, I had introduced a course at the M.Phil. level on women and society in India. This was in 1979, and it is perhaps as much a reflection of the times as of the content of the paper that we had only two students, both of whom were men!

When, in 1984, I moved on to Jamia Millia Islamia's Faculty of Education as a reader (associate professor), I introduced a topic in an optional course on the equality of educational opportunity debate with special reference to women, Muslims, the scheduled castes, and tribes. Muslim students were interested in finding out why their community remained educationally deprived, and this included girls as well. At Jamia there was practically no scope for the introduction of a separate course in women's studies. Today the situation is very different, and all three universities in the capital—Delhi, Jamia Millia Islamia, and Jawaharlal Nehru University—have papers in women's studies in various departments.

A couple of years later, I took a leave of absence and joined the Center for Women's Development Studies. I have not gone back to teaching again, a matter of occasional regret. At the same time, while I had enjoyed my ten years as a university teacher, I never really got involved with introducing gender as an issue at the departmental policy level. Nor is this as yet an easy task. Conversations with former colleagues indicate that they, too, have had to struggle to get their courses accepted by academic and departmental councils; nonetheless, it is interesting that whereas in the past courses on women, and later gender, would have been rejected out of hand, senior academics are prepared to listen to suggestions for change. I remember a time in 1981 when, during syllabus revision meetings at the

Delhi School of Economics, the view that women in the family, or differential socialization patterns, should be considered separately was dismissed peremptorily. On the other hand, at the postgraduate and independent research levels, there was, and continues to be, a far greater flexibility; supervisors are prepared to give their students a fairly long rope in choice of dissertation topics, approaches, and methodologies.

During my later years of teaching I often thought about new research areas. It became increasingly clear to me that contemporary studies of inequality and poverty were not enough to explain the deeper roots of gender divisions. My readings in the sociology of education—a paper I taught for several years—made me feel that delving into history may be useful. Among other things, it would help me overcome my own personal sense of inadequacy that had followed the study of sweeper women. There was something reassuring about looking at data where respondents were not going to be around to ask uncomfortable questions. A number of reasons, one of which was a distinct nagging feeling that I could not enter into another exploitative relationship, took me to a completely different area of study; as a middle-class woman with an interest in her roots, I was curious to find out what role education had played in the lives of early pioneers, that is, of nineteenth century women. I felt that archival research in this area would help me to understand better the sociohistorical genesis of unequal gender relations.

1986 onward

As I was turning these ideas over in my mind, I was encouraged by Vina Mazumdar, by then director of the Center for Women's Development Studies (CWDS), to think of a study that would look at women's self-perceptions as expressed in writing. Accordingly, I wrote up a proposal to work on nineteenth century Bengali women's narratives. When I joined the center in 1986, it was to work on my study as well as to help Vina Mazumdar coordinate the cross-national project, Women's Work and Family Strategies in South and South East Asia. My individual study was one of twenty-two to be undertaken by scholars in different parts of the region. I remember looking forward to my new area of research—at least I would not have to face uncomfortable questions that threatened my confidence as a social scientist and as a human being! At the same time, I was aware that I was now stepping into a new intellectual field: that of interpretation of texts, theories of discourse, and reading. In order to cope better with my material, I also started reading in and around postmodern theory. My area of study clearly lent itself to something more than just straightforward descriptive analysis. I was not looking at the texts in isolation but, rather, as part of—if not symbolic of—a period of change when identities were being re-thought. Clearly, then, an analysis of this kind required a sociohistorical contextualization as well as attempts at understanding why women wrote and why they wrote what they did.

By the middle of the last century, Bengali upper-caste, upper-class women had begun writing essays, poetry, fiction, and about their own lives in a growing number of journals and magazines. All except a handful wrote in Bengali. A few of these were published as independent books. While women were familiar with a number of literary genres, for my study I mainly concentrated on autobiographical writings, which I call personal narratives, and an important body of work that can only be classified as exhortatory literature. Written as poems, stories, and essays, these compositions had the express purpose of reminding the readers of their basic responsibilities in a changing environment. Many also emphasized the role of education in promoting new ways of viewing the world. On the whole, by the later decades of the nineteenth century, morality as a value in public and private life acquired an exaggerated importance. Several views on the matter were increasingly voiced by the Bengali middle class. In part this can be explained by the social reform movement, which drew its strength from a belief in some fundamental moral and religious values.

Almost four hundred works by Bengali women were estimated to have been written between 1856 and 1910. These ranged from short poems to full-length novels and autobiographies. During the same period, to cater to a growing readership, twenty-one periodicals, which dealt primarily with women's issues, were being published. Interestingly, women were associated with these publications in various editorial capacities. More specifically, over the last century, there is a record of at least fifty autobiographies and autobiographical sketches written by Bengali women. These personal narratives, a term which encompasses the more formal, full-length, structured autobiography, personal letters, newspaper and journal articles on one's life, as well as the musings of a daughter at the death of her father, made fascinating reading. As my aim was the re-creating of women's lives and not literary analysis, I used a somewhat nonpurist definition of personal narratives. Accordingly, readings of the texts are essentially a reflection of a personal point of view. This, in turn, influenced my choice of texts and my methodology. An acquaintance with the recorded history of the period, a reading of women's writing in Bengali, as well as the relevant work of social anthropologists, historians, psychologists, and other scholars working in the growing field of women's studies provided an overall context of changing colonial relations.

While writing my first draft, I was acutely aware of the fact that I was treading on difficult terrain; nonetheless, I persisted in a manner which I felt would best represent my understanding of the texts. My work with the Balmiki women had left me feeling that the acts of interpretation, analysis, and writing are basically exploitative in nature. Though I did not go through the same degree of guilt while reading and analyzing the writings of nineteenth century women, I certainly experienced moments when I wondered whether I was not imposing my late-twentieth-century views on a group of women who could no longer defend themselves. While contemporary trends, which state that a work lives through its reader, are attractive, they are also enchaining: they put the onus of representation in writing or reading on the individual. Are we then heading towards multiple readings, understandings? If we are, how do we tackle an apprehensive and powerful awareness of oneself as being center stage? At some point, I came to terms with this dilemma and decided to go ahead and write. That *Voices from Within*[7] emerged at the end of two very different drafts is proof enough of the fact that it has not been easy.

Like many other fieldworkers, I am still bewildered by the entire process of attempting to understand and give expression to other realities. In the process of looking for a context where I feel more comfortable with myself and the subject of my research, I have also moved from active engagement with respondents to a cocooned existence amidst moth-eaten texts, re-creating the lives of individuals long dead. I have moved from interviews and participant observation to the less emotionally wearying analysis of texts and policy documents.

If this essay has read more as an exegesis on fieldwork methods, it is because this very process has been essential for my search for space. I knew many years ago that I enjoyed fieldwork; what I did not know—or did not know well enough—was that being in the field involves a dialogical process, a renegotiation of categories. As I found, it was not easy to adjust to different and, at times, conflicting realities. But it would be less than honest if I did not add that the creation of this space has had implications for my personal life as well: increasingly, commitment to a more equitable society, based on questioning rather than merely accepting existing assumptions, has led me to re-think my role as wife, mother, daughter, and friend. It has given me the self-assurance to reach out to a range of individuals and to cope with complex situations. A decade ago I would have shied away from these, afraid of my vulnerability. I am still vulnerable—after all, who isn't?—yet, I feel stronger within myself to face what I would earlier have shunned, if not looked away from defensively. I feel that much of this feeling is an outcome of intellectual conviction in a particular ideological position: for me, personal beliefs have much to do with a process of reasoning, of attempting to work things out in logical, systematic steps. Since 1975, the Indian women's movement has gone a long way in identifying problems, campaigning for solutions, and getting them implemented.[8] Coincidentally, these were also the years when I withdrew from fieldwork into the reassuring portals of libraries and the homes of the nineteenth-century elite. Yet, by 1990, I felt a restlessness to go back to the field once more. In part, this restlessness was an anthropologist's craving to be with "real" people. But only in part.

If the last fifteen years had not been so rich in methodological and conceptual debates, I'm not sure that I would have felt confident to get back to the field. My choice of research methods had, over all these twenty-five years, been pointing me in a definite, unbroken direction. While the naivete of a twenty-three year old later gave way to a more systematic mode of enquiry, my emphasis has consistently remained on hearing many voices. I have not been alone in my dilemma, nor in my search for an appropriate methodology. When one's private anxieties find a reflection in public discourse, clearly there is scope for articulating and moving back to the field again. A novice's apprehensions at encountering an uncharted terrain are today viewed as vital in the construction of new realities. No matter what adjective one may use, thinking, interpreting, representing, or writing about another's life is a tricky business. It is useful and reassuring then to share with others that "the actual expertise and language of women is the central agenda for feminist social science and scholarship."[9] Feminist researchers have, over the last decade, been increasingly emphasizing the need to hear the voices of women.[10]

By the end of 1989, I was ready to go back to "real" people. My present project on violence against women has so far looked at how the police and counseling centers deal with the voices of women asking for justice. In so doing, they are defining and redefining themselves and their psycho-physical boundaries. For it is clear that aggression and violence, physical, emotional, or otherwise, are all-pervasive phenomena in most heterosexual relationships. It is there in the process that persuades a young woman to be a respectable school teacher rather than a surgeon, as well as in the tension-ridden, inter-caste relationships in villages and slums. Its ubiquity makes it an important area for research and debate as it underpins social and personal constructions of femininity and masculinity. Thus, as I proceed with my present project, I see a continuity with my earlier work.

My confidence also grew in large part because of the knowledge of the ease with which women are willing to share, to speak, and to create their lives again. Before I ventured back to the field, I had many encounters of mutual sharing and trust that assured me that a context is not impossible to create and even re-create anew. For the fieldworker has to tell the story of many lives, one of which is surely her own. And when those voices she wishes to hear speak to her with a poignancy and an almost crystal-clear honesty, she works hard to suppress too many questions on her role and the problems of interpretation, understanding, and so on. Fifteen years ago I felt threatened, pained, inadequate, by that honesty and the reaching out for answers. Today I find it easier to cope with, not only within myself but also because the scope of child care, employment, domestic conflict resolution mechanisms, and so on has increased and been legitimized. I can at least try and work toward some solutions to the age-old problem of wife abuse with battered women: with the Balmikis I did not even have the courage to ask the question, not only because I felt that it would be an invasion of privacy, but also because I did not know how to deal with it.

It is an exciting time to be a social anthropologist with a commitment to women's studies. I have found it particularly challenging to map the trajectories of feminist theory and anthropology with that of postmodernism. Feminists claim the right to contribute to knowledge creation, often by "deposing" reigning canons. So do postmodernists. But for the former—as for anthropologists—the context is of vital importance. Anthropologists in the field are talking to and writing about human beings in a variety of situations. Feminist theorists base many of their sensibilities and observations on the lives of other women: women in poverty, in struggle, in situations of oppression and exploitation, and in joy and victory. It is in these contexts where the stories lie and give strength to those who reach out. The quest for new realities is firmly rooted in women's experiences and their expressions of these experiences.

It is also a challenging time to be a mother of a twenty-one-year-old son searching for himself and a daughter of seventeen who is caught in several dilemmas. Whether one likes it or not, compromises with one's commitments are battered down with the relentless "Why can't I?" or "How shall I?" And yet, as one enters into another endless round of arguments, one still feels that it's worth it. I think back to a youth where one listened and reflected within oneself but did not question too much.

I grew—as we all do—at varying paces and due to different influences. I was a Beauvorian dutiful daughter, but I don't think that either my sister or I had the same kind of symbiotic relationship with my parents as I have with my children. It is a relationship which asks for much, as well as nurtures. And I feel sure that my responses have much to do with an involvement with the women's movement and women's studies. They have taught me to accept individual differences, as well as hold out for ultimate benefits for the collectivity. My children may balk at my occasional flights of rhetoric; but ultimately they know that there is space for other ways of looking at the world. Early exposure to a range of our friends—professional colleagues, Rassundari Debi, Jane Austen, and Ismat Chughtai—has taught them that learning is not only what the texts teach them, it is also the capacity to look for what lies beyond.

Today women's studies is on the threshold of new directions, exciting challenges, and a few long battles. Debates on validity, legitimacy, and differing voices are increasingly commonplace. There is no one women's movement, but several intermeshing issues, aspirations, and demands that spread across geographic boundaries. The points of similarity are many, but so are the differences. This is true within a country as well as cross-nationally. The notion of sisterhood is often enough a symbolic bonding, melding together a range of women from disparate life situations at the level of consciousness, if not reality. For material, social, and ethnic differences cannot be wished away, nor can gender be the great equalizer. And yet, with each passing day, there seems more and more to share.

As I journey along, I am aware of the information and vocabulary revolutions which are a growing part of the women's movement. Violence, new reproductive technologies, environmental protection, wasteland development, grassroots empowerment, and networking increasingly compete for space with the concepts I learned when I was initiated into women's studies. The excavatory phase of looking for hidden voices and invisible faces is now being overtaken by the quest for a sharing of power and authority with the hitherto powerless and unknown. Academia and activism join hands, albeit cautiously, at symposia and conferences. And protagonists argue their positions doggedly. The search for voices continues as does the clamor around me. The women's movement has given an authority to those who had earlier only been expected to listen and obey. The self-confident new generation has inherited a rich legacy of political, legal, and social reform. And as more voices join in, and more demands are articulated, I feel the need to stand back and take stock. The social anthropologist in me remembers the need for self-analysis and introspection even as new issues and agendas tempt, as well as overwhelm.

Notes
1. A. Myrdal and V. Klein, *Women's Two Roles: Home and Work,* London: Routledge and Kegan Paul, 1956; and V. Klein, *Britain's Married Women Workers,* London: Routledge and Kegan Paul, 1965.
2. The title of my M.Litt. dissertation (1970) was *Career Orientation and Commitment of School Teachers: A Study in the Sociology of Professions Amongst Women Teachers in Six Delhi Schools.*
3. Based on the findings of my thesis, I published a paper entitled "Professionalization of Women School Teachers," *Indian Journal of Industrial Relations,* (July 1975), p. 55.
4. *Towards Equality, Report of the Committee on the Status of Women in India,* New Delhi: Ministry of Education and Social Welfare, 1974.

5. E. Boserup, *Woman's Role in Economic Development,* London: George Allen and Unwin, 1970.
6. *Poverty and Women's Work—A Study of Sweeper Women in Delhi,* New Delhi: Vikas Publishing House, 1982.
7. *Voices from Within—Early Personal Narratives of Bengali Women,* New Delhi: Oxford University Press, 1991 (Pb, 1993).
8. See for instance, K. Sharma, "Shared Aspirations, Fragmented Realities—Contemporary Women's Movement in India, Dialectics and Dilemma," New Delhi: CWDS Occasional Paper No. 15, 1989; and Nandita Gandhi and Nandita Shah, *The Issues at Stake—Theory and Practice in the Contemporary Women's Movement in India,* New Delhi: Kali for Women, 1992.
9. B. Du Bois, "Passionate Scholarship: Notes on Values, Knowing and Method in Feminist Social Science," in G. Bowles and R. Duelli-Klein, *Theory of Women's Studies,* London: Routledge and Kegan Paul, 1983, p. 108.
10. Some of these authors and books are: R. Duelli-Klein, "How To Do What We Want to Do: Thoughts about Feminist Methodology," in G. Bowles and R. Duelli-Klein (eds.), op. cit.; M. Karlekar, *Voices from Within—Early Personal Narratives of Bengali Women,* New Delhi: Oxford University Press, 1992; A. Oakley, "Interviewing Women: A Contradiction in Terms," in H. Roberts (ed), *Doing Feminist Research,* London: Routledge and Kegan Paul, 1981; J. Stacey, "Can There Be a Feminist Ethnography?" *Women's Studies International Forum,* 2, no. 1 (1988); and L. Stanley and S. Wise, "Back into the Personal or Our Attempts to Construct 'Feminist Research'," in Bowles and Duelli-Klein (eds.), as well as B*reaking Out: Feminist Consciousness and Feminist Research,* London: Routledge and Kegan Paul, 1983.

Noemi Alindogan-Medina
Philippines

NOEMI ALINDOGAN-MEDINA is Professor of History at the Philippine Normal University. She has been associated with a number of women's groups and is Secretary of the Women's Studies Association of the Philippines as well as co-founder and overall coordinator of URDUJA. She has also published a number of articles and poems on women.

Women's Studies:
A Struggle for a Better Life

The awakening

How did I ever get into women's studies? What was it that hit me so hard, so deep in my heart, roused my consciousness, and made me see things beyond pleasant domesticities? What motivated me to join the women's movement in the Philippines? These questions come to mind when I seek to recall how I became a feminist.

Women's studies and feminism—I was a stranger to both until 1987, when I was sent as a representative of the Philippine Normal College to attend a national consultation on women and education sponsored by the National Commission on Women in Quezon City. I went with great reluctance because its first day happened to be the day of our college commencement exercises, at which President Corazon Aquino was the guest of honor, and I did not want to miss the chance of seeing her in person. Not surprisingly, I reported at the venue of the seminar with little enthusiasm and no curiosity.

The seminar was attended by more than a hundred women teachers and administrators from all over the country. After the introduction and the keynote speech, the participants were divided into small groups, and each participant was asked to reflect upon and share with others a situation in her life that had placed her in a disadvantageous position as a female teacher. I wondered what the facilitators were up to, involving us in such a futile exercise. As far as I knew, women, especially those in education, were neither disadvantaged nor oppressed. I knew Filipinas were considered the most liberated among Asian women and that there were no visible signs of oppression among us. The small-group discussion ended without any contribution from me. For one thing, I was by nature too reserved to discuss personal matters, especially with people I had just met. Also, I preferred to keep things to myself, rather than talk about people who had oppressed me in any way.

Things turned out unexpectedly, however, during the plenary session that afternoon. It was like seeing for myself how much the house needed cleaning, and I couldn't deny the glaring reality that indeed things were not in their proper place. Much dirt had been swept under that beautifully designed carpet for too long a time, and I needed to do something about it at once. In other words, I fully agreed with the presentation made to show how education and media reinforce one another to bring about oppression in different forms among Filipino women. I began to see how we were being projected in films and television as well as in the educational system—in its curriculum, textbooks, and audio-visual materials and in our teaching processes, policies, and administrative practices, which collectively influenced the thought and behavior of students, teachers in particular, and the family and society in general. The nature and extent of the gender issue in education and its relation to the larger society were made clear to us. It was only after more than twenty years in the teaching profession that I became aware of the hidden implications that teachers have unconsciously enforced and perpetuated through generations. This had indeed caused enough damage and I felt that we had to do something to rectify the errors of the past. Now we have to make students aware of how certain laws, some aspects of our history and culture, as well as our educational system have stunted the growth and progress of women and curtailed the full development of our talents, potentialities, and capabilities. With this realization, I committed myself to integrating feminist concepts in my social science courses and to gradually introducing women's issues in the curriculum. I felt that my efforts could have a multiplier effect as some of our college students would become teachers who could also introduce such concepts to their pupils.

Before the break on the last day of the seminar, we were given pieces of paper on which we had to write down the insights we had gained from the activities and our evaluation of the seminar. When I wrote down my thoughts, what came out were statements in poetic form which were well received when I read them before the assembly. The chair of the convenor's group of that seminar reacted by quoting again what feminism aspires to: "a more caring society that gives not only to men but also to women, both bread and roses, poetry and power." Some participants called me a poet and one of them asked for a copy and my permission to have the poem published in their magazine. I was overwhelmed not only by the recognition given me but by my own discovery of a talent of which I was not fully aware. Still unbelieving that I could really write poetry, I tried writing again when I got home. Two poems emerged during the night, which I immediately delivered to the office of the National Commission on Women. Six months later, one of the poems came out in *Ani,* the literary journal of the Cultural Center of the Philippines; the other was published in the *Philippine Journal of Education.* This gave me more self-confidence and encouraged me to write more poems on women.

Growing up

It is said that someone has to plant the seed; that if the seed is buried in fertile and moist soil it will grow into a plant. Others will come and help take care of that plant so that it will grow fast and bear flowers and fruit, from which new seeds can be taken for others to plant again. This, in a way, is how I see myself in my growth and development as a feminist. That first seminar on women was followed by similar seminars sponsored by women's groups. Invitations came and, every time, I would beg our dean of instruction to designate me to attend the seminar. Considering my previous lack of interest, my present eagerness must have surprised her.

The second seminar that I attended was on women and development in the teaching of the social sciences and the humanities, sponsored by the Women's Working Group, held at the Maryknoll College Foundation from 20–22 August 1987, almost five months after that first seminar. It was there that I learned more about women's studies and how women's issues and concerns can be integrated in teaching certain courses in the social sciences.

The third seminar was held in the summer of the following year. It was a national teacher-training workshop sponsored by the Women's Resource and Research Center, St. Scholastica's College, Philippine Women's University, the University of the Philippines, and the De La Salle University, held in Los Banos, Laguna, in May 1988.

On the first day we talked about the definition of women's studies, which places women's own experiences at the center of the process that establishes women's reality. This was followed by the sharing of personal experiences in small groups, in which we discovered how disadvantaged we were as women. Now that I fully understood that experiences shared by group members form the basis of analyzing women's oppression, I was no longer hesitant to open up and share even those thoughts that I had kept to myself for a long, long time. It was still a difficult thing to do, to dig into my innermost thoughts and deepest feelings about people whom I have loved but whom I now saw as the cause of my oppression. It was doubly difficult to break away from the deeply embedded belief which said we should love and respect our parents as we owe our life and whatever we have now to them, and this love and respect can best be manifested by keeping to ourselves our bitter memories of them.

My oppressive past

I grew up in Resurreccion, a small barrio along the sea, under the municipality of San Fernando, a town on Ticao Island, roughly 128.9 square miles in area, in the province of Masbate, Philippines. I was the third child, but the second daughter, in the family. Our eldest sister was taken by our grandmother to live with her in another town, so I became my mother's helping hand, so to speak, as two brothers immediately followed after me and four other children came thereafter.

I was in fourth grade in elementary school when my mother gave birth to another baby girl. I can still remember how I used to wash the diapers and baby dresses at lunch break before going to school, while my brothers just played around. I was the one who cooked our food for breakfast and for supper. Often I would fetch water from an open well about a hundred yards away and gather firewood under the coconut trees before I could start cooking. The boys were nowhere to be found.

After a year, my father went into the fishing business while my mother opened a small grocery store. Early in the morning, when my father's fishermen returned from overnight fishing, my mother would assist him in gathering the catch from every boat that came ashore. At such times my mother would ask me to look after the store as well as my baby sister. She preferred that I should tend the store in her absence rather than my playful brothers. There were times when the catch was plentiful and I would help sell the fish in the village. All this was routine work for me during out-of-school hours. Weekends were scheduled for washing and ironing the week's clothes. As it was more difficult to wash by the deep well, the women in the village preferred to walk a kilometer along a dirt road to the knee-deep stream. With some women neighbors, my mother and I would start very early in the morning on foot, the big bundles of dirty clothes on our heads. We would wash them the whole morning, then spread them out on the grass to dry. We ate our packed lunch at noon and, if we finished early enough, I also had fun swimming with friends in the cool, fresh water of the stream. After gathering the dried clothes we would walk homeward with the big bundles on our heads.

On Sundays, while the women were again busy ironing clothes, the men would usually have some relaxation. Some of them would preen their gamecocks or play cards. Others would drink *tuba* or cheap bottled liquor while exchanging stories of adventures during their youth. Most often the drinking session would end only when they felt groggy; their legs wobbly as they went home. No wife would dare remind her husband to stop drinking and go home, as that would be a sign of being controlled by a mere woman and would start a quarrel in public. Once the husband reached home, it would be the duty of the wife to attend to his needs and make him feel better and superior.

Among his pastimes, my father preferred drinking *tuba*, although he would do it only occasionally. Whenever he joined such a group, my mother and all of us children would be very nervous at home, as if we were waiting for the arrival of a strong typhoon. We knew what would happen, as it had happened often in the past. Usually, the moment he got home, my father would start talking in a loud voice. My mother would be very careful in her responses. Sometimes she preferred to keep quiet while giving him a warm sponge bath. Even then, Father would shout and bang things about with his fists, something which made us tremble under our blankets. We would come out of hiding only when he finally started snoring. Next morning, everybody, including the neighbors, would pretend that nothing out of the ordinary had taken place. But they talked about it in whispers, for if the subject of their conversation found out, he would remember it the next time he got drunk. Almost the same things were going on in other homes as well. Women and children could do nothing but suffer in silence, even when they were physically hurt. In some cases where a wife was battered, the old folks openly talked about it, but usually placed the blame on the wife for not knowing her husband's true nature and for not giving in to someone who was "not in his proper senses." It is from the old folks that I learned what is expected of a "good wife": that it is the duty of a wife to serve her husband, to give in to his wishes, even his whims, and to attend to his needs; to preserve his name and dignity, and therefore to be loyal to him in thought, word, and deed; to sacrifice everything for the family and accept thankfully whatever kind of husband God has given her. To rebel against these strictures was to question God's will.

As a mother, the woman should therefore train her daughters to do household chores so as to prepare them to be good wives. The daughters should also be reared in docility and passivity, reared to sacrifice so as to carry the whole burden that God had placed on them. Such "words of wisdom" strongly influenced the thoughts and behavior of the girls and women in the community and were transmitted from generation to generation. These old folks had been influenced by their Spanish parents or grandparents and by the teachings of the Spanish priests who had stayed on the island for many years. In fact, my parents have traces of Spanish-Mexican blood in their veins.

These norms, however, did not find acceptance in my young mind, and I swore to myself that I would rather not get married to a man from our locality, as every man there seemed to be doing the same dreadful things. I did not want to relive the experiences that my mother and other women in our village were going through. I also promised myself that never would I allow my future children to live in such a place or to go through the same experiences that had been so traumatic for me.

And so I went on with my studies until I graduated with the highest honors from grade six in 1957. In high school, however, I did not make it to the top, although I remained a good student. I knew I would not be able to keep it up as I did not have much time to compete with those students who lived closer to the school, which was four kilometers away from our home. Most often I walked to school and back, as there was only one minibus in the entire island. My older brother was allowed to study in another high school in Masbate Island, where there were board and lodging facilities. That was not possible for me as my parents would not want me to stay elsewhere.

After graduation, I was eagerly waiting to be sent to Manila for my college education when my father decided that I should stay at home as it would be useless for me to study further. He believed, as other fathers did, that women do not need a college education as they only get married and have children. My brother was allowed to leave for Manila because he was a man and, when he married, he would be the breadwinner of the family. I begged my mother to intercede on my behalf but her ominous silence meant that we could not do anything but follow my father's decision. We did not even have the nerve to question the wisdom of his decisions or to prove him wrong as he had the final say in everything. For a whole year I led a virtually useless life at home, doing the usual household chores.

Luckily, a visiting aunt from Manila convinced my father to let me go with her so that I could take a college degree. My father was apprehensive of what city life might do to a young woman, but my aunt promised to take charge of me. Taking his silence as a sign of assent, my aunt began asking me what course I wished to take. I answered "journalism." Suddenly, my father told my aunt to forget about it, as he would rather see me without a college education than working with men late at night as a journalist. He believed that journalism was a man's profession. When I settled for an education course and promised to study hard, to disregard any distractions, and to come back to our barrio to teach, my father finally agreed to let me go. Indeed, I took up elementary education even though I did not like it then. True to my promise, I went back to teach in our barrio school. Every paycheck that I received was immediately turned over to my parents. Then, after two years, I married and left our island for good.

It can be said that, for a husband, I intentionally chose a man from a far-off place. Marriage for me was, in a certain sense, an escape from the autocratic ways of my father and from the stifling lifestyle in our community. Looking back on my married life today, I can say that it was not really a complete escape from the claws of oppression. In the first place, my husband is also a product of a community which has its own idiosyncrasies evident in the values and beliefs of its people. At the same time, he is an army officer who faithfully follows the saying that a soldier is married to the service 99 percent, and to his wife only 1 percent, even if he loves her very much.

No, I had not planned to marry a man in the military. I was in my last year in college and he was then a law school graduate when I accepted his love. I was already teaching on our island when he wrote to say that he had entered military service and was assigned to Mindanao. After two years he came to our island to propose marriage. Learning that he was an army lieutenant, my parents and friends warned me that I may not be able to cope with the demands and pressures of army life. They also thought I was a worrier and that I might not last long with a man whose life could be in constant danger. As I had already made a commitment, my father gave his consent on the condition that I take along my younger sister and see her through high school.

After our military wedding in Manila and honeymoon in Baguio City, my husband took me to Taal, Batangas, to meet his family and relatives. Although he had warned me about his sister, it still hurt when I heard her say to a friend: "My brother should have married Nancy, who is much fairer. Besides, how much is a teacher's salary? I can earn that amount in one day with my business." I was thankful to get away to Davao City in Mindanao where my husband was posted.

In Davao, we lived in a rented cottage in a thinly populated town about two kilometers away from the army camp and fourteen kilometers away from the heart of the city. As there was much work to be done, my husband told me that the wife of one of his soldiers would help me with the laundry. She came with two others, but once the introductions were over, they talked among themselves in Cebuano, which I happened to understand. Just like my sister-in-law, they too noticed my complexion and were greatly disappointed. As if, to be an officer's wife, it is essential to have fair skin. After that first visit not one of them came back. I learned that they worked for an officer's wife whose skin was "like an American's." We stayed in Davao City for three years, after which we transferred to Camp Aguinaldo, Quezon City. With two small children to take care of, I still managed to get a teaching job in an elementary school in Manila. I also enrolled for a master's degree at the Philippine Normal College, where I was taken in as a faculty member after graduation.

Assessment

My experiences and my exposure to feminism raise many questions in my mind. Looking back, I cannot help wondering what my life would have been like had I not gone to college. In a wider sense, what happens to daughters who are not sent to college? If they look for jobs, where do they work? Do they become domestic labor, victims of discrimination? Do they get less pay for doing the same job as a man? The last to be hired and the first to be fired, do they suffer sexual abuse and harassment on the job? If they ever get married, what are their chances of having an understanding husband, a man who would be responsible and worthy of raising children who can be useful citizens of the country?

If we dig deeper into my case—and it could well be the case of many other young women from a similar background—there are still a number of questions that need to be answered. For instance, why are daughters not given preference for a college education? Even if daughters are allowed to go to college, where are they sent? Do they have the freedom to make their own choice of a career or vocation, to make their own decision as to what they want to do with their lives? How many opportunities are denied to daughters whose lives are controlled by their fathers and whose mothers cannot do anything to defend their daughters' aspirations? How does culture typecast women? The same culture that makes fathers the sole decision makers of the family? How does a highly patriarchal setup affect the daughter's performance when she has to face the world by herself?

In my case, as I have realized only recently, I cannot overcome my fear and inhibitions in expressing my thoughts and feelings, ideas and opinions in the presence of someone who is an authority on the subject. Why can I not be assertive enough in pursuing a certain goal? Why do I always think that I cannot make it because I am weak, because I am only a woman? How many chances of early success did I let go of because of my cowardice, my inability to speak out? What held me back? Why am I like this?

Why do some women think that the wife of a military officer should be fair complexioned and look like a half-breed to be considered beautiful? What kind of orientation and education did these women get out of the system?

Growing strong

The next live-in seminar workshop that I attended was quite different in the sense that the participants came mostly from the grassroots level. There were only two of us who were teachers; the rest were health workers, church workers, women from poor urban communities, farmers, peasants, fisherfolk, and factory workers. This was my first exposure to women from such a wide variety of backgrounds. It turned out to be one of my most rewarding experiences. It was here that I realized that these women—all without college degrees and only elementary or high school graduates—could speak authoritatively on the realities of life, the hardships and difficulties that life offers to us women, who give and nurture life. They called for change not for our own sake anymore but for the generations to come, perhaps because as women and as mothers we have more concern for the future.

Before the three-day workshop was over, I came to know more about women from the grassroots, their thoughts and aspirations, their dreams and wishes, which they were actively striving to fulfill. And I could not help but compare them with the women of the same level in our island. The island women seem to entrust their lives and futures to the men of the family for whatever it brings them and their children. They are inexorably tied down by old customs and traditions to the roles they must perform. They might constitute a vital force in shaping the future of an ideal barrio or town on our island or elsewhere but, without empowerment, are unable to do so. Having grown up on that island and having retained my roots there, it bothers me to no end that the island women should suffer in this way. I keep thinking about what I can do to empower the women in our town so that they, too, can determine the direction their lives should take.

My new experiences reinforced my conviction that there is indeed a great need for change in the role and status of women in the country, and this can be systematically introduced through education. It may be a long and arduous process, and the results may not be readily manifest, but I feel something must be done right away. I have to do my share in this collective endeavor.

Another seminar I attended was the 1990 National Conference and Festival on Women, spearheaded by the Women's Resource and Research Center (WRRC) and supported by the Institute of Women's Studies, the Women's Desk of the Cultural Center of the Philippines, the Association of Philippine Medical Colleges Foundation, and the Women's Desk of the Philippine Council for Development. It was held in February 1990 at the Manila Film Center. This was the biggest workshop

I have ever attended as almost eight hundred representatives of different sectors from all over the country converged for the national consultation, with the theme "Women's Power in Us: Reflecting on Philippine Feminism." This time I was also invited to be one of the resource persons for the education sector and I shared with the group how I, along with some colleagues in the college, joined the call for feminism.

I also joined group discussions on various topics, and one of them was on the militarization of women. One resource person shared her experiences about what some soldiers did to her when she was suspected of working for the rebels in their area. She narrated the dangers encountered living in a place where a military operation was going on. During the open forum I could not help but react to her story in my attempt to make it clear that women, whoever and wherever they are, are the real sufferers of military operations, which are obviously conducted by men in uniform.

I shared with the group my experiences during the coup attempts that were made before daybreak, and each time we were always caught unprepared. Before we could even confirm its veracity, all the gates of Camp Aguinaldo would be closed, making it very difficult for us to evacuate to a safer place. Our cottage inside Camp Aguinaldo is quite close to EDSA, across Camp Crame. This area was considered a war zone during the EDSA Revolution in 1987 and the August 1988 and December 1989 coup attempts. This was where the real action took place, but in all these uprisings nobody seemed to give attention to the safety of the families living inside the camp. With all attention concentrated on the enemy forces, the lives of military dependants were virtually forgotten.

To leave the camp on our own was risky and impossible. We couldn't do anything but lie flat on the floor or seek cover under tables every time war planes or helicopters flew over. It was like being caught in a crossfire, and we didn't know where to go. It was indeed a traumatic experience since I was alone with my children all the time. Even during a lull we hesitated to get out of the house as uniformed men were all around, and it was not easy to identify the rebels.

We have to consider the root causes of all these happenings. Why are Filipinos fighting each other? Why do some of them become rebels? Who suffers the most as a result of their action? In the case of soldiers or a husband who died during encounters, who is left behind to take over the family responsibilities? Who is left behind to suffer humiliation when the husband-turned-rebel is killed or imprisoned? Who is left behind to explain to the children why their father behaved the way he did?

The flowering

Back in college, I started sharing the insights I gained from my experiences with six colleagues who also happened to have participated in similar seminars and workshops conducted by other women's groups. Together we formed an organization of college women and called it URDUJA. Urduja was a Filipina who held a prestigious position in her tribe during the pre-colonial period. She was a beautiful and intelligent princess who was also a brave warrior and freedom fighter. Her name, therefore, represented a cherished ideal for the women in this country.

The newly formed group then identified their objectives: to develop awareness of women's issues and concerns among faculty members and students; to identify specific content areas where women's studies could be introduced or integrated; to develop strategies and techniques for introducing, integrating, and teaching women's issues and concerns in different subject areas; to improve one's level of consciousness through sharing knowledge and information from seminars and readings on women's studies; and to collect, collate, and reproduce instructional materials for women's studies.

From then on, the core group continued to meet whenever necessary to discuss ways and means of carrying out our set goals. As we did not have the funds to support our needs, we decided to coordinate with existing organizations at the college to cosponsor the following activities:

• A panel discussion on women's studies with three resource speakers from WRRC, Lucia Pavia-Ticzon, Josefa Francisco, and Lorna Israel. They talked on women's issues, why there is a need for women's studies and for integrating women's studies in the curriculum, as well as how women's studies can bring about change in a person's life. The discussion was well attended by faculty members and college students, most of whom probably learned something new about themselves, as was evident from their reactions. This activity was cosponsored by the Philippine Association of University Women— PNC chapter.

- A panel discussion, "Women's Rights: A Step towards Relevant Education," was held 10 February 1990, with the PNC Graduate Assembly as cosponsor. The guest panelists were Aurora Javate-de Dios, Aida Maranan, and Lyn Lee. The audience, numbering more than two hundred graduate students from different specializations, learned much from the topics discussed. There were plenty of questions asked even after the discussion was over, as some students still made follow-up inquiries while the guests were having a snack at a nearby canteen.

- A lecture forum on women in history and religion, which had Sr Kristia Bacani of St Scholastica's College as guest speaker. This was cosponsored by the undergraduate Freshmen Assembly and was attended by more than five hundred college students. Many questions were raised by the students on the role of women as chronicled in the Bible, especially those which were being given different interpretations by their priests in homilies in the church.

- A symposium on sexual violence and rape, which had the Social Science Club as a cosponsor and ten members of WRRC and Women's Crisis Center as resource persons. Again, this was attended by more than five hundred college students who showed much interest in the topics discussed. They were also given a demonstration on how to defend oneself in case of sexual harassment.

- A seminar on the psychology of Filipino women overseas workers (Japayuki, domestic helpers, and mail-order brides), which was cosponsored by the Pambansang Samahan sa Sikolohiyang Pilipino. Aurora Javate-de Dios presented the life of Filipino women in Japan who work as dancers, commonly known as Japayuki. Gina Alunan-Melgar and Vina Bugayong, of the Kanlungan Center for Migrant Workers, talked about Filipinas as brides for sale in Europe. I presented the results of a study I had made of domestic helpers in the Middle East. This activity was also attended by faculty members and students of other colleges and universities.

All these activities were intended to raise the level of consciousness of faculty members and students on the status of Filipino women. At the same time, they were meant to test the water, so to speak, for us to know how open and receptive our administrators are to this area. After the first two activities,

URDUJA came up with a proposal to offer an introductory course on women's studies for the summer of 1990. Luckily, this was approved by both the Dean of the School of Social Sciences and the Vice President for Academic Affairs. Although the announcement came out quite late, twenty graduate students enrolled in the course which I was handling. I also invited Lucia Pavia-Ticzon of WRRC to meet the students and conduct a session with them. The course was again offered in 1991, but I was obliged to leave it when I had to go to the United States with my husband.

Between 1990 and 1991, six other faculty members joined URDUJA. With this development, I requested WRRC to conduct an orientation session with the twelve of us, especially as we had many questions we wanted to ask. There was also the need to understand fully the theoretical framework of women's studies. Two other similar sessions followed when we decided to come up with a course outline on women in history, which we wanted to propose as an alternative to a Spanish course.

Sr. Mary John Mananzan, who chairs the Inter-Institutional Consortium, also contributes a great deal to the effort. She conducts a Gender Fair Education Seminar-Workshop at least twice a year for members of the consortium, of which Philippine Normal College, now a university, is a member. So far, eight members of URDUJA have attended these seminars and workshops, which deepened their understanding of and commitment to the cause of women.

In consonance with our goals and objectives, members of URDUJA try as much as possible to integrate women's issues and concerns into the different subject areas taught at the college. We watch out for possible entry points through which women's issues can be discussed. Given the right techniques and strategies, we feel the lessons can bring about a change in the level of consciousness of the students. After a year, we saw the growing enthusiasm of the students for joining us in the organization. This brought about the birth of the students' organization which we call the Kabataang Urduja. The organization was formally introduced to the academic community on 19 July 1991 in the presence of our college administrators. On 3 August 1991 we conducted the first seminar-workshop for the members of Kabataang Urduja, with the support and assistance of Lucia Pavia-Ticzon and two other members of WRRC. This was attended by 118 of the initial 135 members of this new students' organization.

The members of URDUJA have also increased to twenty-one faculty members representing the following departments: history, social sciences, psychology, education, value education, child study, mathematics, natural sciences, language, and literature, as well as the Research Center and the Students' Affairs Office.

As agreed upon, a number of us are recording our respective experiences in integrating women's issues and concerns into the different subject areas. Our goal is to come up with instructional materials from these journals, or diaries, that we are striving to maintain. This should help guide other teachers who would want to venture into the same area.

On a more personal note, my involvement in seminars and workshops on women inspired me to write poems, which have been compiled in book form called *Ugat,* or Roots, published by WRRC. I have tried out most of these poems with my students and have found that they are effective as consciousness-raising activities in and out of the classroom. Most of them can also be used in introductory lessons in women's studies or as springboards to introduce women's issues into different subject areas.

I am also at present working on my dissertation on women in the military. This entails a lot of hard work, time, and patience but I am slowly pushing my way through in spite of my jobs at home and in college. I believe I can make some contribution in raising the status of women in the military. The result of my study could perhaps form a basis for revising some obsolete policies that are discriminatory to women.

Another area we are trying to explore is that of research. Some of us teach a course called Research Designs. In my two classes, for instance, I have encouraged my students to come up with studies on women for their mini-theses which form the main requirement for this course. The following topics have been chosen by the students, and their research efforts were presented for oral defense: women in media, women as breadwinners, single parenthood, women in the integrated national police, domestic helpers, Japayuki, women behind bars, and life histories of women of three generations (grandmother, mother, and daughter). For supplementary reading the students made use of the reading materials collected by URDUJA members for their office and library. Yes, URDUJA now has an office, given to us by the Dean of the School of Social Sciences, perhaps in recognition of our efforts. Our modest library is also a realization of one of our prime objectives: to collect, collate, and reproduce instructional materials for women's studies. The inclusion of our organization in the Directory of WRRC has helped us greatly in collecting materials from various sources. From time to time we receive magazines, and even books, sent by other women's groups, locally and from other countries.

The future lies before us

Once we start work on women's studies, we cannot merely limit our energies to a certain area. We cannot simply concentrate on curricular and materials development without paying attention to the possible result of this: the growing need for students to organize themselves and to find answers to the many questions that spring up through these consciousness-raising activities. The process of seeking the answers leads students to conduct research on women's issues.

For our part, we would not have been able to handle these demands and the challenges that come along the way without the support and cooperation of friends in the movement. As the overall coordinator of URDUJA, I have gathered much strength and encouragement from Lucia Pavia-Ticzon, Josefa Francisco, and the staff of WRRC, from Sr. Mary John Manan-zan and the Interinstitutional Consortium, and from friends like Aurora Javate de Dios who support our activities. In all this I see the importance of women's solidarity in the attainment of a common goal: to make life worth living for half of the country's population.

So what made me get into women's studies? As I see it now, it is my very life which is, in itself, a spectrum of experiences that I once recalled with bitterness and resentment. Such experiences were caused by people around me who had lived, thought, and believed that the essence of life and virtue lay in abiding by the rules of a patriarchal society. Their lives were dictated by norms set by people who had been colonized both in mind and body. They based the roles of men and women on schoolbooks and rules perpetuated by the old folks who, in their unlettered wisdom, told the young to obey these rules, so as to be accepted members of the community.

What made me get into women's studies, then, was the realization that something has to change in the way things are, that women should act together and resolutely evolve a better life not only for a few but for all women in all sectors of society. It was the awareness of the necessity for sharing and learning from one another; for examining minutely the factors that chain us and control our hearts, minds, and bodies within the walls of an invisible cage; and for coming out with a concrete effort to free ourselves from our fetters so that we may explore all possibilities of discovering and utilizing our talents, strengths, and resources. Only in this way may we become worthy trustees of the riches of our country. Truly, women must work together to bring about "a more caring society that will give not only to men but also to women, both bread and roses, poetry and power."

Freedom for all

I lived with eyes closed in an invisible cage
Like any other girl of my time and age
Blindly I acted the roles traditions dictate
Women are slaves to men, and thus nurture hate.

Household chores have sapped me of initiatives
Restrained me from exploring possibilities
Circumscribing my world and my perspectives
To discover my talents and potentialities.

As I face the world and life's stern reality
I felt the effects of piled-up insecurity
Inferiority, inhibitions gnawing at me
Getting out of my cage was a difficulty.

I bolted out of my cage: yet long did I know
The claws of oppression followed me through;
Church and school only emboldened the forces
That chained me to mere pleasant domesticities.

Now with my eyes open I desire and strive
To cut off the chains so I can stay alive:
I have discovered my true worth in life
No more a slave of traditions, and less strife.

Let me be free as a bird, not controlled like a kite
Let me soar through the sky with my own wings and
*   might*
And let this be so for all women in cages of distress
Let us all feel freedom, equality, happiness!

Nora Lan-hung Chiang (Huang)
Taiwan

NORA LAN-HUNG CHIANG
(HUANG) (b. 1946) teaches in
the Department of Geography,
National Taiwan University and
has published widely, both at
home and internationally. In 1985
she founded the Women's Research Program (along with three
other professors) and was its Coordinator for four years. She has
also coordinated a number of
seminars on gender studies in
Taiwan.

A Personal Essay

A s I look around me, I find many middle-aged Taiwanese women who fit the stereotype in Norma Diamond's paper, "One Step Forward, Two Steps Back."[1] In it she describes Chinese women who were educated but who did not engage in occupations outside the home. In my neighborhood of academic families, many women of my generation gave up their jobs after marriage or when they had children. Typically, they did housework, entertained friends and relatives, and participated in rituals of ancestor worship. Occasionally they would accompany their husbands to conferences or trips abroad. Such women went together for community activities such as art, aerobics, and flower arrangement classes. There were the occasional attempts at taking paid work, but almost all failed to continue for various reasons. I have never heard of anyone who went back to school.

Our middle-class women seem to live the kind of life described in Betty Friedan's book on American women in the 1960s and 1970s; yet I do not hear any open expression of boredom or complaints from them. Maybe this is because of our culture, which socializes women to accept their place at home. In the early 1970s, there was a strong stigma attached to a woman who took paid work outside her home while her husband "brought the bread home." A man would "lose face" if his wife had to work. This applied to all women, especially the middle class. Today a working woman is socially very acceptable, although she is expected to place her work as secondary to her family responsibilities.

Attitudes towards women taking paid work have changed rapidly in the past few decades. More and more women want to take up paid work because they marry later and they are better educated than their mothers. The earlier stigma towards women working was due to patriarchal values that discourage women from being active outside their homes and assumed that full responsibility for the home lay solely with the woman. Now, even though the woman has full-time work outside, she is supposed to have another full-time responsibility at home. In some young families, however, husbands today participate in doing minimum housework and help take care of small children. Working-class women have always worked, formerly in factories, now more and more in urban services. There is a large female population that is self-employed or doing piecework at home, but it often does not figure into statistics.

Seventeen years ago, when my son was born, I was asked by my mother-in-law to quit my university teaching job and to sacrifice my own interests for my family. She herself went back to school and took work after widowhood, but expressed ambivalence toward other women who worked. Had I followed the cultural norm of Taiwan in the 1970s, I would have been like the "selfless" women I see in my neigborhood, but I would have been very unhappy and frustrated. I have always liked my work and never even dreamt of being a full-time housewife. I have resisted the oppression of the pervasive cultural and social environment and have emerged as a confident and assertive person. The struggle which began in the early 1970s, when I started my career, continues to this day.

Growing up with a good education

As I was born in China after World War II, I experienced better economic conditions than my two older sisters. My mother did not express her disappointment at having a third daughter, but when my brother was born four years later, he became the most favored and the most spoiled among us! However, as far as education was concerned, my father treated all of us equally. We all went to good schools run by missionaries and subsidized by the Hong Kong government. I still remember the good teachers I had in the Methodist Primary School, which I attended as a child. It was coeducational and was attended mostly by middle-class children. After graduation I entered a government-run middle school for girls, where we had excellent teachers. Most teachers were graduates from universities of mainland China and the University of Hong Kong. My first role model was the school principal, Mrs. K.E. Cheung, who spoke beautiful English and appeared confident and graceful when she spoke to us formally every week. When I graduated from high school in 1963, she recommended that I should continue in Maryknoll Convent School to prepare for the matriculation examination for university admission. This decision changed my life, since it was not my father's design to send me to a university; higher education was expensive to support on his small income as a university lecturer. Apart from Mrs. Cheung, whom I consider my first mentor, there were two other persons during high school who were important role models: Mrs. Ruth Fok, who taught typing, and Mrs. T.N. Chiu, who taught geography. I was fascinated by geography as a subject and had started to like it in Form IV, when I was sixteen. From Mrs. Chiu I learned to study the subject analytically and systematically and did very well in class. I attended a more prestigious high school for my matriculation examination later on; however, I never developed the same kind of respect for teachers in the first five years of high school at Ho Tung Technical School for Girls. Classmates who graduated in the same year did not enter the university, but most of them became very successful career women in Hong Kong.

The University of Hong Kong, where I was a student between 1965 and 1968, was like a playground for young men and women who came mainly from upper-middle-class families. Most had studied in reputable English-medium schools. To my great disappointment, the intellectual environment of a university was missing here. Students were allowed to take very few courses and had long vacations to study on their own or to earn wages by teaching part time in secondary schools. Both British and Chinese teachers at the university were aloof and "colonial" toward their young adult students. As a student who was spoon-fed with lecture notes read out by the instructor, I had no chance to ask any questions. Luckily, there was a good university library to study in, and, due to an honors system at graduation, students competed fiercely in their assignments and examinations. Geography was a popular subject because of the British tradition and attracted the best students in the Faculty of Arts. This factor possibly accounted for the cultivation of self-esteem in geography students, who later took up graduate studies, taught in high schools, or went into government service.

My interest in graduate studies was partly derived from reading all available material in major geography journals; moreover I wanted to go to the United States, where my parents and the rest of the family had migrated. In 1969 I was admitted to the graduate program at Indiana University for a master's degree with an assistantship. I found that geography there was quite different from what I had learned in the undergraduate years, which included a considerable amount of regional geography. Since there was a lot of ground to cover, I took two and a half years to obtain the master's degree. My thesis was on transportation geography.

In the first year of graduate school, I met my husband, Dr. Men-Fon Huang, who was a young professor in mathematics. When we decided to get married I did not expect to come back to Taiwan with him, but his decision to do so was very firm. His reasons were that as he was the only son of a widowed mother he had the sole responsibility of caring for her, and he did not want to teach in the United States anymore. It was a hard decision for me and my parents as I had ideas of continuing to study for a Ph.D. and settling down in the United States. However, it was the convention for a woman to move with her husband wherever he went. That was the only reason for me to pack up and come back to Taiwan in 1972. I was totally unprepared for the new environment, which is different from Hong Kong culturally, socially, and politically. Back in the early 1970s, Taiwan had a very undemocratic government, which one could not criticize openly. If one did, one risked one's life. So I was constantly afraid that I might say something wrong in public or even in the classroom. In spite of this, teaching students gave me a lot of joy and psychological satisfaction.

When I came back to Taiwan with my husband I was stunned to discover my subservient status within the extended family, where daughters-in-law did not eat with the menfolk and spent all their time caring for the family. The attitude of the older generation to those younger was patriarchal and condescending. It was very oppressive for someone used to living in a freer society. I began to realize that I would need to struggle if I wanted to keep my identity intact and be different from other women. This was particularly so with respect to my work. I did not adjust well and was constantly angry and frustrated. I also felt humiliated. However, I was luckier than many Chinese women at that time as I was living in the city and not with the extended family. Nowadays, it is common for a young couple to live by themselves when they first get married.

Becoming a professional geographer

A turning point in my life came when I left Taiwan in the summer of 1973 to attend a seminar on population. Among young international scholars, I regained my confidence and self-worth as a person and was attracted by the intellectual environment of the East-West Center and the University of Hawaii. I was admitted to the Ph.D. program at the Department of Geography, University of Hawaii, in 1970. Hoping to be closer to home across the Pacific, I did not apply to other universities in the U.S. mainland.

My decision to leave home for further studies had my husband's full support. I had two full-time maids (whom I regarded as helpers) to help take care of my two-year-old son and to do the housework. My mother-in-law, who taught in a college quite far away, came to live with my family to help out as well. In addition, my parents' moral support was very important. My mother had played an important role in my education all the way. Not having as much education as she desired because of the war and the migrations in China when she was young, she wanted all her children to be well educated. What she said to me was of critical importance for my educational experience: "If you get an education, you will never lose it. No one will be able to rob you of what you have learned. Do not depend on your husband for economic support. You will get more respect from him if you don't." In my family, my mother is the wise, personable, and artistic person whom every child likes. My father is much more distant, obstinate, and authoritative.

Getting a Ph.D. is like moving a big mountain. Apart from my feelings of homesickness and guilt at leaving my family, I was aware of the critical views and curiosity of my friends and relatives toward a woman who went abroad to study without her family. The Chinese students' wives at the East-West Center were very concerned, as in those days women only accompanied their husbands who went abroad to study. It was often the case that husbands went without their wives and came back after three to five years with doctorates. My own unconventional behavior naturally made people wonder. At the University of Hawaii I met several other Asian women doing the same as I, and my only source of moral support came from female students and colleagues. Between 1974 and 1976, when I completed my course, there was no woman faculty member in the department of geography. When I presented my proposal to the all-male committee, I was initially persuaded to change the study of female migrants to a comparison between men and women: it took me a while to convince them that previous studies had never been on females alone and, quite often, studies of men were used to represent all migrants. I was the first student in the department to focus on women in my dissertation, although there were quite a few studies on women completed in other disciplines. For the first time in my graduate studies, I came across a wide spectrum of literature on women's studies.

From 1978 to 1979, I obtained a grant from the Rockefeller Foundation's Research Program on Population and Development Policy to carry out my research on female migrants. Since the study covered both the rural areas from which migrants had moved and the urban destination, Taipei, I carried out extensive fieldwork both in villages and in the city. Later I established a new tradition in field studies in human geography, which I taught for twelve years. Since in-depth interviews were not emphasized in other courses, students who participated in the collection of data found it a new and exhilarating experience. I also approached research problems analytically and taught students to be creative, which was traditionally not encouraged. Combining research for my dissertation and teaching was the way to continue my work to finish the Ph.D. Between 1976 and 1980, when I came back from the University of Hawaii, data collection, teaching and research, family life, and readjustment all blended very well. In order to use my limited time and energy for all these, I had given up vacations, sacrificed time with my family, and sometimes missed all social life at my workplace. In the process I became even more isolated from my relatives and friends in Taiwan.

While gathering data and writing my dissertation, I had the opportunity to attend three conferences on women, which were very important for my involvement in the Women's Research Program later on. These were: "The Role of Women in Population Re-distribution" (Sardinia, Italy, 1982); "Impact of Multi-national Corporations on the Socio-Economic Status of Women in the Third World" (East–West Cultural Institute, 1978); and "Working Group on Women and the Cities" (East-

West Population Institute, 1979). All bore fruitful results in networking and publication as well as a broadening of an understanding of questions on women in Asia.

Those whom I had studied for my dissertation represented a good cross-section of working women who had moved to Taipei with husbands or alone.[2] By participating in various types of urban industrial work, they acquired an economic status that might not have been possible in the villages. Even with very low incomes, they were daughters who sent back money to their parents and helped their brothers and sisters with further education. I have not found the exact equivalent of the words "filial piety" in the English dictionary, nor could I explain to my dissertation committee what it meant in Chinese culture. From a Western point of view it could mean exploitation of daughters by parents if they send back money to them, even out of love and respect. It was the first time that I became aware of the possibility that earlier studies on Chinese women by Western scholars may carry a cultural bias. While my study was on the physical movement of women from rural to urban areas, it involved an understanding of the cultural dimension of women's liberation. Although industrialization and urbanization did not result in a rise in the general social status of women, they were still able to acquire more autonomy and were emancipated from traditions, such as the control of parents and the institution of arranged marriages. It was possible that women who migrated from the Hakka villages were more likely to combine their jobs with schooling; if they did not have the opportunity for further education after nine years of free schooling back home, they would want to continue in the urban areas.

For myself, the years I spent combining family obligations and academic life, which included teaching and earning a degree, were the most difficult years of my life, both physically and psychologically. Having finished the first draft of my dissertation at about the same time that my second child was born, I found it impossible to concentrate on the revisions and do a good job. Between 1980 and 1982, I left home again for one and a half years to finish writing my dissertation at the University of Hawaii. My one-year-old daughter was left with my parents in the United States and my son, who was seven and a half, stayed with my husband in Taiwan. In all, I spent seven years on my Ph.D. I know that I would not have done it through sheer energy and persistence alone: the assistance and support of many people were vital in the process. Dr. Roland Fuchs, chairman of the Department of Geography at the University of Hawaii, used to visit Taiwan almost every year between 1974 and 1984 and helped me a great deal by reminding me to turn in the chapters to him whenever he visited. His constructive comments, his recommendations of literature on female migration, and his provision of logistical support from the Department of Geography were very important in helping me reach my goal. Without his moral support, I could have been yet another of those graduate students who never completed their research.

When I was asked by friends the point of having two Ph.D. degrees in the family, I really could not provide them with a satisfactory answer. My father derived great satisfaction from seeing me follow his path of a university professor. The greatest reward, however, was my personal growth in confidence and assertiveness, which I would not have gotten otherwise. An unforseen—but most welcome—outcome was my husband's growing closeness to his children, which developed in my absence. The "abnormal family" that my friends might have envisioned turned out to be quite normal after all those years!

Establishing a career in women's studies

The realization that many years of struggle in graduate studies were justified came several years later, when I became executive secretary in the Population Studies Center at the university. Although I had not continued to do research on women or demography, I had kept up an interest in the literature on women in Taiwan. Before the mid-1980s, there was very little serious work in the area except in history and anthropology. Besides a few dissertations and papers written by Western scholars, most papers published in Chinese were not to be found in academic journals. In the early 1970s, a woman by the name of Lu Hsui Lien was writing articles in the newspapers, calling attention to the discrimination against women in law and the double moral standards that operate in society. She introduced the ideas of feminism prevalent in the United States. I was attracted to her thought-provoking writing, creativity, and courage in attacking traditional values in public. In view of the undemocratic climate, any criticism of traditions was outlawed. So was Lu's one-woman feminist movement. Getting herself involved in the anti-government political campaign in

Kaohsiung in 1979, she was tried by the martial court and jailed for five years. Lu was the leader in the earliest stage of the feminist movement in Taiwan, and she was instrumental in the formation of the Awakening group in 1982 by her followers. Coming across a group of like-minded and educated women, I joined the Awakening group, but did not find it rewarding intellectually. My moorings were firmly in academics; and I could not share as much commitment to feminist issues as other members of the organization. Thus, instead of continuing to participate in the activities of the Awakening, I began collecting articles on women as a hobby and as a preparation for my study of women in Taiwan.

Having finished my Ph.D., I was free to do what I wanted academically. I was drawn to research projects related to environmental conservation—on people's perceptions of slope hazards,[3] environmental impact assessment, and tourist behavior in national parks.[4] The range of my research topics was due to the nature of human geography, which applies itself well to the variety of environmental and social problems in Taiwan. The rise in GNP in the last fifteen years has, at the same time, brought about immense environmental problems and social costs. The Taroko National Park was threatened by the scheme of the Taipower Company to build two major dams for generating electricity on the river that holds the life-blood of the Taroko Gorge. There were also plans to have a cement plant built near the park to make use of natural resources close by. Though my paper, appealing to the government and the public, to save the gorge was a shot in the dark,[5] it was a powerful input among the efforts to preserve our natural heritage. My article caught the attention of conservationists the world over who sent letters to the newspapers in support of the appeal. The decision to prevent the building of such dams was made soon afterwards. This was the first battle which I had won over a public issue, with the support of my own research. During this period, other than public service, I was mainly engaged in teaching and research and was promoted to full professor in 1983.

Ever since I returned from the United States, I had not continued to carry out research on female migration because of the demands of several other research projects sponsored by the government. My association with the Population Studies Center began in the late 1970s, as the chief of the resource materials section and then as executive secretary. Formed in the early 1970s, when fertility levels were high in Taiwan, the population studies center was like a forgotten child in the university as interest on fertility subsided. Although ten departments were represented at the center, they served as supporting members and were not involved in the planning and administration. The core group that ran the center consisted of a director, an executive secretary, three section chairs, and only one full-time assistant. Financial support from the university was minimal and there was only one full-time staff member to help with administration, publications, resource materials, and other research activities. This was one reason why the Women's Research Program found a home.

When the representative of the Asia Foundation, Dr. Sheldon Severinghaus, came to visit the center in 1984, he suggested the possibility of a women's research conference. Very soon the center's staff formed the organizing committee and started arranging the conference agenda. Seventeen papers were to be presented. Seeing the shortage of personnel at the center, the Asia Foundation agreed to provide a part-time assistant for the preparation of the conference who was also to work with me on a bibliography of women's research in Taiwan. This was during the ten months prior to the conference. In March 1985 the first women's research conference was held in Taiwan. Called "The Role of Women in National Development," it proved to be a great success. It was attended by over two hundred established and young scholars, government officials, and leaders of women's organizations. There was a lot of coverage in the media, which helped in its publicity and the dissemination of information to those who did not attend. Supported by the Asia Foundation and the National Science Council, proceedings in two volumes[6] were published in six months' time. With Ms. M.C. Hsu as an assistant, I also had a bibliography[7] compiled in time and an English report written on the conference to disseminate the information abroad. I was surprised how well this turned out, since it was my, and also the center's, first experience in running a conference all on our own.

Moreover, it was due to the suggestions at the concluding session of the conference that we started to think about having a women's research program at the center. With the support of the Asia Foundation and space available at the Population Studies Center, three other professors and I together founded the program in September 1985. All of us were women and from different disciplines—anthropology, English language, rural sociology, and, of course, geography. As the executive secretary of the center, I was appointed the coordinator to represent the program. Though this was a new experience for all of us, the program was founded on previous and ongoing work that each of us did on women's issues, our contacts with women's studies scholars, organizations we visited, and conferences we had attended abroad. Two researchers, Dr. Bih-Er Chou and Professor Yenlin Ku, donated their valuable time, commuting from their institutions; they had to cover greater distances than Dr. Elaine Tsui and I, who are from the National Taiwan University. This was an extra commitment on the part of each member because all of us had full-time university teaching and research jobs. I soon found that, being the coordinator, I naturally had to take up a large share of the work, although other team members all shared in the planning and responsibilities. I also knew that I had to put more effort into the program because women's studies was an area new to me academically. I learned very quickly to sort out my priorities and gave up accepting research projects on environmental conservation in the Geography Department. I found the work for the program fascinating because it not only related to my own experience as a woman, but also gave me opportunities to meet new people. Working with an all-female group was another new experience. I found more equal sharing of work among the team and had a more caring relationship with my colleagues—definitely a more humane experience than that in the male-dominated Geography Department or even within the Population Studies Center itself.

We had a full agenda to start with at the beginning, including publications, preparation of resource materials, special lectures, and seminars. We published a bulletin every three months to inform the academic community and the public about research activities in Taiwan and abroad. We went as far as organizing seminars with other universities, such as the Institute of Sociology and Anthropology of Chinghua University. This led to the publication of *A Report of the Summer Seminar on Gender Studies* in 1988 and *Gender Roles and Changing Society* in 1989. No matter how hard I worked, the mountain of work kept getting higher because of increasing publicity of the program. Our members were consulted on research problems and women's questions during office hours and were invited to give public lectures frequently. We were regarded as an established women's organization at the time when many others were formed. From 1985 to 1989, about two thousand visitors came to use the library, talked to us about research, and attended our lectures. Within the Population Studies Center, the program was almost like a women's research center, as it was administratively independent.

I will never forget the experience of our group's sharing of so much ingenuity and creativity to produce something that was beneficial to the academic community, and which won so much public acclaim! Our easy association with each other was symbolic of the breakdown of the patriarchal structure in the university, which was based on domination and hierarchy, with people being assigned places and allocated power or privilege related to that position. Despite the fact that, later, different people came into the program, the tradition with which we began still holds firm. Working almost like a women's studies association, we have tried to involve as many research scholars (both male and female) as we can and have attempted to make our resources accessible to the public. The library was open to all, for instance, and the bulletin was free. A special grant was set up for young women research scholars to help them with research for their degrees. Between 1985 and 1990, up to twenty-eight scholarships were given to twenty-six students and two professors to carry out research projects on women. The program served to fill a void in the mainstream of knowledge so successfully that its credibility as a women's research institution was well established by the third year. Obviously, the demands of society were overwhelming. When they began to feel a need, government agencies found it awkward to address themselves to the problems of women as they lacked a policy on the subject. At such times, the program's resource materials were relied on heavily by the non-academic community.

From 1985 to 1990, more than ten women's groups were formed. A law that did not allow two organizations of the same kind to be formed (so as to ensure that the government could control the public from joining together) meant that women's organizations could only exist if they agreed with the ideology of the ruling party. Traditional women's groups are not geared toward individual growth or consciousness-raising, nor do they challenge the subordinate status of women in law and politics. Although a great amount of social service was performed by these groups, their focus was on reinforcing the role of women in the family. In 1986, after martial law was lifted, the political climate started to change. It provided the background for well-educated women, who were aware of their subordinate positions in society, to form themselves into groups. In these groups they discussed their frustrations and problems, pursued activities that encouraged self-worth and growth, as well as looked at social ills and issues beyond the family. Newly formed women's groups included the Warm Life Association for divorced women, the Women's Rescue Association to help young prostitutes, the Homemaker's Association to help clean the environment, to support consumer rights, and advocate better education for children, etc. The galaxy of women's organizations formed between 1985 and 1989 was well after the UN Decade for Women, which understandably had had only a limited impact on Taiwan. Communication and contact with other women in the world may have brought in new insights; but the change was mainly due to the new crop of women intellectuals born after the war who looked at the sociopolitical situation much more critically than the older generation. Although much smaller in scale than the environmental movement, or consumer movement, these women's groups were a new social force that sensitized the public on women's issues. Since 1985 there has been a much more active calendar of events each year produced by women's groups on International Women's Day. Coverage of women in the newspapers now includes subjects such as working women, single parenthood, and international women. Besides the Women's Research Program at the National Taiwan University, the Gender and Society Program was formed at Tsing Hua University in 1989.

Economic growth in Taiwan has helped the Women's Research Program to continue by getting support from local foundations, though, unfortunately, funding was not available from the university. However, almost all the initial activities have continued with outside funding, along with the publication of the *Journal of Women and Gender Research* in January 1990. A new course for undergraduates, Gender Relations, is to be started by the program and will be cosponsored with the Public Health Department. The purpose is to raise the awareness of students on the many issues concerning women in our society. This will be a first attempt to introduce gender issues into the general studies curriculum from a multi-disciplinary perspective. We hope such an undergraduate course will become a model for the liberal arts curriculum of the other universities, which will work to transform students' educational experiences in the long run.

An unfinished liberation

My experience as a promoter of women studies in Taiwan has been an exhilarating one. Compared to the first battle I fought to save the Taroko Gorge, this work is rewarding on a different scale and may have a long-standing impact on women students, as well as on the academic community, in Taiwan. Although I have a commitment to feminist issues in society, (by which I mean approaches to women's experiences that question patriarchal modes of domination in all areas of life as defined by Charlotte Bunch),[8] I can only devote my time and energy to feminist research within the university. This "vested" interest will be parallel to my two other areas of research: population and environmental conservation. It is now time for the government to conduct policy-oriented research—one such research project being undertaken is on the quality of life and welfare needs of women factory workers. Apart from attending several international conferences to present papers on women, I am a member of two international groups of academic women on feminist studies. I am also a member of the Committee on Women's Studies in Asia and the Geography and Gender Research Group of the International Geographical Union.

These international contacts will, I hope, help me strengthen resources to build women's studies in Taiwan; this is the third battle I have to fight in the future. The discipline will serve to provide the theoretical background to support the women's movement in Taiwan, on the one hand, and future policy issues related to women on the other. The slow growth of the discipline here, as compared to other countries, may be due to the absence of full-time research scholars working on women and the low priority given to humanities and social sciences in the universities. Even though a good number of students have written their theses on women, they may not continue their research or further studies in the future. It will take some more years for young women with Ph.D. degrees to take the lead in the academy and to have a larger voice in important matters.

After resigning from the program as coordinator in September 1989 for health reasons, I began devoting more time to reading, thinking, and formulating questions. It has become clear to me that the program will have to continue to demonstrate the power of knowledge and excellence, of the scholarship of individuals, so that women's studies will become a prominent field of study.

The chances of introducing feminist geography are still very limited because geography as a social science is underdeveloped in Taiwan.[9] The geography department where I teach is male-dominated, oriented towards physical geography and computer applications. As the only woman faculty member with an interest in feminist geography, it seems odd to advocate a new dimension and claim for it "scientific" status in the department single-handedly. Fortunately, feminist geography has been developing rapidly internationally.[10] The extent of concern has included a study of gender differences and gender inequalities in spatial patterns, environmental perception, and women's role in environmental change. At the present moment, the most I can do is to integrate a feminist perspective in the courses I teach, especially in research methods and social geography.

My "liberating" experience still continues on two different fronts—in the family and at work. Today I am the director of the Population Studies Center. The Women's Research Program is still vigorous, coordinated by Dr. Cheuh Chang, an associate professor in public health. Other researchers include scholars from the fields of medical sociology, anthropology, geography, and sociology. My struggles as a human being and especially as a woman in a patriarchal society are constant; the challenge that remains is how one can be fully liberated from the designs of a society loaded with such values.

Notes

1. Norma Diamond, "The Status of Women in Taiwan: One Step Forward, Two Steps Back," in Marilyn B. Young (ed.), *Women in China*, Ann Arbor: Michigan Papers in Chinese Studies, No. 15 (1989): 211-242.
2. Nora Chiang (Huang), "The Migration of Rural Women in Taipei," in James T. Fawcett, Siew-Ean Khoa, and Peter C. Smith (eds.), *Women in the Cities of Asia—Migration of Urban Adaptation*, Boulder, CO: Westview Press, 1985: 247-267.
3. Nora Lan-hung' Chiang, "Adjustments to Hazards on Slopeland— A Case Study of Keelung City, *Journal of Engineering Environment*, (1984): 1-12.

4. ——, "A Study of Attitudes and Behavior of Tourists in the Taroko National Park," *Science Report*, Department of Geography, National Taiwan University, no. 12 (1985): 151-176.
5. ——, "Save Taroko Gorge—Our National Treasure," *The Economic News*, Tourism Special No. 2895, (1984): 36-37.
6. ——, "The Role of Women in the National Development Process in Taiwan, Report of a Conference, March 14-16," Population Studies Center, National Taiwan University, Taiwan (1985).
7. —— with Mei-chih Hsu, *Bibliography of Literature on Women in Taiwan, 1945-1985*, Taiwan: Population Studies Center, National Taiwan University, 1985.
8. Charlotte Bunch, *Feminism in the '80s: Bringing the Global Home*, Denver, Colorado: Inkling Press, 1985.
9. "Feminist Geography in Taiwan," *Arena, Journal of Higher Geographical Education* 3, no. 1 (1989): 94-96.
10. Janice Monk, "Feminist Geography: Theory and Practice," *Bulletin of the Geographical Society of China*, no. 16 (1988): 89-102, and Catharine Stimpson, "Women's Studies in the United States" (A Report to the Ford Foundation), Ford Foundation (1986).

Thanh-Dam Truong
Vietnam

THANH-DAM TRUONG was born in Dalat, Vietnam in 1949 and has lived most of her life in exile. She studied political science and development studies at Ohio University, the Institute of Social Studies at the Hague, and the University of Leiden. She has worked for the United Nations and is currently part of the Women and Development Programme at the Institute of Social Studies. Her interests include issues related to women and the North-South question, feminist theory and epistemology, and women, ideology, and culture. She also writes poetry.

Passage to Womanhood and Feminism:
Bridge over Troubled Water

E very human life is a kaleidoscope of experiences, a tapes-
try of feelings and consciousness. To write about my own
life and how I became a feminist is, to a certain extent, an
effort to reconstruct the past in the light of the present, something that is unavoidably selective. For this reason I must stress
that I only wish to share the events of my life that have moved
me most deeply and contributed to shaping its course. What I
want to avoid is to tell a story about feminist consciousness in
a predetermined way, as if in my tender years, or in those full
of calluses, I really knew what was happening to me. To me,
consciousness is an unfolding process and its beauty is the fact
that it does unfold itself and therefore enables one to feel, experience, and reflect on life in a kaleidoscopic manner.

Growing up in Vietnam
Growing up in Vietnam in the middle of a war notorious for
the nature of its many conflicts, my childhood was inevitably
affected by their visibility. A rather shielded life had made me
a spectator most of the time to these conflicts until pain taught
me what conflict really meant.

Born as the second youngest child in a family of six children, I hardly knew my father as a child. We were brought up
by my mother single-handedly as my father was away most of
the time studying, at work, or involved in other activities. My
mother was a strong-willed woman who ran a maternity clinic. She was highly disciplined in her work as well as in the daily
routine of her children. With my mother, the "dos" and "don'ts"
were always clear because of the penalties and rewards. Her
discipline turned my father into a loving saint every time he

191

came home for a visit, usually on festive occasions. During these short periods of time, my parents would carry on a power struggle about what should be the rules for the children. In my father's absence, my mother was both authoritarian and caring. And in his presence, she was nobody. In such an environment I developed no sense of fairness, although I enjoyed the festive atmosphere when my father came home.

In my father's absence, my mother always talked about how we should not disappoint him. "Don't ever bring shame on him," she said, "or I'll be blamed." The kind of shame she feared the most was unwed motherhood. She amazed me with her strict control over the mobility of my then teenage eldest sister and, at the same time, her compassion for unwed pregnant women who came to her for shelter and care until delivery and adoption. My sister would be beaten sometimes or sent to bed without dinner for coming home late (when the light was switched on).[1] Yet my mother would be very supportive to unwed mothers. She taught them nursing skills and even employed some of them until they moved on to better pastures. I was puzzled by her double standards. I wondered how she could accept others' wrongdoings while fearing that her daughter might do wrong. Little did I understand the complexity of social roles and their contradictions.

The pain I experienced throughout the long procedures of my parents' formal separation turned my consciousness of conflict from that of a spectator to that of a participant. My own identity came into question, something to which I could provide no answer. My father was to take care of two young children, still in their teens. My brother and I were to live with my father, stepmother, and their three children for the sake of our own "education." During that time, my mother could not afford to pay the expensive fees of the French private *lycee* as the clinic was closed down due to her illness. We would visit her regularly, only to witness the slow destruction of a strong-willed woman, alienated from her family and friends; a price she paid for taking my father to court for polygamy, something which conventionally should have been settled within the family.

Often I heard my paternal relatives discussing my mother, how her regional and family origins were different from "ours," how "those northerners" were strict, tough, and not as easygoing as "we," the southerners were. After all, those who migrated down south had lost their roots. In particular, my mother had lost her feminine character because she dared to fight my father and his relatives. I never knew where I belonged as the "they" and "we" became more and more polarized. This divided sense of loyalty and belonging was perhaps the first kind of pain I experienced; it taught me what conflict meant.

Undoubtedly to reassure me that there was nothing wrong about a woman fighter, as long as she defended her children's interests, my mother often told me about the story of her grandmother. In the nineteenth century, at the age of sixty, this widowed woman dared to travel on foot from the Ha-Noi region to the Imperial court in Hue to file a complaint against her husband's family about the unfair application of inheritance laws to the detriment of her children's and her own interests. It took her six months to reach her destination. She lived in the vicinity of the Forbidden City (the Imperial Palace) where she disguised herself as a petty trader selling tea to the guards. For months, she played the sweet old lady to gain the guards' trust so as to be more mobile between the different gates. One afternoon, when the guards were napping, she ran straight into the inner courtyard, put on her "proper"[2] robe, and rang the gong, a highly protected royal object which, once rung, meant a call for the emperor's personal attention. Few ever succeeded in getting past the guards, and those who dared to ring the gong without a substantiated cause might be condemned to death. The "sweet old lady" was not condemned to death. On the contrary, her complaints were tended to personally by the emperor, who sent her back to her village in a royal carriage accompanied by guards and an administrator to settle her affairs. I always found this story amusing and inspiring, particularly when my mother mumbled between her giggles: "Women are no fools."

Outside the boundaries of the home, I became aware of the "they" and "we" in multiple forms. They could mean the government and we the people. They could mean the communists and we the nationalists. They could mean the Americans and we the Vietnamese. They could mean the Catholics and we the Buddhists. They could mean the bad women who prostituted themselves and entertained American soldiers, and we the good women who maintained tradition to the point of refusing to wear Western clothes. For the first time, I was bewildered by the terms *Ben Nay, Ben Kia* (this side and the other). Growing up in a Buddhist family with its old traditions, where socialization always stressed harmony and oneness, even in the midst of conflict, I always wanted things to be "one." However, my wish was not what society desired.

Between 1963 and 1965, when there were demonstrations, explosions, and arrests almost daily, the merry-go-round of the entertainment industry for American soldiers kept turning. At school, we were told not to join the radicals at the university and go on strike. They were all sent to jail and created a lot of problems for their parents. We were only in high school, and we should not be influenced by ideas of "solidarity" among students. At home, the adults would gather around the radio to follow the events of BBC news while street fighting was going on right in the middle of the city. Quietly, I used to toy with the idea of escaping all conflicts. I did not like them. They were, for me, like an army of ants eating out my heart.

I could not solve conflict. But at the personal level, marriage often crossed my mind as an escape. My eldest sister had chosen this route. But then I thought she had gotten herself into new kinds of conflict. I wanted to be able to travel far away. Then I could escape all conflict, I thought. Since education has always been so highly valued in our society, it was difficult for anyone to find good reasons to stop me when the means to pursue higher studies abroad were available, namely, a scholarship. What mattered was the field of study chosen, which must meet with parental approval.

Pharmacology was the favorite field for women because it allowed them to combine family chores with the management of their drugstores, said one of my teachers. Pharmacology had never inspired me, nor did other natural sciences. I wanted to do something bold and adventurous. And I love to write. I had written poetry since I was thirteen as my way of escape. So I wanted to become a journalist. "What? You want to tell lies, lies which bring money and power? You haven't the character for this!" *Nha bao noi lao an tien, noi lao co tien, noi lao co the,* my mother said. I suppose being a journalist was stereotyped in our society as "the paper scrapper," or the rich and powerful lies-teller at either end of the spectrum. I wasn't too surprised at my mother's reaction. My father's view was that I should enter the field of education if I did not like pharmacology. Being a teacher was also proper for a woman. But I remained stubborn in my desire.

Finally, suppressing their doubts, my parents agreed that I should leave for the U.S.A. at the age of eighteen to enroll as a university student. Until the last minute, my mother was of two minds. On the one hand, she was proud of my achievements in school; on the other, she resented that education was taking me away from her once more. Marriage would have kept me home and she would not have "lost" me. I saw her crying at the airport, and I almost ran back because I understood what my departure meant to her. My parents made me promise to write them one letter a day and to keep all their letters in a file. I was to consult the file from time to time so as to prevent myself from going astray in a foreign land and culture.

Conflict and benign radicalization

Landing in Ohio in 1968, I soon discovered that my way of escaping conflict had thrown me into another major one. I was exposed to this almost daily throughout my stay in the U.S.A.: the students' rebellion which included protest against the Vietnam war and the sexual revolution. Debates on campus about corrupt South Vietnam and the glorification of the regime in the North touched me very directly. Such debates initially made me feel ashamed for coming from the South, made me question my class background. As I belonged to the patrilineal feudal class, I was therefore categorized as the oppressor and the corrupt. I always thought my family were "nice" and "correct" people. Members of the extended family were on either side, North and South, government and people. Where was I, what should I stand for?

More particularly, the debates about sexual freedom, safe contraception and abortion, and opinions expressed about prostitution in Vietnam made me aware of double-edged arguments, with both racist and sexist undertones. Sometimes discussions were loaded with layers of insinuation, which were culturally and personally offensive to me. When I said so, the response would be: "Ah, but you are different, you have become one of us." I did not appreciate being identified with the "us" in this case. Confronting the self was a matter of survival, which prevented my gradual absorption by other people and their ideas.

Often I felt moved by the pictures of my country bombarding the television screen at every hour of the day. My life had been too protected so far for me to be fully aware of the scale of destruction my country and its people were experiencing. Often my heart cried at my ignorance. But deep inside myself, I questioned some of the interpretations about the conflicts in my country. Too sure of my own ignorance and too uncertain of my own opinions, I wrote poetry when I found debates futile.

I marched with others in demonstrations for peace, never once questioning whether we were anti-war or pro-Vietnam. There was something romantic about holding a candle, walking with the crowd around the campus singing John Lennon's "Give Peace a Chance." I could feel the romanticism while, at the same time, the television screen reminded me that more unfortunate people were simultaneously experiencing extreme forms of suffering. Moreover, students' yearning for peace quickly ended up with Nixon's order to bring the National Guard onto our campus to restore discipline and civil order after the incident at Kent State University. The constellation of feelings, events, and rationale of action was, for me, an absurdity hard to take. Real tears were with tears jerked out of my eyes by gas.

By the time I was halfway through my studies, I stopped filing my parents' letters, particularly my father's. Somehow I resented always being reminded that I musn't forget my studies and my family, and that I should be conscious of how I behave. "Follow the Buddhist way," he said, which implied, for me, "seek harmony and don't be a fighter." The value of his words somehow had no space in a young mind full of conflicts. I must have caused him a lot of pain when I wrote to him that I was old enough to be myself and to know my own way. The torments I felt at the time used to give me the most dreadful nightmares. One night I dreamt that I was floating on air. On earth, a funeral was proceeding. I recognized the people in the funeral, they were my family but I could not communicate with them to ask whose death it was that caused them so much grief. Then I saw my own body. I woke up bathed in sweat. I suppose that every growth process must involve deep convulsions that bring one to a different kind of consciousness and being.

My journalistic career began in 1971, as a twenty-one-year-old trainee in the Paris office of the Westinghouse Broadcasting Company. I was guided by a mature and gentlemanly journalist, with a long international career, and assigned to assist him with the reporting of the peace talks between Vietnam and the U.S.A. at the Kleber Conference Center. Everyone in the press corps was unimpressed by the appearance of the negotiators and their spokespersons, who had been stepping in and out of their limousines since 1968. It was commonly expected that at the end of the day all of them would end up saying nothing about peaceful settlements; only mutual accusations about violation of international norms and accords would be made. Coming to Kleber and waiting for the weekly press conference was, for many, a routine check so as not to miss any new declaration that would make "news." I wasn't unimpressed. I was a beginner, thrilled to be in the vicinity of the "big shots" during their stopovers in Paris for their "shuttle diplomacy." Amongst them, Madame Binh, of the National Liberation Front of South Vietnam, touched me deeply with her toughness beneath a veneer of extreme simplicity of conduct and speech. To me, she was the ideal woman.

Being too much of a contemplator throughout my traineeship, I was never quick enough for action—the kinds of action required in this profession. It was as if one must always be a predator for news, a hawk perched on his branch awaiting the first thing that moved. A small event or comment can be captured and skillfully framed in a context that "makes news." Being a journalist required one to be close and to be far at the same time, like a zoom lens. One cannot put across one's opinion, but one can "make news." News and opinions must be differentiated and there are proper places reserved for each category. In between my boss's advice and explanations, my mother's comment about my choice of journalism crossed my mind. I understood the reasons for her stereotyped image. Yet I also discovered, through my boss and teacher, that there was much else in journalism. Not all forms of journalism have the same professional implications. I wanted the kind of writing with room for depth. I did not want to just "make news." My choice failed me or I failed it.

Desert and development

Being inspired by development issues, I went back to the U.S.A. to complete my master's in international relations. After all, if ever peace came to Vietnam, that would be needed, I thought. Shifting away from U.S./Vietnam politics, I found myself a post as consultant in the Information Division of UNICEF and eventually UNDP in New York City between 1973 and 1975. There I was assigned the task of helping to prepare for the International Women's Year, first planned to be held in Bogota, but later shifted to Mexico City. I could not escape from "making news," this time not about my country but about women in the Third World.

One of my major tasks was to show in writing what the UN had done or not done for women in its development efforts. "Stay away from declarations, get to the project level," I was advised. Project level? In the head office? That meant consulting tens of meters of files in the cabinets! Out of this jungle of information, I tried to weed out the word "women," only to have its marginality as a budget item confirmed. My report was quoted by Senator Charles Percy in his speech to the UN Assembly in preparation for the introduction to the Percy Amendment, an amendment which required all USAID projects, regardless of their nature and scope, to take into account women's interests. Marginality made "news" in this case, thanks to the women's movement. In contrast to this marginality, I discovered in the audio-visual department of the UN an enormous collection of films and photographs of women toiling in the field, building roads and dams, and peddling their wares in crowded streets. Two levels of reality came to my mind. The reality of fund raising and the reality of fund spending. I wanted to experience the second reality.

My application for a field post was accepted and I was assigned to the UNDP office in Upper Volta (now Burkina Faso) in West Africa as the coordinator of the UN volunteers program. I had no previous knowledge of Africa except through films and files. Being briefed that Upper Volta was situated in the Sahel and drought-stricken lower belt of the Sahara, my ideas about the country were formed with pictures of dying cattle and people—skin and bones—who were trying to make another day liveable. They brought back memories of the suffering and destruction of Vietnam. "Are you sure you want to leave the New York office for Upper Volta? You must realize that it's a hardship post for a young woman like you," said one of my bosses. It can't be different from where I come. All destruction, whether caused by war or ecological disaster, must bring the same suffering and loss to people, I thought.

I left New York two months before the fall of Saigon in 1975. On the eve of my departure, the television screen showed scenes of the American evacuation of Cambodia and the chaotic outflow of Cambodian refugees. For no obvious reason, I was certain that the political settlement in Vietnam would be different and therefore had no worry about being cut off from communication links with my family once I was in the Sahel. After all, I wanted so much to go to Africa and to "give two years of my life to development," as the slogan said in one of the posters recruiting volunteers. Little did I know what lessons life had stored up for me!

One such lesson was the futility of my certainty about my own life. During the first twelve months, I followed the news about my country on the radio with great anxiety but received none from my family. Being in the desert at that moment had existential implications for me: emptiness, being devoid of the presence of loved ones, and not knowing when there would be a time for reunion. One could never be certain of such things. I went back to the file of my parents' letters. For me these have become the most precious living memories of my people, of where I belong, of "us." Never disconnect. You never know when a connection becomes a source of life for you.

The vulnerability of intellectual certainty (being cocksure about one's own point of view) was another precious lesson that made me realize the difference between a slogan and reality. What did two years of my life mean for development? For the people whom I came to "help?" The arrogance of such certainty became more explicit as I became more involved in my work. "What this country needs is . . . ;" such was a common saying among many "experts." One was left free to fill in the empty space according to one's whims, whether the issue concerned ecology, women, or the informal sector. Those who were more sensitive to the fragile social fabric would tell me different stories and showed me areas in which male outmigration had severely affected agricultural production. Only women and the elderly were left to till the soil, sometimes with their bare hands. Yet, our support to women took the form of the construction of a "Maison des Femmes"[3] in Ouagadougou, the capital city. Even for local women, such "white elephants" counted as significant. I suppose material objects must give people a sense of concreteness and certitude of "right" action.

In addition, the very existence of a Ministry of Tourism and Environment was too striking an example of the discrepancy between policy discussions in air-conditioned rooms and the needs of the country. While I did not question the second function of this institution, I was puzzled by the "whys" of tourism in a country pressed by drought and food shortages, where limited food and water supplies were being diverted to hotels hosting a handful of tourists and, mostly, foreign "experts" on missions. And, of course, the classic and naive question often raised by young people involved in volunteer programs did creep into my mind: "What's the meaning of development?" I never thought that, after an M.A. and about three years of working experience, I would find myself back at square one.

Identity politics and feminist consciousness

My pursuit of the perplexing question of development in the latter half of the 1970s brought me to the Institute of Social Studies (ISS), in The Hague, subsequent to my assignment in Burkina Faso. My experience there was very different from the years spent at the graduate school in the U.S.A. For one thing, development theories had radicalized me, or at least I was exposed to more controversial perspectives about development and underdevelopment than before. The benevolence and neutrality of the international system of aid and cooperation were often exposed as myths and contrasted with its commercial and manipulative nature. In particular, the poignant discussions of the effects of development policy on women had helped make my latent interests, evoked from field experience, more pronounced.

Soon after I completed my training on international relations and development policies at the ISS, my interests turned to the phenomenon of sex tourism in Southeast Asia in the early 1980s. This shift had been somewhat unavoidable for several reasons. First, the information obtained from travel brochures and in newspapers about sex tourism generated in me similar reactions as did the discussions on prostitution in Vietnam a decade earlier. One could not query the facts and their offensive nature, but there was something that put me at odds with the interpretations. I wanted to work out my own interpretation. Second, with a course on women and development starting in 1978, many women at ISS took up the issue as part of their struggle against male dominance and the exploitation of women. Protest campaigns were organized in front of travel agencies and at the airport against such tours, in collaboration with Dutch women's groups. A two-pronged approach emerged: within the Dutch context, women's organizations took their campaigns into parliament and government buildings, demanding protective legislation for victims of sex trafficking and the banning of sex tours; within ISS, sex tourism was brought into the classroom for debates and was taken up as a research topic by a number of participants.

Fortunately, positioned as a lecturer in the Women and Development Programme, which by then had become a full-fledged M.A. program, the first of its kind in Europe, I was able to discuss with women committed to the movement, from many regions of the world, aspects of prostitution as well as my most conflicting inner reactions to it. Not only have such interactions been crucial for me to overcome some of the barriers I had encountered earlier, but they also fostered a sense of solidarity and understanding among women activists concerned with the issue.

I started my doctoral research,[4] basing my thoughts, with some hesitation, on the notion of "male social power" that has guided feminist action groups against prostitution and pornography. To face a prostitute and ask what she thought and felt was the next step that could no longer be kept away from my thinking. During fieldwork in Thailand and the Philippines, my assumptions about male power were both confirmed and challenged. The information gathered through unstructured discussions with clients, prostitutes and their managers, travel writers, and government officials, as well as the emotions evoked from this experience, led me to raise more questions than I had planned to when I had initially started the project.

Some questions were latent and some were new. The latent "whys" of tourism came to the fore and added to the question of what such tourism did to women. This newly added element to my question was partly provoked by the contradictory feelings I experienced during fieldwork. How could I feel sympathy and disgust at the same time for what I heard, saw, and read about prostitution? The "why" of tourism made me probe deeper into the rationale of tourism as a development strategy. The "how" of such mixed feelings about prostitution made me recognize the significance of differentiation and the power of discourse. Of particular importance to me then was the differentiation between prostitution and prostitutes, the differentiation among prostitutes, and the differences between the moral position adopted by officials and the practices they followed.

Subsequent to this field experience, I became involved with organizations set up by prostitutes themselves in Western Europe and, to a lesser extent, in the U.S.A. and Canada. Although the involvement was of short duration—mainly during the first and second World Whores Congresses in Amsterdam and Brussels—I soon discovered that differentiation ran much deeper. I felt compelled to understand its deeper roots. Fieldwork, as well as armchair research, have evoked so many feelings that educated me on differentiation, while the literature on theories of power and feminism that I have consulted hung somewhere in my subconscious. Emotions such as anger, guilt, embarrassment, and despair have been part of the process of looking, finding, talking, reading, thinking, and writing. Experiencing these emotions has helped me grasp the meaning of power at its center as well as at its extremities.

Anger, evoked from an awareness, motivated me to wrestle with the topic in as many dimensions as possible as I began to recognize the power of scientific discourse, of which I have become a part. I have also felt guilt for having reproduced the many biases and assumptions (as learned) during discussions with and about women who have confided in me and for having caused them pain. I was at times the carrier of the very biases that I sought to destroy. Through being embarrassed by men who had mistaken me for a prostitute during fieldwork, I also learned about my own threshold and the threshold of sisterhood. I felt the urge to prove that I was a researcher and not a prostitute. Yet, simultaneously, I also felt embarrassed for having pretended that the "dichotomy between madonna and whore" could be erased through supportive action and embarrassed at being awoken to the fact that there are prostitutes who can do without researchers or activists. The glimpse I had of certain aspects of power in prostitution, as well as women and development issues, has also influenced my process of becoming an aware researcher. By this I mean the ability to recognize complexity and to note the selectivity of advocacy. In my mind, feminist consciousness encompasses this recognition.

In this regard, I consider the challenge facing the Women and Development Programme at ISS, and therefore myself, as being directly related to the objective the women's movement has set for itself in its struggle to gain space within academia: to transform science in order to deal with women's issues more adequately. This objective places feminist scholarship between two relationships that are not necessarily smooth; that is, the relationship with academia and the relationship with the movement.

Given the general recognition of the element of power inherent in the relationship between science and society (for example, the control of knowledge and the control over women), feminist scholarship cannot escape being politicized. The scientific definition of women's problems (who defines them, what is included and what is excluded), and explanations provided, as well as their practical implications, cannot be treated as neutral issues. The tremendous upsurge in feminist scholarship in the last two decades, the charge and countercharge that goes on between various segments of the women's movement and within academia (for example, Western hegemony, feminist imperialism) are clear expressions of the lack of consensus regarding objectivity, analysis, explanation, and prescriptions for change. To me, this is a *cri de coeur* warning us about the assumed liberating potential of theory built about and by women, its capacity to reproduce oppressive stereotyped images, and ineffective strategies for change. More importantly, this *cri de coeur* questions the place of feminist scholars in the process of social change and the convergence of the intellectual and political objectives of the women's movement.

Owing to its social origins,[5] it is impossible for the Women and Development Programme to turn a deaf ear to the *cri de coeur*. So far our response has been on the methodological and didactic front, namely, to account for the experience of participants in curriculum development and learning processes. In the area of theoretical development, this *cri de coeur* remains a critical challenge. Having torn down male partiality in the human sciences, feminist scholars have become increasingly aware that to construct a feminist alternative requires another round of tearing down of our own assumptions about the universal category of "woman" and the qualities we assigned to it. In my experience as a lecturer, this basic question of what constitutes "womanhood" is unavoidably prone to conflict. The different experiences of womanhood along the lines of class, ethnicity, and generation imply the need to provide space and understanding for such experiences. The question is how to create and use that space without falling into the trap of cultural relativity.

While aware of the significance of the new space needed, I have also recognized how important it is for us to critically assess all forms of knowledge, the labels assigned to their producers, and to accept the contradiction between the legitimization of one form of knowledge and its contestation as part and parcel of the same process of knowledge construction. In this regard, as a scholar I realize that I am only a translator of social reality. My texts try to be faithful to the original meaning of what I have observed, but I will always be unable to capture all the colors and their nuances. This brings me to the next challenge: if I accept the boundaries of theories in the human sciences as mainly a carrier of a message (translation of an experience into a coherent sequence of thought), then what is the place of theory in social change (how far can we tie theory to action)? Many feminists, including myself for some time, understand the function of theory as two-dimensional, namely the provision of explanations and guidelines for practices. In other words, we converge our intellectual and political activities. This convergence obscures the role of feminist scholars in social change and is a potential point of conflict between feminist studies and the women's movement. We need to reassess this convergence and our own roles.

For many women activists, the function of theory in explanation is appreciated to some extent. But there is also a disdain and outright rejection of particular kinds of theory due to their limited relevance. There is a preference to build strategies on the basis of practical experiences, something that may be reflecting a process of separation between theoreticians and practitioners, rather than of weaving the crucial insights offered by the academy and the movement. The very recognition of the need to build a regional perspective on the women's question (Asian, African, and Latin American) and the various research and teaching networks that have emerged in this context are a clear indication of the tension between the global nature of sexual inequality and its particular expressions. Such networks reflect both the divided world we live in as well as the need to take a pragmatic approach to such divisions rather than relying on false universal claims of solidarity.

As women, we are differently positioned in society in terms of class, ethnicity, political affiliation, learned traditions, all of which have implications as regards our thinking, and access to resources and facilities to participate in building a feminist science. Such positions also define the boundaries of our political action. The plurality of our existence implies a richness of experiences and perspectives, which do not have an equal opportunity to be expressed and utilized. For this reason, to assign to theory, and thereby the scholars who produce it, a position of political authority, is to favor one facet of the women's movement over another, one group of women over another. I remember a comment made by Renate Klein, whom I had the pleasure to meet during my visit to Japan: "We should not speak as priestesses, or avoid being put in a position where we have to speak like a priestess." I fully agree with her. We should resist being pontificated to, as well as being cajoled into pontification. Perhaps through this awareness and practice, some vision of a feminist democracy, through validation of self and others, can emerge.

As a feminist scholar, I do not see my role only within the boundaries for change of curriculum building and knowledge dissemination. I must also question the knowledge I produce, its relevance, and the foundations from where I took off. Lenin's vision of the "vanguard intellectual" or Gramsci's version of the "organic" intellectual, however powerful, have shown their painful limits in the socialist emancipatory project. If we believe in the lessons of history, this is perhaps the most precious and costly lesson to be digested.

Imposed socialism and maimed ideals: return to Vietnam's quagmire

Over the years of my active involvement in women's studies and the movement, I have come to identify myself more and more with the socialist-feminist perspective. I appreciate its attempts to bridge the existing gaps in the areas of sex, class, race, generation, and the fact that it does address the North-South question. Simultaneously, at a personal level, I have also been confronted with the painful realities of my country's trials and errors to construct a version of socialism.

In the course of the first five years of socialist experiment in my country, I found myself as the only income-earning member of my direct family. For their daily survival, the women were forced to sell everything they owned, from family valuables to functional objects such as clothing, furniture, and kitchenware. Apart from this, the extended family survived on the remittances of relatives and friends living abroad who pooled their resources to ensure regular and equal support to all concerned. In many instances, such remittances only helped the women to finance their long trips to the "re-education"[6] camps in the North to visit their husbands and sons. While these trips could take weeks due to the poor means of transport, as well as the location of the camps in hills and mountains, the women were allowed a short visit of only fifteen minutes. Those who could make such a trip once a year were considered lucky because they could supply their male folk with essentials and could be assured that the men would come back alive. My father and one brother came back after four and eight years respectively. They were in such a dreadful state of mental and physical health that, to me, "re-education" could not be regarded as a version of socialist "reconstruction" of the human subject but, rather, its destruction. One brother never came back. Nobody had a chance to visit him. They did not know where he was. Six years after his detention for "re-education," one of his campmates who fled abroad met a family member and informed her that he was no more.

The next five years I witnessed the painful fate of boat refugees, joined by several old and young relatives. For ten years, the process of "redistribution" was going on without any income-generation, except occasional and modest support from family members and friends living abroad. Some would argue that it is a class war after all, isn't it?

During my short visit home in 1985, having witnessed the realities of people, close and distant, fighting for every inch of their daily existence, I often wept. The image formed in my mind of my country and its people was that of a basket of crabs clinging on to each other's claws until these eventually fell off. Still caught in the basket, the crabs had no way to crawl out of it. I remember an American diplomat once told me at a reception in New York in the 1970s: "So the North Vietnamese think they're tough with their determination to win the war? We'll put them in their place. We can either flood the country with dollars and eventually everyone will be corrupted, or let the country bleed to death, they will turn to fight amongst themselves." A chill ran up my spine then. Now, I understand the power of diplomacy and its reality. Our tragedy was not just a class war. It was also a case of arrogance built on absurdity. Never mind the human costs. War has no room for compassion, only for winners. Even losers try to show that they have won. Peace has no room for reconciliation, only domination. Development has no room for social costs, only for grandiose projects and "white elephants."

Wrestled down to its last claw, Vietnam is revising its policy and socialist project. It has no resources, only a vision of a new path of liberalization, the vision of the "Four Tigers" (Singapore, Hong Kong, South Korea, and Taiwan). The IMF has blessed its "good" behavior, compared to its erratic policy in the late 1970s and early 1980s. Businessmen are building up their confidence to invest and profit from a highly skilled but dirt-cheap labor force. And, of course, to join the "civilized" world community, reforms are needed. Freedom of expression and association are still too dangerous to be allowed. But beauty contests, a seemingly harmless "cultural" reform, are promoted. The first beauty contest was organized in early 1989, paving the way for the marketing of female sexuality with tourism development on the policy agenda. By default or design? It is difficult to tell, as always.

Prostitution flourishes around newly opened bars and clubs and becomes a parameter for foreign journalists to assess the degree of openess and liberation. On the other side of the globe, the media are busy commenting on the premiere of a musical play by mega-producer Cameron MacIntosh, "Miss Saigon," featuring the romance between an American soldier and a Vietnamese prostitute. The tragedy of a nation is now being caricatured for profit-making fantasy. There is something to be said and done about patriarchy and its reproduction. Sometimes the power of poetic expression helps me to channel the feelings and perceptions that analytical reason fails to capture.

A cry of Vietnam

One hundred years,
Or maybe more.
I have been dressed
As a whore,
Vested with guns
As an angry warrior.
I have allowed
The violation
Of my dignity,
And
The manipulation
Of my sexuality.
I have spied
For many sides
Of the liberation.
I have satisfied
The many needs

Of the foreign legions.
I have put my faith
In the many faces
Of emancipation.
I have swallowed my pain,
My bitterness and shame
For a tomorrow.
It is barely
Tomorrow.
Already I see.
Another me:
"Miss Saigon"
In her new clothes,
Getting on
With the fever of growth,
And trapped
In
The promising romance
With the fancy Fifth Tiger
I shiver
At the brutality of greed,
And the logic of need.
Only heaven will know
How much more sorrow
Must flow
To the Southern Sea
Before I could be
ME.

Me

I exist in relation to others. I am an aggregation of my interaction with others, a flux of forming, being, and decaying. The skin I wear is part of my roots, which I still feel in spite of, or perhaps owing to, my life as an expatriate. My roots grew in a pot rather than in the soil where they were seeded, like a bonsai. Not too much water, and make sure that the roots don't outgrow the pot. Try to take the bonsai out of its pot and put it back into the natural soil. It probably will die. It longs for its pot.

I feel like a bonsai every time I am told how well I have done in adjusting myself to different cultures and ways of life. My earth will probably never receive me again, or perhaps I will not be able to adjust myself to it: deformed growth, but growth nevertheless. Some may even find a sense of aesthetics in deformation.

I don't want to be identified as a bonsai or a wild tree. I don't want to be sentenced to my present form of existence. As a human subject, I am expressing continuously the life that flows through me. I have limited control over what flows through me. But I have ample space to grasp its meaning, to learn, unlearn, and relearn. Beyond my present form of existence, the world is wide open and free. Nobody, no boundaries, can imprison my consciousness. In my work as a scholar, I am forced to categorize others and their social life. I am imprisoning people and their reality. Yet in my personal daily life I find being categorized distasteful. Where is the room for understanding of self and others? To me, this room can never be created in a "scientific" or "political" way where only logical reasoning and rational action will survive.

I value the room provided for me in this book because it allows me to express my yearning for understanding of self and others in a different way than my work has conditioned me. In my life, I don't know how many times I have been fearful of understanding something which is at odds with me, mainly because I may have to accept it. Not knowing all the consequences, it is better not to give room to understanding. I have discovered that acceptance is not necessarily the logical consequence of understanding. Sometimes one does not have to be accepted. Just understood. Once something is understood, there is no longer room for fear but ample space for compassion. The feared consequences are no longer deduced products of logical reasoning. They reside in the heart.

I come from
A world
So fragile.
Dolls with broken arms.
The warmth
Of one embrace
Must last one thousand years.
The sparkle of one smile
Must light
One thousand nights.
I come from
A world

Where the horizon
Is too hazy
Distance between people
Too far.
That world
Has taught me
The fragility
And meaning
Of kindness
In
A world
A look
A touch
A thought

Notes

1. The light was switched on at home when it got dark, around 6 P.M. But "light" also has another meaning: clarity, transparency. Coming home in the dark can mean that there is something to hide. It is very difficult to defend oneself from neighbors' gossip because it all "happened in the dark." To prevent such gossip, it is better for women to move in and out of the boundaries of the home in full daylight.
2. To have an audience with the Emperor, the subject must wear the right shape and color of clothing.
3. The Maison des Femmes is a multi-purpose building financed by UNDP for women's use. It has a library, meeting rooms, and some offices. The idea is to promote women's issues through the creation of facilities that enable women to interact more with each other. In itself it was not such a grandiose project, but in relation to the general socioeconomic conditions of women in Burkina-Faso, such a meeting place was, to me, more of a display of support than an attempt to meet women's needs.
4. T.D. Truong, *Sex, Money and Morality: Prostitution and Tourism in South East Asia*, London: Zed Books, 1990.
5. See T.D. Truong, "Feminist Studies in International Education: The Experience of the Women and Development Programat the Institute of Social Studies in The Netherlands," in *Proceedings of the International Seminar on Global Perspectives of Changing Sex-roles*, 23-26 November 1989.Saitama, Japan:
6. Re-education is a socialist version of social engineering. Members of the former South Vietnamese government and army, regardless of ranks and professions, were considered unfit for a socialist society. In 1975, they were to undergo a training program referred to as *Hoc Tap* (re-education). They were informed that the learning

process would last only a few weeks for the low-ranking officials and a few months for those of higher rank. They were instructed to bring the necessities (clothing, blankets, and toilet articles) for that period. Many people, including my family members, had registered voluntarily for re-education rather than change their identity and try to flee. They saw their future in Vietnam and not elsewhere. They realized that they had to come to terms with the principles of the new system. No one expected the trauma that followed.

Yasuko Muramatsu
Japan

YASUKO MURAMATSU is a faculty member at Tokyo Woman's Christian University (TWCU) in Japan. A development economist, she has undertaken a number of research projects on the economic status of women in Japan, including pioneering and award-winning work on women in small- and medium-scale industry. She is a member of the Tokyo-based International Group for the Study of Women and chaired their third Intenational Symposium on Women in an Age of Science and Technology. She also served on the original steering committee of TWCU's Center for Women's Studies where she has continued to serve in administrative and advisory capacities.

An Exploratory Journey

⟩•⟨•⟩•⟨•⟩•⟨

W hen did I become "positively" involved in women's studies? It is difficult to retrace my journey and much depends on how I define positively. However, for the moment, let me begin by identifying my involvement in three interrelated spheres—research, teaching, and administrative activities. Of these three, research on women and work and Women in Development (WID) have taken up most of my energy and time.

An economist's introduction to women's studies

Even after women's studies was introduced in Japan in the early 1970s, I did not immediately relate my research to it. I took the position: I will retain an interest in it, but women's studies is not for me. This was primarily because of my professional training in conventional economics and partly because of my ignorance of the very meaning of women's studies, especially its significance for women. I will return to this first reason later. As to the second, during the earlier phase of women's studies in Japan, I was a little discouraged as I felt that most of the work was descriptive in nature and lacked solid methodological and theoretical foundations. I subsequently realized that this was a very premature evaluation, although it is still true that theory building is an urgent task for women's studies scholars.

My very first piece of research in the field of women and work was carried out as a three-year project of the Center for Women's Studies at Tokyo Woman's Christian University (TWCU), in collaboration with my colleagues in the Department of Sociology and Economics; the subject was on the so-

213

cial and economic status of post-war Japanese women.[1] As a woman economist, as well as one educated in the "democratic" social atmosphere, I had become aware of the unequal status of women long before the days of women's studies in Japan. But I was unable to comprehend the situation in terms of the structures and systems of our society. This is not a problem peculiar to Japan. There are built-in, sociocultural, political, and economic institutions in each society that work against women in similar ways.

The reasons I decided to carry out my initial research on women and work were twofold. Although I did not intend to specialize in women's studies, I wanted to support our newly opened center by not only participating in its efforts through research, but also broadening its base by involving as many colleagues as possible. Also, to make the research interdisciplinary, I needed their cooperation. A more professional reason was that by investigating the social and economic status of Japanese women in a historical perspective, I intended to identify implications of the roles of women in the course of Japanese post-war economic growth. My research gave me a valuable opportunity to gain a better understanding of Japanese women and my society.

It was from this research that one of my hypotheses on women's labor, to be tested in future studies, was derived: traditionally female labor has been viewed as "peripheral" to male "core" labor and analysed in the short-run framework; for example, as a "buffer" labor force at a time of recession. In this research, however, we examined the long-running trend of women's labor participation rates. When the trend was studied carefully against the structural changes that took place in the post-war Japanese economy, we found a continuous downward trend of female labor participation rates. This was until the first turning point in the economy, after which the movement was in the opposite direction. This suggested that Japanese women as workers facilitated a structural transformation of the Japanese economy and led the way to successful rapid post-war economic growth. This hypothesis was tested and proven by my later work.[2]

A conference entitled Career Counselling Service, organized by the Asian Women's Institute, an Asian-based consortium of colleges, of which TWCU was a member, was a breakthrough for me. There I met women deeply concerned with women's development regardless of their "narrowly" defined professional disciplines or fields of work. At the time, without quite knowing what awaited me, I had agreed to participate in the conference in Singapore, simply because I was the only TWCU faculty member competent to write the required paper on Japanese women's employment and its related problems. I thought that career counseling was somebody else's field, not mine. But after attending the meeting and discussing women's issues and possible ways of working for women's empowerment, it was almost imperative for me to become a women's studies practitioner. While continuing with development economics as my major field of work, my growing commitment led me into the larger area of women in development.[3]

A new commitment: women in development

Nineteen eighty was a memorable year for me; I was asked to join the International Group for the Study of Women (IGSW), an interdisciplinary women's studies group in Japan with a cross-cultural perspective. The members of this organization formed themselves into several research subgroups to carry out research projects concurrently. The themes of these projects were to eventually become the basis for workshops at international symposia on women, organized every five years by the group. At that time I did not consider myself a women's studies researcher; I only meant to join a subgroup on women in small- and medium-scale industry. However, the research process itself, both the subject matter and discussions with colleagues, made me increasingly interested in women's issues. I ended up as a coordinator for the 1988 Tokyo symposium, Women and Communication in an Age of Science and Technology.[4]

Our work on women in small- and medium-scale industry in Japan is of a pioneering nature. At the time we initiated the project, there was no serious study on women in this sector of the economy from a women's studies perspective. In Japan, family sociologists and labor economists have had a long tradition of analyzing women in the family and the labor market. Women in the labor market were, and often still are, characterized as peripheral workers, while men were viewed as core workers. Nor were there many detailed studies that examined women's diversified work experiences by differentiating them according to the sectors where they worked. A few researchers had pursued projects focused on women in the government sector and with higher educational attainments. None, however, had attempted to focus on women's experiences in the sector we chose, despite the fact that the majority (roughly 80 percent of Japanese women) were and are employed there. Furthermore, we were eager to gain a better understanding of these women in a cross-cultural perspective, particularly in the Asian context.

We interviewed nearly one hundred women executives and managers on the basis of a semi-structured questionnaire, with the aim of asking them to share their individual stories and experiences as freely as possible; we tried to avoid imposing our preconceptions on them. Questions were asked about parents, upbringing, education, career paths, business philosophy, management styles, and so forth. At the same time, we sent out a questionnaire to two hundred male presidents of small- and medium-scale companies, asking how they perceived female executives, managers, and workers, both in and outside their own business enterprises.

We have published a book on the basis of our work entitled *Women in the Small- and Medium-Scale Industry.*[5] This is not the place for me to elaborate further on our findings; but let me say that many male businessmen still have a fairly conservative evaluation of their female counterparts and subordinates. This is illustrated in the following quotation from the book:

> Our research findings reveal that the small- and medium-scale industry allows a wider range of career patterns for women and men than the big business sector does. The big sector has only afforded young people who have newly entered the labor market opportunities advantageous to their business careers. Whereas the small- and medium-scale industry offers even those who have entered the business in later stages of their lives the chance to be successful not only as entrepreneurs but also as executives and managers.
>
> Moreover, differences were found in the ease with which women can be successful according to the type of business they are involved in. No female entrepreneurs were seen among our subjects involved in heavy industry, an area considered a "male" arena; although there were women who became company presidents as successors to male family members. In contrast, many women initiated their own business when it involved apparel, food-processing and service industries related to information. Of these female-initiated areas, the first two are traditionally considered to be "female" arenas, whereas the last is a new area where

younger, highly educated women are found to be presidents and managers. This last area is an industry still in the trial and error stage, but is the most important industry in this age of information. Men and women stand at the same starting line here and our subjects felt that women have no handicaps in this industry.[6]

At present we are carrying out a study of the impact of technological changes on women in manufacturing, banking, and software development industries. Our preliminary findings suggest that Japanese women suffer adversely from the introduction of new technologies when they decide to stay in the labor market for a long period of time (at present they work for about four years). This is because new technologies introduced in recent years were generally capital intensive and labor saving, which enabled businesses to substitute unskilled women's labor with machines. The shorter duration of service for women, as a result, helps the economy maintain low unemployment rates (2.8 percent as of November 1990) despite rapid introductions of new technologies.[7]

In this context it must be remembered that in Japan women are still considered to be primarily homemakers. Thus, the patriarchal family and social system encourage women to retire from the labor market once they are married and ready to bear children. How did I free myself from this traditional social norm? I had one of my junior high school female teachers and my own mother as role models, who actively encouraged me to develop myself fully and become self-reliant. It is vitally necessary for Japanese young women to have a wide range of role models before them, from which they can choose a life style that will be truly satisfactory and rewarding.

Thus in the process of my struggle with the identification of women's problems, I encountered Women in Development (WID), a new interdisciplinary field in social sciences which focuses on women in the process of development in the Third World. I was already working with mainstream development economics, but clearly I was not quite comfortable with its theoretical bases. It failed to explain why women gain proportionally less from the fruits of development than do men; or why the development process often has an adverse impact on women.

As I see it, the insensitivity of mainstream development economics toward gender issues arises from the following methodological deficiencies:

First of all, it assumes that people are homogeneous and therefore does not differentiate them by class, gender, age, ecological environment (for example, irrigated rice land in case of rice farming), and so forth. As a corollary, it also assumes that top-down development policies do have a "trickle-down" effect.

Secondly, it does not take social institutions into consideration. For example, it neglects the existing patterns of the sexual division of labor. The displacement of women from rice harvesting in many Asian countries when new agricultural technologies are introduced is a classic case in point.

Thirdly, it assumes that the husband is the head of the household; that he is a benevolent, altruistic dictator; and that a household has a joint production and utility function. All these unrealistic assumptions help to explain why women and children often get a smaller allocation of household resources and income.

Fourthly, its concepts and definitions are inappropriate for analyzing women's "economic" activities. Many of their activities do not bring them monetary rewards, since they often work as unpaid family workers. Women are also primary providers of the family's basic needs, but their labor is not considered as productive. In order to shed light on this area of women's work, WID introduced the method of time allocation studies, a great breakthrough in highlighting the nature of women's work.

Mainstream development also ignores the political aspects of the development process. The low socioeconomic status of Japanese women can be traced, among other things, to their lack of political empowerment. Empowerment of women, therefore, is an area of major emphasis in WID, which also considers an interdisciplinary approach essential to research on women.

A fresh look at development concepts

Of course, WID is not yet a firmly established academic field and there is room for elaboration and expansion in its analytical scope and framework. Development, *per se,* neither guarantees women's liberation nor improves their status. As such, there is no reason to exclude women in "developed" countries from WID research. Although some dialogue between researchers from the south and north has been stimulated, researchers from developed countries generally do not identify women's issues in the Third World with those of their own. Unless we overcome this problem, we shall not be able to answer the much more complicated methodological problem of subjectivity and objectivity. Also, the WID approach may be perceived as isolating women from national or global concerns and it is important to find ways to integrate WID's "bottom up" approach with broad-based development planning. In my own work, I have been able to combine my interest in development economics and women's studies. I am now ready to carry out a new research project—which excites me greatly—in a Central Javanese rice-growing village.

My aims for this particular project are manifold. One is to broaden the analytical framework. Rather than treating them as a homogeneous group, I plan to differentiate women by individual characteristics (age, education, marital status, etc.), household characteristics, environmental conditions (fertility of agricultural land, availability of water, access to transportation, and so on), and class (access to agricultural land). I also intend to integrate women's issues with development economics in my research and analysis. Isolating women's issues from the broader context of their lives, I feel, cannot provide a total picture of economic and other realities. Through these new directions in fieldwork and theory, I hope to be in a better position to identify women's living conditions, their changing roles, and patterns of sexual division of labor in the process of development. Studying the overall impact of development on women in terms of employment opportunities in rural settings is another of my aims. In addition, my research will focus on those factors which lead to the serious problem of migration of women from the rural areas to the cities.

The researcher as teacher

My research has naturally influenced my teaching. I teach economics at Tokyo Woman's Christian University. The university has two four-year colleges located on two separate campuses, with roughly four thousand students. Some departments offer both graduate and undergraduate courses, while my department, the Department of Sociology and Economics, offers only undergraduate courses. Although we have a very competent faculty in our department, we do feel that young women should receive their graduate training at larger schools where they can learn more from their contemporaries as well as from the faculty.

I teach courses on economic theories and development. By now it has become clear that economics is gender blind. Some people feel that it is gender neutral, that it only distinguishes between "skilled" and "unskilled" labor, which can mean both male and female labor. "Consumer" can mean men as well as women. However, is the discipline really gender neutral? Women are usually identified as unskilled labor because of their lack of education and/or adequate training. Also, the understanding of "short-term" workers is based on the assumption that with marriage and/or child-bearing women will withdraw from the labor market. But economics does not question why women have lower educational attainments than men. New family economic theories state that men have comparative advantages in paid work, women in unpaid domestic work.[8] But why this is so is not questioned. Sexual differences are taken care of merely in quantitative terms. For instance, a male worker is automatically paid twice as much as a female worker on the assumption that his skill level is twice as high as hers. There is little discussion, however, on why women continue to remain unskilled. This is what is meant by being gender blind—a point of view which conceals women's roles. Another example of the gross limitations of mainstream economics is that it implicitly assumes decision making is done either collectively or by the head of the household, who is always a man. There is also the problem of the conceptualization of terms such as production, income, productivity, and work.

I teach a purely theoretical course, Principles of Economics, which deals with standardized concepts and theories. In Japan, familiarity with and knowledge of conventional economics are absolutely necessary, for example, for the civil services examination, for being admitted to a graduate school, and even for recruitment by large corporations. I cannot avoid the traditional method of teaching and the introduction of a certain basic and broadly accepted terminology. However, I have adopted a technique: in my very first class I tell the students about my intellectual conflict in teaching this course. As we go along I take time to explain how I feel about key standardized concepts and suggest alternative ways of defining terms when I can; but there are many concepts which are still at variance with the feminist approach. One of the most crucial concerns of both committed Marxist feminists and non-Marxist economists, for example, is over the introduction of the idea of partriarchy into economics, and finding a link between the production and reproduction of human beings.

When I explain to them the reasons behind my dilemma in teaching mainstream economics, young students (my students are exclusively women) express their anger, saying it is not fair that women are thus marginalized. In reply, I usually tell them, "Yes, it is not fair. But I do not know of any historical case where the minority and powerless groups are empowered and liberated by the majority and powerful groups. What we have to do is to liberate ourselves. Stick to your jobs and speak out whenever you are treated unfairly. Broaden your women's networks so that you have people who support and encourage you whenever you encounter discrimination and problems. I am always with you. Call me up whenever you need my help."

I also teach a lecture course and hold junior- and senior-level seminars on development economics. The situation with courses on development economics is a little more flexible. They are not essential for later career development and the field is still in the process of being explored. Also, it is not only those who are concerned with women and children in developing countries who have raised critical questions on conceptualization, definition, and built-in biases within the system, but also those concerned with North-South problems in general. The aim is to find better approaches to development. Therefore, there is room for me to develop methods to introduce women's issues into discussions in classrooms. Students in these courses have the opportunity to share findings from my own research.

Meanwhile, I am hoping to develop a curriculum for WID for our university. I intend to do this during my field research in Java as an integral part of my project and, subsequently, in my year in the United States following the fieldwork in Java. I am planning to visit and discuss the issue with WID researchers in the American academy as well as those in Asia. Japan has been seriously suffering from a lack of Official Development Assistance experts with a WID perspective. Developing a WID curriculum would help to support women-oriented planning for development in the long run.

In the process of socialization and upbringing, Japanese society tends to marginalize young women.[9] Women often view themselves as inferior to men and are likely to confine their areas of activities within the "women's domain." As a women's studies practitioner in the academy, I feel strongly that I should lend a helping hand to my students in developing the powers latent within them and exploring fully their potential as human beings. I am acutely aware of the need to act as a role model for my students as well as to encourage them to take on the challenge of professions or activities that are perceived to be solely men's domain. Of course there are always some students who do not appreciate my point of view, but I have been fortunate in meeting young women in my classes who are confident of challenging existing structures and working for change.

In 1976 the Center for Women's Studies at Tokyo Woman's Christian University was opened in response to a resolution of the newly formed Asian Women's Institute, which decided to initiate women's studies programs at each of their nine higher educational member institutions. Thus, our center was started through an external decision rather than by internal choice. The administration decided to place the center under the umbrella of the existing Institute for Studies of Comparative Culture—a clever choice—since the institute had a firm foundation both within and outside the university, while the time was not really ripe for women's studies to be part of mainstream education. The director and associate director of the institute automatically served as director and associate director of the center; further, the center did not—and still does not—have even one full-time professor or researcher. Instead, there is a single full-time research assistant. Courses called Women's Studies are taught by part-time lecturers, while some full-time university women professors offer such courses as Heroines in American Literature, Family Sociology, and Mass Media from a women's studies perspective.

In April 1990, the center became independent from the institute and automonous in its decision making and budget. It now has a full-time secretary. Ever since 1983, the center has organized and/or sponsored numerous lectures on women and has been offering a couple of series of five-session seminars annually. It also provides financial support for a new, three-year research project each year. Thus there are three projects running concurrently each year, and in the fourth year a research report is published. By late 1990, the center had supported thirteen research projects, and nine research reports had been published. One of the new programs initiated since April 1990 is a

Visiting Fellow Programme in which a few researchers from a-broad will be invited to come to carry out a short-term research project at our center. So far, we have accepted three fellows.

In 1986, the Nao Aoyama Award was established at the center with funds willed by the late Professor Nao Aoyama, a former teacher at the university. The prize is awarded annually for an outstanding piece of work on the history of women, a field in which the late Professor Aoyama was eminent. This year the prize was awarded to an extremely interesting and fine work on women's history in Okinawa by a woman poet and researcher. The subject of her research was a local women's movement against a custom, hated by women, of washing and cleaning human bones exhumed after several years. Recently we had a special lecture on the work by the author and were deeply moved by what she said. Since 1987, the center has also used some of these funds to encourage graduates and students of the university who are doing promising research in the field.

My involvement in and association with the center began when I became a member of the original steering committee. The steering committee is responsible for setting up programs, most of which were approved by the Council of the Institute for the Studies of Comparative Culture and are now approved by its own council. When the center began, both the director and the associate director of the institute and the center were male. Some people in women's studies outside the university felt this was inappropriate. In a sense, this was true, and a few of us shared this sentiment, but at the same time, at least I felt that it was all right if *we* could actually formulate and implement programs and *they* were responsible for the budget! I also thought this was an appropriate survival strategy for the newly established center, particularly in terms of crucial decision making.

It was during my second term as a member of the steering committee that I participated in the Career Counselling Conference in Singapore, which I mentioned earlier. At the end of my second term in 1980, I decided not to continue on the steering committee. I believed that the center should recruit as many new members as possible—both women and men—so as to increase its familiarity with faculty within the university. Even after I withdrew from the steering committee, I continued to be associated with its activities in various ways: giving lectures, participating in seminars, carrying out the center's research project, writing papers for it to submit to the AWI, attending conferences organized by the same body and its related organizations, and so on. However, I was not involved in decision making. There was another reason behind my decision: a senior colleague in my department told me that he wanted to read more of my papers on development and "economics" rather than on women's studies. Implicitly he was criticizing me for being active in women's studies as I had been employed to teach economic theories and development. So I decided it would be a personal survival strategy to stay away from the steering committee. Further, there was a more serious reason. At that stage of my career, I was not yet ready to commit myself fully to women's studies. As I said earlier, I have now solved this problem by identifying WID as the area of my greatest interest; but it took me some years to reach this position and level of commitment.

The teacher as administrator

In April 1988, I was appointed associate director of the Institute for the Studies of Comparative Culture and the center. My specific responsibility was to prepare for the center to become an autonomous institution in April 1990. What struck me most when I accepted the position was the fact that there was an assumption that autonomy could come merely by making minor changes in the center's provisions. By this time I had moved a long way from my earlier ambivalence: I was no longer afraid of identifying myself as a women's studies practitioner as well as a development economist; consequently I was able to fight to restructure the activities of the center with more than a doubled budget. My inclination was to foster the university's full commitment to women's studies. There were more people deeply committed to women's studies by then, whose expertise had not yet been linked directly to the center's activity. I immediately formed a task force committee, preparing for its independence. I really wanted to see the center become a focus for women's studies scholars and practitioners, not only those within the university, but also those outside. I began this work by setting up a forum for providing opportunities for those who were seriously interested in women's studies to get together and discuss mutual concerns. Two such meetings were scheduled for that year. I believed that no matter how small my attempt, it would become the seed for a big harvest in the future. In April 1990 I again came back to the center as a member of the steering committee. We now have a new director and associate director; and, needless to say, now women are assuming these offices. As I look to the future, women's studies today presents a great challenge. It is not only rich in data but is also moving toward strong theoretical underpinnings. Personally, it means that I have begun to think about myself and my work, explore new possibilities, and search for a common field for women to restructure society toward a more equitable world.

Notes

1. Yasuko Muramatsu, "Socio-Economic Status of Women in the Post-War Period in Japan" (mimeo), Tokyo: Center for Women's Studies, TWCU, 1982.
2. See Yasuko Muramatsu, "Absurdity and Promises," in Erik Aerts, Paul M.M. Klep, Jurgen Kocka, and Marina Thorborg (eds.), *Women in the Labor Force: Comparative Studies on Labor Market and Organization of Work since the 18th Century,* Leuven: Leuven University Press, 1990, pp. 63–75.
3. I discuss this in more detail later in this paper.
4. The proceedings of the symposium have been published as Yoshiro Kawakami, (ed.), *Women and Communication in An Age of Science and Technology.* Tokyo: International Group for the Study of Women, 1988.
5. Hiroko Hara, Yasuko Muramatsu, and Chie Minami (eds.), *Cushokigyo no Onnatachi* (Women in the Small- and Medium-Scale Industry), Tokyo: Miraisha, 1987.
6. Ibid. pp. 395–6.
7. Somucho (ed.), *Fujin Rodo no Jitsujo* (Present Situation of Women Workers), Tokyo: Okurasho Innsatsukyoku, 1989. p. 8 (Appendix).
8. Gary S. Becker, *A Treatise on the Family,* Cambridge: Harvard University Press, 1976.
9. Japanese women's labor participation rates still show an M-shaped curve, with the trough at the age group of 30-34.

The Feminist Press at The City University of New York offers alternatives in education and in literature. Founded in 1970, this nonprofit, tax-exempt educational and publishing organization works to eliminate stereotypes in books and schools and to provide literature with a broad vision of human potential. The publishing program includes reprints of important works by women, feminist biographies of women, multicultural anthologies, a cross-cultural memoir series, and nonsexist children's books. Curricular materials, bibliographies, directories, and a quarterly journal provide information and support for students and teachers of women's studies. Through publications and projects, The Feminist Press contributes to the rediscovery of the history of women and the emergence of a more humane.

New and Forthcoming Books

Always a Sister: The Feminism of Lillian D. Wald. A biography by Doris Groshen Daniels. $12.95, paper.

The Answer/La Respuesta (Including a Selection of Poems), by Sor Juana Inés de la Cruz. Critical Edition and translation by Electa Arenal and Amanda Powell. $12.95 paper, $35.00 cloth.

Australia for Women:Travel and Culture, edited by Susan Hawthorne and Renate Klein. $17.95 paper.

Black and White Sat Down Together: The Reminiscences of an NAACP Founder, by Mary White Ovington. Edited and with a foreword by Ralph E.Luker. Afterword by Carolyn E. Wedin. $19.95 cloth.

The Castle of Pictures and Other Stories: A Grandmother's Tales, Volume One, by George Sand. Edited and translated by Holly Erskine Hirko. Illustrated by Mary Warshaw. $9.95 paper, $23.95 cloth.

Challenging Racism and Sexism: Alternatives to Genetic Explanations (Genes and Gender VII). Edited by Ethel Tobach and Betty Rosoff. $14.95 paper, $35.00 cloth.

China for Women: Travel and Culture. $17.95, paper.

The Dragon and the Doctor, by Barbara Danish. $5.95, paper.

Japanese Women: New Feminist Perspectives on the Past, Present, and Future, edited by Kumiko Fujimura-Fanselow and Atsuko Kameda. $15.95 paper, $35.00 cloth.

Music and Women, by Sophie Drinker. Afterword by Ruth A. Solie. $16.95, paper, $37.50, cloth.

No Sweetness Here, by Ama Ata Aidoo. Afterword by Ketu Katrak. $10.95, paper, $29.00, cloth.

Seeds 2: Supporting Women's Work around the World, edited by Ann Leonard. Introduction by Martha Chen. Afterwords by Mayra Buvinic, Misrak Elias, Rounaq Jahan, Caroline Moser, and Kathleen Staudt. $12.95, paper, $35.00, cloth.

Shedding and Literally Dreaming, by Verena Stefan. Afterword by Tobe Levin. $14.95 paper, $35.00 cloth.

The Slate of Life: More Contemporary Stories by Women Writers of India, edited by Kali for Women. Introduction by Chandra Talpade Mohanty and Satya P. Mohanty. $12.95 paper, $35.00 cloth.

Solution Three, by Naomi Mitchison. Afterword by Susan Squier. $10.95 paper, $29.95 cloth.

Songs My Mother Taught Me: Stories, Plays, and Memoir, by Wakako Yamauchi. Edited and with an introduction by Garrett Hongo. Afterword by Valerie Miner. $14.95 paper, $35.00 cloth.

Streets: A Memoir of the Lower East Side. By Bella Spewack. Introduction by Ruth Limmer. Afterword by Lois Elias. $19.95, cloth.

Women of Color and the Multicultural Curriculum: Transforming the College Classroom, edited by Liza Fiol-Matta and Mariam K. Chamberlain. $18.95 paper, $35.00 cloth.

Prices subject to change. Individuals: Send check or money order (in U.S. dollars drawn on a U.S. bank) to The Feminist Press at The City University of New York, 311 East 94th Street, New York, NY 10128. Please include $4.00 postage and handling for the first book, $1.00 for each additional. For VISA/MasterCard orders call (212) 360-5790. Bookstores, libraries, wholesalers: Feminist Press titles are distributed to the trade by Consortium Book Sales and Distribution, (800) 283-3572.

DATE DUE

OCT 2 0 199?			

Demco, Inc. 38-293